Czech New Wave Filmmakers in Interviews

Czech New Wave Filmmakers in Interviews

ROBERT BUCHAR

foreword by Antonín J. Liehm

McFarland & Company, Inc., Publishers

Jefferson, North Carolina, and London

LIBRARY OF CONGRESS CATALOGUING-IN-PUBLICATION DATA

Buchar, Robert, 1951–
    Czech new wave filmmakers in interviews / Robert Buchar ;
foreword by Antonín J. Liehm.
    p.   cm.
    Includes bibliographical references and index.

    ISBN 0-7864-1720-X (softcover : 50# alkaline paper)

    1. Motion pictures — Czech Republic. 2. Motion picture
producers and directors — Czech Republic — Interviews. I. Title.
PN1993.5.C89B83   2004
791.4302'33'09224371— dc22   2003019550

British Library cataloguing data are available

On the cover: (clockwise from top left) Jiří Menzel, Stanislav Milota, Jan
Němec *(photographs by Robert Buchar)*, Drahomíra Vihanová *(courtesy
CINEART TV Prague, photograph by Vlastimil Malaska)*, Karel Vachek
(photograph by Bob Barnes), Ivan Passer *(photograph by Morton Zarcoff)*;
(background) Věra Chytiltová *(photographs by Robert Buchar)*.

Manufactured in the United States of America

McFarland & Company, Inc., Publishers
  Box 611, Jefferson, North Carolina 28640
  www.mcfarlandpub.com

Contents

Foreword

ANTONÍN J. LIEHM

The history of Czech film started immediately after Edison and the Lumière brothers. Czechoslovakian cinema flourished during the silent era, taking full advantage of international collaboration between Prague, Vienna, and Berlin studios. This all ended when sound film arrived and raised the language barrier, which pushed Czech cinema towards provincialism. But Czech film didn't go away. Thanks to a tradition of good professional craftsmanship, we still watch many of these films from the 30s on television and buy them on video. We don't do that just because of their historical nature or nostalgia.

But some filmmakers wanted to do more than just make entertainment films for a small local market. They wanted to make art films that could reach the whole world. The Second World War and German occupation didn't suppress this movement. On the contrary, it had the opposite effect. The occupation and subsequent cutbacks on production of Czech films surprisingly raised awareness of film as an important part of the nation's culture. It was then that the concept of a nationalized film industry was born. The idea was that a nationalized film industry would free filmmakers from dependency on the market and the box office and move film closer to art. When the war ended in 1945, a nationalized film industry seemed possible. *The Siren* received a Gold Leo Award in Venice, Jiří Krejčík made his film *Conscience* and Jiří Weiss *Stolen Borders*. But in 1948, the period of brutal Stalinism interrupted this and it wasn't until

1

the mid–50s that Czech film was able to make a turnaround. Many of the old dreams were fully realized in the 60s when Czechoslovak cinema became, for a short period of time, honored worldwide. The Soviet invasion in August 1968 abruptly ended the "Czech film miracle," and the period of so-called normalization that followed after 1968 wiped out everything. The "Velvet Revolution" in 1989 didn't just fail to build on the best from Czech history but returned Czech cinema to the provincial misery of the pre–World War II era.

This is a brief, schematically condensed history of Czech film you have to know before you begin to read the following text. Robert Buchar, a Czech cinematographer who for many years has taught at Chicago's Columbia College and remembers this history very well, interviewed a number of Czech filmmakers a couple of years ago in front of his video camera. He focused his attention on the creators of the "Czech film miracle" of the 60s called "Czech New Wave." (Unfortunately, Slovak filmmakers who played an important role in the movement are not included.) He added Jan Svěrák, Jr., and Saša Gedeon as successful representatives of the "Velvet Generation." When Czech television refused to broadcast this extraordinary documentary, the author made it available in the literary form so we all can read it.

The book version has two advantages. First, it's more complete. Everything that didn't fit into the two-hour television format is here. If you see the film, you will understand how important this is. Second, the interviews in the book have a raw taste of the unpolished spoken word. It adds a drama and complexity to individual interviews, often surpassing the fascinating authenticity of the audio-visual recording. The consecutive lineup of individual interviews fully supplements direct confrontation created by the editing in the film.

Thirteen years after the November turnover, Czechs have an Institute for Contemporary History and many others. They are shooting films — mostly fictions and non-fictions made for television about the horrors of Stalinism. But until today, nothing worthy was shot about the real history of 20 years of normalization, or about how the Czechoslovakian society in the 60s tried to find a way out of the darkness of Stalinism. But Czechoslovakia lived through this history, slowly but steadily recuperating from the Stalinist terror and consciously (or unconsciously) trying to follow up with better traditions of the past history. It's not difficult to guess why. The 90s, like the era of Stalinism, were years of ideology: years of denouncing the past and celebrating the present and the future. The more distant the past is, the more comfortably you can dig in it. The 60s and normalization were much more complicated times. In the 60s there was an energy to life, or something coming alive. It's better not talk about this here because the younger generation, which didn't experience it, could get an idea. In order to assess the normalization period it would be necessary to explain and document how 15 million people "suffered and fought against communism" while a handful of dissidents pretty much "sabotaged" this process. To explain this would be much more complicated and much more difficult than to denounce the terror of Stalinism.

And this is exactly the point where these filmmakers enter. They candidly and without self-censorship describe this landscape — a landscape full of lions and many white spots on the map of recent Czech history. They openly talk about the spirit of the 60s, about the Czech New Wave film movement, about the challenges they faced, and about their hopes. The fact that none of them was a member of the Communist party makes their confession even more credible. They are aware that those they called "Bolsheviks" during normalization included at least half a million people expelled from the Communist party after September 1968 and fired from their jobs because they opposed for years the reality of that fraudulent dream. But this is not about words but about the fact that they are saying out loud, on camera, what many others think but are afraid to say in public. Are they brave, courageous? I don't believe that any of them thinks about it. They simply stayed faithful to their own beliefs, paid for it dearly during the normalization period, and are not willing to compromise today. The question is, how long they will remain an exception?

But more important are their opinions about the normalization and present times. Their candid confessions reflect the character of the time period that lasted four times longer then the Nazi occupation. During this period, the risk was much smaller than during the World War II, barely two thousand out of the fifteen million people in the nation publicly stood up in opposition. Historians, sociologists, philosophers and artists owe us answers to the questions these facts present.

A few of those who speak here are opening Pandora's box, letting us see images of demoralization, moral relativism and egoism that grew (and continue to grow) through the society and left scars much deeper than a decade of barbaric Stalinism. Milan Kundera once wrote that Stalinist socialism allowed us to see sides of human character we sometimes sensed but haven't seen or refused to see. This experience deeply influenced Kundera's growth and all his work. But Czech literature, film and theater didn't even start to think about what the normalization period did and revealed to us. We are hiding behind the word "Bolshevik" calling every day from the grave the ghost of communism. But one day those who show us a mirror reflecting normalization, its legacy and ourselves will come. And then we will be able to breathe again.

A few artists who have been gone through it and survived this trial with clean heads, who stood tall, put this mirror in the way of a small fragment of Czech reality called film. And as Czech films in the 60s, and films of the New Wave especially, draw out of individual stories, like under a microscope, an image of the whole society, their statements in this book reflect an image of all of us, regardless of how and where we were living.

Even more interesting and more important is how all this stretches out into the following post-communist era. How everything we learned during normalization became handy after the November 1989 revolution: adaptability, conformism, a fear not from police persecution or a prison, but from losing our own well being (not accidentally, Jiří Menzel talks about Karel Čapek). A small greed became a big greed. The art of small cheating became the art of big cheating. The lack of responsibility for our own work and the results of that penetrated deeply under our skin. "Only take care of yourself" became a slogan written in the subconscious. I could go on and on. What we were doing in the past, because we were forced to and because of the circumstances (or we were justifying our actions that way), we are doing today freely and with great applause. Cinema is now just an insignificant fragment of the big picture. This statement, this truth, is not just spoken by those who, after November, "were not invited to the feast," but we can hear it also from the successful Jan Svěrák, Jr., who probably in reality does different things than he frankly talks about on camera. But I am getting ahead of myself here because at the time these interviews were recorded, *Dark Blue World* wasn't shot and Jiří Krejčík didn't have any idea that Barrandov Studios under the ownership of Třinec Steel Corporation would make billions, out of which the Czech film industry will never see a penny. Czech films aren't shot at the Barrandov Studios anymore because Czech filmmakers can't afford to pay as much as foreign producers can, sucking the best professional craftsmen away from the production of Czech films.

Was all that really necessary? I am afraid it was. A handful of dissidents fascinated by their own status and mostly certain about the permanency of the communist regime were not ready for the downfall of communism. They didn't generate a new political, economic or cultural elite which would be able to follow up with the best from history, creating a sort of Czechoslovakian model of transformation. The power fell into the hands of characters who were mostly just a mirror image of those from the past. Stalinist-ideological economists, politicians acting like Forman's firefighters, but driving Mercedes limousines and wearing Hermes ties. Not to mention those in charge of developing links between society and culture. And so the empty pocket of Czech culture and its present state is, again, a result of a commonly known situation: Who is responsible for it? "Bolsheviks," of course.

But it's not just about vigorously opening Pandora's box (many strong arms will be needed to lift its lid). The book you are about to read is hiding another surprise: It's a collection of uniquely truthful self-portraits. The individual authors here are sincere, not afraid to speak up and point fingers. Director Jiří Krejčík has used the word "criminal" as long as I've known him. The fact he sometimes repeats himself is not a surprise. He's done it for decades. It's part of his character and his strength. We can't imagine the last 50 years of Czech film history without him. His bursts of indignation didn't fade with age.

Or Věra Chytilová. The conversation with her is a great self-portrait by itself. Nobody will make a better one and I don't believe that Czech television even noticed. Drahomíra Vihanová and Jan Němec are upset and concerned, and nothing will make them indolent. A reader will realize here that without this anger and passion, they would never be able to make their films, which are now a part of Czech history and Czech culture. On the other hand Jiří Menzel and two-and-a-half-generations-younger, Jan Svěrák are calm and thoughtful. They understand everything and they became wise a long time ago. Ivan Passer, a tramp forever, is also calm and thoughtful but in a different way. An American producer in Hollywood once told me that Passer's *Intimate Lighting* is one of the best films of the 50s. "Fortunately, he didn't have to make this film in Hollywood. You would have kicked him out the door with his script," I replied. Jaroslav Bouček is sympathetic because he describes simply and without any emotions how Barrandov Studios were privatized and Czech cinema wiped out.

They lived the best years of their lives under "Bolsheviks" and that doesn't seem to go away. During the hard years of "normalization," it was not a bloodthirsty dictator wrapped in a flag of utopia, but a grotesque, ridiculous, evil, sadistic, stupid policeman who stamped out everything he could do for Czech cinema and Czech culture. But this "policeman" didn't take from them, and couldn't take from them who they are and who they were. And they are painting for us a missing picture of present times. It's like a tragic cartoon where present and past are interlaced. Once upon a time I was thinking of Gogol while watching Miloš Forman's firemen. Now the same thought comes to my mind. Because it's not only about "what," but also "how." And not just because of that.

Did nothing good, original, arise during normalization or after November's fall of communism? Something that could measure up to the success of the past? Maybe. Actually, I don't know. The interviews in this book — this documentary — don't mention it.

But very often the question of a theme comes up. In the 60s, there was a big theme. And not just one. Those ill-fated, who had to live and are still living without a theme, are saying this to those who lived through that period. It seems odd to me. The whole world, including ours, was shook up in the 90s and now all topics have disappeared? Maybe it's because, in contrast to our neighbors, communism had fallen accidentally on our heads and we can't get over it. Adam Michnik once wrote that you can make soup from the water in an aquarium, including the fish, and if you get really hungry and spice it enough, maybe you will eat it. But nobody has figured out yet how to make this soup into an aquarium with live fish again. He thought that this is a great new theme, quite original, and not just for one generation. I agreed with him. But I forgot that this theme is alive and uncharted. It has no steady shape as, for example, Stalinist's socialism had. It's constantly in motion, once hot, the other time icy cold. You can easily slip, get in trouble, break your neck. Didn't this apply to the 60s' generation as well? Sure, but they were different. They survived the period of Czech Stalinism, didn't get through 20 years of Normalization yet, didn't and couldn't think about money, and they were fearless. They didn't worry about politics or political correctness, about being different. They didn't care about a box office success. To make films, television, and literature as well for the mass audience has become now once again a slogan adapted from the Communist establishment. This curtain is hiding everything and it is not advisable to look behind it if we don't want to see what is back there — conformism, opportunism and the unattainable craving for money, the lack or total absence of talent. All this because of conditions created not just in the film industry.

And so not only a great theme of our times leaks through our fingers, but many smaller topics with big metaphoric potential as well. But the present times are not favorable to metaphor. The generation of contemporary filmmakers literally strolls through a deep forest of topics, crossing over what is in front of them. They don't want to see — not even mentioning their producers — and they are busy proclaiming, "There is no theme, there are no topics!" The idea that film, or art, can change the world, or at least influence reality, is gone. But maybe not so. Despite plenty of new film and television propaganda — very much like in the 50s or during normalization, but with the opposite polarity — Czech Communists are doing better and better. Even this sounds like a great theme! And this book is filled with themes.

Introduction

In the 1960s something interesting happened in Czechoslovakia. Artists started to realize that the aesthetics of social realism contrasted with the realities of their everyday lives. This became reflected in Czech art, literature and film. The films of the so-called Czech New Wave rose as a movement in response to the political and historical reality of Czechoslovakia. The movement (at that time called "the Czech Film Miracle") started in 1963 with the special premiere screening of Stefan Uher's film *Sunshine in a Net* [*Slnko v sieti*] in Prague. This film became a symbol of upcoming changes and opened the door for a new generation of filmmakers such as Věra Chytilová, Jiří Menzel, Miloš Forman, Ivan Passer, Jan Schmidt, Jan Němec, Ester Krumpachová, Jaroslav Papoušek, Antonín Máša, Evald Schorm, Zdeněk Sirový, Jaromil Jireš, Drahomíra Vihanová, Pavel Juráček, Hynek Bočan, Juraj Jakubisko, Dušan Hanák, Ello Haveta and Juraj Herz. They, together with some directors of the older generation (Vojtěch Jasný, Jan Kadár, Elmar Klos, František Vláčil, Ladislav Helge, Karel Kachyňa, Jiří Weiss, and Jiří Krejčík) produced during a period of five years some 60 outstanding films, put Czech film on the map of world cinema and generated two Oscars for Best Foreign Film. The credit also goes to the new generation of cinematographers that had arisen together with the new directors. Names like Bedřich Baťka, Jan Čuřík, Jan Kališ, Jaroslav Kučera, Igor Luther, Miroslav Ondříček and Jaromír Šofr became an inseparable part of the movement.

In 1963, films of the young directors showed up in theaters. Miloš Forman shot his first film, *Black Peter* [*Černý Peter*], Věra Chytilová *Some-*

thing Different [*O něčem jiném*], Pavel Juráček and Jan Schmidt directed *Josef Kilian* [*Postava k podpírání*], Karel Vachek *Moravian Hellas* [*Moravská Hellas*] and Jaromil Jireš *The First Cry* [*Křik*]. Also, Vojtěch Jasný, the representative of the older generation, shot *Cassandra Cat* [*Až přijde kocour*]. All these films had one thing in common — a lack of everything that the ethics of social realism required. The official critique marked these films as decadent, pessimistic and reactionary. But the genie was out of the bottle.

In the following year, directors Jan Němec and Evald Schorm made their debuts. Němec shot *Diamonds of the Night* [*Démanty noci*] and Schorm *Courage for Everyday* [*Každý den odvahu*]. The script for Schorm's film was by Antonín Máša. Some other directors from the previous generation jumped on the bandwagon. Ladislav Rychman's *The Hop Pickers* [*Česáči*] and Oldřich Lipský's *Lemonade Joe* [*Limonadový Joe*] became extremely popular musicals, and Karel Zeman shot his *War of the Fools* [*Bláznova kronika*] continuing his technique of combining live action with animation.

But the real harvest came in 1965. Miloš Forman's *Loves of a Blonde* [*Lásky jedné plavovlásky*] was attacked as amoral because it introduced nudity. Antonín Máša debuted with his *Wandering* [*Bloudění*], Jiří Menzel shot his debut *Death of Mr. Baltisberger* [*Smrt pana Baltazara*], and Ivan Passer, a close collaborator on Forman's films, came with two films, *Intimate Lighting* [*Intimní osvětlení*] and *A Boring Afternoon* [*Fádní odpoledne*]. These two films immediately made Passer one of the best directors in Europe. Hynek Bočan shot *No Laughing Matter* [*Nikdo se smát nebude*] and Pavel Juráček his second film *Every Young Man* [*Každý mladý muž*]. Also, Karel Kachyňa made his *Long Live the Republic* [*Ať žije Republika*], Zdeněk Podskalský *White Lady* [*Bílá paní*], and Otakar Vávra *Golden Rennet* [*Zlatá Reneta*]. And finally, but most importantly, Jan Kadár and Elmar Klos made their *The Shop on the Main Street* [*Obchod na korze*]. This film, for the first time in the history of Czech cinema, won the Academy Award for Best Foreign Film.

The year 1966 was equally successful. Věra Chytilová shot *Daisies* [*Sedmikrásky*], another milestone in Czech cinema. Together with Ester Krumpachová (script and art design) and Jaroslav Kučera (cinematography), she created a bizarre comedy in the setting of a highly stylized reality. The film used language totally incomprehensible to the Communist establishment. Evald Schorm shot *The Return of the Prodigal Son* [*Návrat ztraceného syna*], Jan Schmidt *The End of August in the Hotel Ozone* [*Konec srpna v hotelu Ozon*], Antonín Máša *Hotel for Strangers* [*Hotel pro ciz-*

ince], Karel Kachyňa *Carriage to Vienna* [*Kočár do Vídně*], Václav Vor-
líček *Who Wants to Kill Jessie?* [*Kdo chce zabít Jessie?*], Otakar Vávra
Romance for Trumpet [*Romance pro křídlovku*] and Jiří Menzel *Closely
Watched Trains* [*Ostře sledované vlaky*] — his most successful film. Based
on the novel by Bohumil Hrabal, this film brought Menzel the Academy
Award for Best Foreign Film, the second for Czech cinema in a few years.
Then Jan Němec came up with the film that shook the highest places in
the government, including President Antonín Novotný — *Report on the
Party and the Guests* [*O slavnosti a hostech*], one of the most significant
films of the Czech New Wave. The film was an allegory of a process common to any totalitarian regime — the pressure to accept official opinion
and the elimination of those who refuse to go along.

One of the problems with the film was the casting. All of the characters were played by well-known personalities of Prague's cultural life.
The whole film feels like a nightmare — regardless of people constantly
talking, the result is indolence and alienation. Antonín Novotný, the
president of Czechoslovakia, went ballistic and the film was banned. It
was released for a short period during spring of 1968 and was then locked
in a vault again for the next 20 years.

In 1967, before the dust could settle, Jan Němec came out with his
new film *Martyrs of Love* [*Mučedníci Lásky*]. While this film wasn't political at all, it had something equally dangerous — it was totally unintelli-
gible to the Communist party officials. The film consisted of three surreal
stories connected by one theme — shy lovers. This lyrical, highly emotional film was the last straw for Němec's career. It was the last feature
film he shot in Czechoslovakia until his return from emigration in 1990.
Miloš Forman shot *Firemen's Ball* [*Hoří, má Panenko!*], a great metaphor
about stupidity, dullness and incapacity, Hynek Bočan *Privat Hurricane*
[*Soukromá vichřice*], Evald Schorm *Saddled with Five Girls* [*Pět holek na
krku*], and Jiři Menzel *Capricious Summer* [*Rozmarné léto*]. From the older
generation, Jiři Krejčík came with two films, *Wedding Under Supervision*
[*Svatba jako řemen*] and *House for Bachelors* [*Penzion pro svobodné pány*],
Jiří Weiss shot *Murder Check Style* [*Vražda po našem*], Karel Kachyňa
Night of the Bride [*Noc nevěsty*], and František Vláčil, after four years of
exhausting work, finished his historical poem *Marketa Lazarova* [*Markéta
Lazarová*]. This film became the most beautiful and most cruel histori-
cal film in the history of Czech cinema, and can be compared with the
monumental films of D.W. Griffith. Another newcomer, Slovak director
Juraj Jakobisko shot his debut *Crucial Years* [*Kristovy roky*].

Barrandov Sudios (photograph by Jiří Antalovský).

Nineteen sixty-eight was a year of great political turmoil and freedom. Offical censorship almost disappeared. The Czech and Slovak filmmakers were riding high and at full speed. It looked like nobody could stop them. Jaroslav Papoušek shot *The Most Beautiful Age* [*Nejkrásnější věk*], Juraj Hertz *The Cremator* [*Spalovač mrtvol*], Dušan Hanák *322,* Jan Schmidt *Lanfiery Collony* [*Kolonie Lanfieri*], Antonín Máša *Looking Back* [*Ohlédnutí*], Jiří Menzel *Crime in the Nightclub* [*Zločin v Šantánu*], František Vláčil *The Valley of the Bees* [*Udolí včel*], Juraj Jakubisko *Deserters and Nomads* [Zbehovia a pútníci] and Karel Vachek his documentary feature *Elective Affinities* [*Spřízneni vlobou*], a harsh but persuasive documentary about the Prague Spring Revolution.

The Soviet-led invasion of Czechoslovakia in August 1968 didn't slow the pace of the film industry. On the contrary, 1969 was the most productive year. Many of the best films of the Czech New Wave were shot then. It was the climax of the whole movement before its sudden death in January 1970. Pavel Juráček shot *Case for Rookie Hangman* [*Případ pro začínajícího kata*], inspired by Part III of Swift's *Gulliver's Travels.* The film, drafted as a dream, was, in Juraček's words, "about the confidence and safety that stupidity gives to fools." Evald Schorm shot *The End of the Priest* [*Farářův konec*], Jiří Menzel *Larks on the String* [*Skřivánci na niti*], Karel Kachyňa *Funny Old Man* [*Směšný pán*], Hynek Bočan *Honor and Glory* [*Čest a sláva*], Otakar Vávra *Hammer Against*

Witches [*Kladivo na čarodějnice*], Vojtěch Jasný *All My Good Countrymen* [*Všichni dobří rodáci*], Jaromil Jireš *Joke* [*Žert*] and *Valery and the Week of Wonders* [*Valerie v říši divů*], Juraj Jakubisko *Birds, Orphans, and Fools* [*Vtáčkovia, siroty a blázni*], Ello Havetta *Party in the Botanical Garden* [*Slavnost v botanické zahradě*] and Věra Chytilová *The Fruit of Paradise* [*Ovoce stromů rajských jíme*], "a symphony of surrealist estheticism," as Antonín Liehm put it.

In 1970, new management was appointed to Barrandov Studios and to the Czech film industry in general. Comrade Jiří Purš became the General Manager of Czech Film, Kamil Pixa was appointed as General Manager of Short Film Studios (Krátký Film) and Ludvík Toman dropped out of nowhere into the Barrandov Studios as a Chief Dramaturg. Only a few films were finished that year — Ester Krumpachová's *The Murder of Dr. Lucifer* [*Vražda ing. Čerta*] and Karel Kachyňa's *The Ear* [*Ucho*]. Other films in production and post-production were stopped and the prints were not made. Many films released in previous years were banned as well. More films were banned in 1970 than during the previous 20 years of communism! There is no official roster of banned films but we can list those not finished, or pulled from distribution. The following films were

FAMU — Film Academy in Prague (photograph by Jiří Antalovský).

stopped: Hynek Bočan's *Reformatory* [*Pasťák*], Ivan Balada's *Pavilon No.6* [*Pavilon č.6*], Ladislav Helge's *How Bread Is Made* [*Jak se peče chleba*], Václav Matějka's *Nakednes* [*Nahota*], Ivan Renč's *Prison Guard* [*Hlídač*], Evald Schorm's *Dogs and People* [*Psi a lidé*], Vladimír Drha, Otakar Fuka and Milan Jonáš' *The Visits* [*Návštěvy*], Zdeněk Sirový's *Mourning Party* [*Smuteční slavnost*], Drahomíra Vihanová's *Dull Sunday* [*Zabitá Neděle*], and Karel Vachek's untitled first fiction film. Many films waited the next 20 years for their premiere. (See complete list of banned films in note 74.)

The creative core of the Czech New Wave had broken apart. Some filmmakers immediately left the country after the 1968 Soviet occupation (Forman, Passer, Kadár, Jasný, Weiss), and some followed later (Juráček, Němec, Vachek). Those who stayed were not allowed to make films for several years. Jiří Menzel didn't shoot his next film until 1974, Hynek Bočan 1974, Věra Chytilová 1976, Zdeněk Sitový 1978, Evald Schorm 1988, Jan Němec 1990, and Drahomíra Vihanová 1994. Others, like Ladislav Helge, Ester Krumpachová and Pavel Juráček, didn't get another chance to make films.

Josef Škvorecký ended his 1970 book *All the Bright Young Men and Women—A Personal History of the Czech Cinema* (Horizont 1999) with the following words: "Barrandov Studios leaves the path, which ten years ago young graduates from the Film Academy took and moved on, following in the footprints of Hollywood. The Hollywood with a Marxist-Leninist coat." He had no idea that 20 years later in 1990, Barrandov Studios would become a shooting stage for the Hollywood film industry and Czech filmmakers would be left out on the street, unable to afford to shoot there any more.

After the Velvet Revolution, the former General Manager of Czech Film from the Normalization era, Jiří Purš, said in an interview, "There were no banned films before 1989. There were only films that the audience didn't have any interest to see."

Antonín Máša

DIRECTOR, SCREENWRITER

How would you characterize the Czech New Wave?

I would characterize the Czech New Wave politically because it is tied up with politics, and because it was in opposition to official film. Regardless if it was Vojtěch Jasný[1] or the generation before us, František Vláčil,[2] the oppositional element against the trends in culture and politics was always there. I also see it as an opposition movement against what was taught at the Film Academy[3] at that time, against how films "should be made." And then some students from the Film Academy got together, and with some filmmakers from the older generation, created a group. What came out of it was later labeled the Czech New Wave. I see it from Vojtěch Jasný and Karel Kachyňa to the youngest Jiří Menzel.

Somebody said that Otakar Vávra was the father of the Czech New Wave.

I don't know who thinks that Otakar Vávra is the father of Czech New Wave. I don't think he is. I believe that he taught his students how to make films well. In that sense, yes. They all suddenly knew how to make good films. Like Evald Schorm,[4] Jiří Menzel and the others. However, Miloš Forman[5] and Ivan Passer, or Jaromil Jireš, were not under Vávra's influence and they were a significant part of the movement as well. So I believe this idea comes out of gratitude from his students (there were five of them) to their professor. But those trends, which led to the birth of the New Wave, they came from other places, from literature, French

Antonín Máša (photograph by Robert Buchar).

cinema and the social movement which lead into the year 1968. It went parallel with the critical spirit of that period — an urgency to express reality, to speak the truth. Otakar Vávra definitely had nothing to do with that.

And then the Soviet Invasion happened with all its consequences.

Exactly. That was the fatal blow for some of us. Because a system of so-called screenings was established which served as a vehicle to knock out some inconvenient filmmakers, directors and producers, like Jaromír Kalista and so on. In these screenings, everybody knew how crucial the attitude toward the Soviet Union was and any opinions on the occupation of Czechoslovakia by the Warsaw Pact Armies. It had to be clearly formulated in writing. There was a specific line for it in the questionnaire — "Your opinion about the entry of armies" — was how they phrased it. Whoever wrote that he disagreed with the entry of armies had nothing more to say. There was nothing more to talk about. He was simply out of the game.

Most people chose some sort of compromise. Like, "I am not thrilled about it, but it's not too bad." This is a historical fact but, of course, today it's not kosher to remind people that it was so simple. But it was exactly that simple. Anyway, whoever stayed at Barrandov Studios[6] at that time answered the question positively, "Yes, I agree with the entry of armies," or he found a way, a smarter way.... I don't know how, to get around it...

Some of them actually hired a lawyer to formulate the answer some smart way — to save both their job and face at the same time. That allowed them to stay at Barrandov Studios. It was, of course, a great dirty trick from the regime — from those new people who rose to power after the 1968 occupation here.

Hotel for Strangers, 1966 — Actors (left to right) Jiří Kodet as Jiří, Petr Štepánek as Petr Hudec, and Jiří Hrzán as Kája. Antonín Máša, director, screenwriter; Ivan Šlapeta, DP; premiere screening March 24,1967; produced by Filmové Studio Barrandov (courtesy National Film Archive Prague, photograph by Josef Janoušek).

How was censorship at the end of the 60s?

Censorship was at work, of course, but as I said, all the way from the top of the party leadership, from the Politburo, the Ministry of Culture, they became somehow uncertain. Some of those in the Politburo, Pacovský, for example, who later signed Charta 77,[7] was on our side while working on the Central Committee of the Communist Party. He supported the new film movement and tried to help as much as possible. There was official censorship, too, but at the time they only watched the dialogue, not the overall concept. They were bureaucrats reading scripts. They had a list of what was prohibited to say. You couldn't slander the Soviet Union or slander the Communist movement, and you couldn't insult the army. Censorship always exists, but it wasn't ideological censorship any more. Ideology was controlled by another authority. Official censorship only watched dialogue, cutting out individual sentences they thought were wrong. The decision to ban a film after it was shot was not made by censors, but by the party leadership. The official censors were just checking the dialogue in films, eliminating individual sentences they thought could be somehow controversial. So there were two parallel things. Because the decision to approve the production of a film or ban it after it was finished was not done by the censors but by the party officials. For example, the film *Place in the Crowd* was made but not released for nine months because they believed it was ideologically wrong. It took many meetings and screenings before they released it to the theaters, but that was orchestrated by a special department of the Central Committee of the Communist Party, not by the censorship department.

Do you mean comrade Müller?
Many different people were there. Müller[8] came in the 70s.

And what then, after the Soviet Invasion?
To follow up on censorship, censorship was gone forever. Official censorship was never reinstituted, but new leaders appointed to all the cultural institutions fully made up for it. And they were very efficient because of people like Ludvík Toman,[9] whose only mission was to watch the film industry, to avoid the production of ideologically wrong films. They also organized and found people willing to shoot politically correct films. I don't know what topics, for example the glorification of [the] Communist party. Evald Schorm refused. He could have easily gotten work if he would have been willing to shoot a film about the Communist activist Zika, who was actually killed during the German occupation. But the script glorified the Communist party. So, he could have paid his dues, if he would have taken the script and made the film. Then he would have been in a position to make other, maybe better films. Adaptations of good literature, etc., but he refused and because of that he was not allowed to work until the late 80s.

There is an opinion that there was nothing wrong with joining the Communist party for the purpose of making good films. What do you think?
That's a very complicated question. I'd like to emphasize that this issue is very personal and I would never dare to write an essay about it or something that would be published, because I have no objective opinion about it.

I can only tell you my personal opinion and I want to say that I discussed this issue back in the 70s with the writer Eva Kantůrková, a signatory of Charta 77 and a strong adversary of the Communist regime, who was banned from publishing. Anyway, she defended the position that a talented artist in any field, poet, painter, filmmaker, has a direct obligation to society to do anything he can to exercise and implement his talent. My opinion was and still is that, sure, it is possible, but in that work, if it is really artwork and not just a commercial film from an assembly line, show business, if it is a work of art, then the artist's problematic morality always comes to the surface somehow and it will show up in his work. Simply put, it hurts the film.

She brought up, for example, our poet Vítězslav Nezval[10] who was — talk about social morals — quite political. He flirted with the Communist party and later became a party official and worked in the ministry. And simultaneously he was writing good poetry. But his poems, which appeared to be good at the time — like Edison for example — didn't look so good a few years latter. They were technically, verbally, nice but the meaning evaporated with time. Now they are just nice poems without a meaning.

On the other hand, Vladimír Holan[11] was a person with high moral integrity. He didn't get involved in politics — except for a few poems in 1945 celebrating the liberators, which was spontaneous and normal at the time. He lived a secluded life and the values in his poems are timeless. Of course, you can't apply this as simply to filmmaking because a film is a product of many people. However, I believe this plays an important role in film as well.

The way one sees the world, how he thinks, what stand he takes against authority — that's what I see as morality — how to act against power, any form of power. It can even be the power of money, the power of capital. In our case it was the power of a totalitarian government and if anyone thought he could cheat his way through... I don't believe anybody fully succeeded.

What is your opinion of contemporary young filmmakers?

I think that young filmmakers know the craft very well. I think they do. But if I look at them as serious authors, artists, then I believe they have nothing to say. It is just filmmaking for the sake of making films, just to do this interesting activity if somebody likes it. But, compared with the 60s or 50s, not only in Prague, but also in Moscow, Poland,

Italy or France, the bottom line was to express something, to make a statement. A personal statement, a subjective statement, or neo-realism which survived into the 60s, let's say objectified that statement. Anyway, it was about saying something, being like a poet, let's say. Today, this is, for good or bad, definitely gone. Films are made today for the audience to like, for entertainment, which is fine, or to succeed in some exclusive film festival. That's how I see it. But this personal involvement of the author is not there. To say at any cost — this is how I see the world. Who knows if the new generation asks themselves these questions? I believe they don't. What is my opinion, what do I want, how do I see this world? They take life as it comes. And I believe that these deeper reflections are missing.

Do you believe that freedom suppressed creativity?
     I wouldn't say that freedom suppressed creativity. Absolutely not. Because as we can see in other areas of art, for example fine arts and music, creativity is flourishing. Very interesting stuff has arisen because of the open contact with the West. The situation in film is more complicated because it costs a lot of money to make a film. A filmmaker is in a different position than a painter who needs just a palette, a brush, a canvas and paint. A painter is pretty much free. A filmmaker has to face limitations. He must find money first. It's true that in the 60s we experienced something that the French or Germans didn't. Socialism suddenly somehow weakened and the ideological control shattered a little — just enough to open a space for a limited form of free expression — but there was no problem as to who would pay for it. The government paid the bill. Once the script was approved there was no money problem. Today the issue of raising money is the bottom line in filmmaking. I believe that the author has more creative freedom when television produces the film then in the situation where private investors are involved because then the pressure to make a profit is much higher. But on the other hand, films produced by television rarely get a theatrical release, they are made just for the TV screen. And the filmmaker must keep this in his mind.

I hear often from young filmmakers here that present times don't offer any theme. There is no appealing topic.
     I believe there is a theme, for young filmmakers especially. I think there are some, maybe a lot of talented filmmakers who want to make narrative films, and this theme is very simple: to speak truthfully about

their generation. A personal story, that's what I am missing. That is their mission. I, as an audience member, don't know and can't know these young people, and nobody is telling me about them, not even the writers. There are no writers here to talk about themselves, about the generation of 20-, 30-year-olds. There are no filmmakers here to do this, and, if there is a film about young people, it is conventional and you can feel it's not authentic. It's not an authentic statement or it's superficial. It would be enough if somebody would just show up, he doesn't have to be a filmmaker as good as Miloš Forman or Ivan Passer, but if he could show young people realistically as Miloš Forman did... Because what was interesting about Forman, what was actually shocking, was the realism of his statement. And that's what is missing today. For example, look at Jan Svěrák's *A Ride*. Jan Svěrák is a great talent. But the film is ... focused too much on effects, the form and so on. But the story about those three people, the statement itself, is superficial.

What would you do if you could live your life again?
I can't tell you what I would do because I am not in that situation. I would know better about what I can expect, what's ahead. However, when one wrote that one didn't agree with the entry of armies or in some other way expressed this opinion, you pretty much knew what to expect and what would happen to you.

Then it is, of course, the question of internal personal freedom. Because I believe that excuses like "the system was not free, it was a totalitarian system..." are just that, excuses. I am saying that even in that system, one could behave relatively freely. Of course, it was risky, but one could behave freely. And I don't like that many people today are blaming the system, using it as an excuse. "We had to participate in the elections," everybody says. It's not true at all. We didn't participate and we were not arrested. I just couldn't make any films. And that wasn't such a great punishment, I would say. And no great bravery was necessary. It wasn't life-threatening. Our son even finished college. So it's only an excuse. People were far too scared for no reason. It is the same as if the Secret Police tried to recruit you to become an informer. It happened to me once. It was horrible, because for that one week they focused on a person, I assume they didn't spend more time on me, they tapped your phone and learned a lot and when they called you in or came to visit you, it was really impressive because they knew everything. "We know everything about you," they said. They learned everything in a week. If you listen to somebody's phone calls for a week, you know whom he meets and so on. In addition to that, they activated agents and asked them, "What about Máša?" And then they impressed Máša, because they knew everything I said the day before in the Film Club. When I said, "No, I will not collaborate with you," then they made threats. None of those threats ever materialized and the promise "If you collaborate, you will be allowed to make films" didn't materialize either when I refused to collaborate. Nothing else happened. The question is if someone could buy an opportunity to make films by this. I believe he could, they would probably keep their promise, and there would be no risk to the children. However, in my case, they didn't follow up on their threats. So it is simply a problem of unfounded fear, and freedom or lack of freedom, internally. But this issue is topical everywhere. As long as humans are around this will be an issue. Today many people are again acting with a lack of internal freedom. For example, when ODS[12] got in power many people started to publicly support them because they believed it would help them to get somewhere. I don't think it help them at all. But they believed in it and they acted like that.

This is always a hot topic. Simply, if I don't want to do something, I don't do it! And if somebody does it and then tries to find an excuse, it doesn't matter what it is… Everybody must bear responsibility for his own actions regardless, or I must say to some extent regardless, of who is in power or what type of regime is in place.

Would you like to make another film?
No, definitely not. I wouldn't have the energy to do it. I gave up on that. But I would like to write a book. That's what I am working on now.

Filmography
ANTONÍN MÁŠA (1935–2001)

He was born at Višňová u Příbrami. Originally he studied at the Philosophical Faculty of Charles University but after he was expelled (together with Pavel Juráček) he worked for a regional newspaper. Later he went to FAMU to study screenwriting with Prof. František Daniel. As a student he wrote scripts for several thesis films which later were distributed in theaters (for directors Zdeněk Sirový and Evald Schorm). After graduating from FAMU, he worked at Barrandov Studios as a dramaturg and in 1965 debuted with his film *Wandering.* He also wrote scripts for TV plays and for theaters.

1990 — *Was It Us?* (director, screenplay)
1989 — *The Silence of Larks* (director, story, screenplay)
1980 — *Vacation That Sucks* (story, screenplay)
1977 — *Why Not Believe in Miracles?* (director)
1972 — *Rodeo* (director)
1968 — *Looking Back* (director)
1966 — *People from Trailers* (screenplay)
1966 — *Hotel for Strangers* (director)
1965 — *Wandering* (director, story, screenplay)
1964 — *Everyday Courage* (story, screenplay)

Jan Němec

DIRECTOR

Unfortunately, Jan Němec declined to give permission to print the interview we shot with him for my documentary film Velvet Hangover. *However, I will try to summarize it because without his story this book would be incomplete.*

Jan Němec's career as a filmmaker was never easy. He always made films that somehow ran into problems, either aesthetically or politically. He shot three films in Czechoslovakia. *Diamonds of the Night, Report About the Party and Guests* and *Martyrs of Love. Report About the Party and Guests* was personally banned by the president and Communist party chairman, Antonín Novotný.[13] Němec was one of a few people who were named as dangerous individuals and he was fired from Barrandov Studios (this was a decision from the Communist party and adopted by the Czech National Council, not the film studio). That's why Kamil Pixa,[14] the General Manager of Short Film Studios[15] (a famous secret police agent who was, despite all that, an interesting and charming man), once told him, "You know, Němec, we can't let you make movies. You are so clever and such a swine. You would learn how to do it better than those who we are allowing to work now, those non-talented cretins. You would build up your position and when the party and society stopped watching you, you would stab us in the back. You are unreliable. Simply forget about making films again."

He was slowly preparing to move out, as Roman Polanski[16] did. In

24

1968 it was possible. He prepared some projects. Němec wrote a feature script with Václav Havel,[17] the president of the Czech Republic in 1989-2003. (It was the only script Havel ever wrote originally for film. This script still exists today but was never produced.) Němec shot the first footage of the Soviet invasion in 1968. Shooting in crowds, he captured the images of the tanks rolling through Prague. On August 21 he smuggled it to Austria for broadcast on Austrian TV and via satellites around the globe. The first pictures the world saw of the invasion were his. It was no fun. His assistant was wounded (Russians shot off part of his face). Němec later returned to occupied Czechoslovakia. Of course, he was not allowed to make any films, and as he says, he stewed in his own juices until 1974 when, after some dramatic moments, he got permission to leave. The Communists let him out of the country in 1974 warning, that if he ever came back, they would find some legal excuse to throw him in jail. So, in fact, he was kicked out. From 1974 to 1989, Němec was wandering abroad.

Jan Němec (photograph by Robert Buchar).

He spent 12 years in America but he didn't make any movies there. He wasn't very happy, and when he saw Communism going to hell in Czechoslovakia he wanted to be a part of it. When Václav Havel became president, he decided to come back. President Havel was his second cousin and they were very good friends. Havel was the best man at Němec's wedding. Němec's thinking was that, if his relative was the president, he would have an open door everywhere. It didn't actually happen like that, but he started to make films again. Since then he has shot two features and some 15 documentaries. He lives in Slapy village and picks mushrooms in the forest near his home. When he was living in California, on the seashore, he got used to being alone. He doesn't go any-where, doesn't socialize, doesn't write articles for newspapers. He says, "I just work quietly by myself, watching everything around me malfunctioning somewhat." Because of pressure from students, he was invited to teach at the Film Academy in Prague. There he teaches documentary filmmaking, not directing, because "too many Communists are still teaching there."

Němec says that if he were to take the present situation seriously, he would be extremely disappointed. Because Czech society is (there is only one way to say it) fucked up. The only honest person is probably the president, and even he is doing plenty of dumb things. But at least he takes it seriously. Havel has character and is an honest man and he is aware that the Czech Republic is not an island, but that it is a part of Europe and the world. The demoralization that started during the short

Diamonds of the Night, 1964 — Based on Arnošt Lustig's fiction novel *Darkness Cast No Shadows*. Jan Němec, director, screenwriter; Jaroslav Kučera, DP; premiere screening September 24, 1966; produced by Filmové Studio Barrandov (courtesy National Film Archive Prague).

Nazi occupation and continued for 50 years under Communism (especially after 1968 during the 20 years of the so-called Normalization[18]) is widespread. People lost all decency. Simply put, people are ripping each other off. Each one is a bigger son of a bitch than the other, and everybody is looking to grab as much as they can. There is ruthlessness and enormous corruption, and at the same time self-indulgence and laziness. Nobody works, nobody wants to work. In the beginning, people were enthusiastic and saying, "Let's get rid of communism" because they believed they would then live like Austrians. They believed a higher standard of living, common in the West, would come immediately. But people in the West achieved that standard because they worked hard. Czechs would like to have capitalism but at the same time they would like to continue to live like they did under socialism — not work too hard, to

Report on the Party and the Guests, 1965 — Ivan Vyskočil as Host (left) and Jan Klusák as his adoptive son Rudolf (center). Story by Ester Krumpachová, script by Ester Krumpachová and Jan Němec; Jan Němec, director; Jaromír Šofr, DP; premiere screening December 30, 1966; produced by Filmové Studio Barrandov (courtesy National Film Archive Prague, photograph by Karel Jesátko).

cheat, to steal from others. So presently they have the worst from both systems there and most disgusting of all is the political scene represented by those two idiots-criminals Zeman[19] and Klaus.[20] They are criminals. They are worst than Communists because people elected them in free elections, gave them their trust, believed them, and now these two make fun of the whole nation, replacing each other in the government and paying themselves big money. All the important party posts are appointed the same way as during the one-party system. State property was stolen. By so-called coupon privatization[21] it was given away to specific crooks. Worst of all, the most important strings in the economy are in the hands of people from the old system — KGB[22] and StB[23] (secret police). And all this is with the silent approval of these so-called political representatives. After ten years, this country is heading for disaster; they will probably accept Albania into the EU sooner than the Czech Republic. People are bitching but they don't care. The demoralization of the people, the way they think, and their attitude is pretty bad. Němec doesn't believe he will live long enough to see better times, when people realize that they can't move forward by acting like clowns, tipping off one another and being spineless. He just can't talk about the situation seriously because it's horrible. But at the same time, he is not pessimistic. As he says, "I just see everything as it is. I don't have any illusions and don't look through rose-colored glasses. I learned how to survive, the art of surviving."

Němec describes the Czech film industry's present situation as "worse then ever." During the Nazi era, Czechs produced many films. Under the Communist regime, they produced even *more* films because the government supported the production of Czech films and was aware it was an integral part of the Czech culture and Czech tradition, and an expression of Czech talent. Because Czechs have more than football players, or Jaromir Jagr[24] and Dominik Hasek,[25] to look up to — they also have filmmakers with a tradition going back to the invention of cinema. After 1989, the new government declared itself a capitalist, market economy, and stopped its financial support of film production. Of course, films are being produced every year. "Desperate people always find money somewhere," Němec says. But it's obvious that these films are shot under desperate, half-amateurish conditions. One decent film may come along over every three years. It's a pity because in the best of times, 30-40 films were made every year. If the government would finance five good films each year, it would be sufficient. But it's not happening. So the situation is hopeless and when films like *Kolya*[26] or *Cozy Dens*[27] come out and everybody is celebrating, it makes it all worse. These films are stuffed with everything from politics to emotions to sentiment. They are actually artsy-looking pieces of kitsch. Films like these neglect the language of film and film culture. Actually they are TV plays — soap operas. Němec believes that contemporary Czech film doesn't exist!

The future.

Unfortunately, films cost a lot of money to make. You can't make a film without money, you can't draw it on a piece of paper. Němec believes that the reason nobody makes "art films" today is not because a lack of interest from filmmakers or the audience. It's because of the present economic situation. A civilized society should support production of these films. People always find a way to survive without being a servant, liar or informant. One day a better government will arise (like in France for example, which spends eight percent of the budget on the film production) and more and better films will be produced. It would be enough if the Czech government would spend 0.1 percent of the government's budget on film. This must happen one day and then students from FAMU will have an opportunity to make their films. But it will take some time.

Němec imagines that in the future there will be no Communists, no Nazis, but there always will be plenty of crazy people, dangerous people, terrorists and madmen. There will be no new ideology, for which people would be willing to kill themselves by the millions. People will find a democratic, progressive system like, for example, in America. Hopefully it will happen one day in Europe, too.

Filmography
JAN NĚMEC (born 1936)

He studied directing at FAMU and graduated in 1960 with his film *A Loaf of Bread.* His film *Report on the Party and the Guests* (1966) was personally banned by the president of Czechoslovakia, Antonín Novotný, and Němec was kicked out from Barrandov Studios. In 1974 he was forced to leave Czechoslovakia. He went to Germany, France, Holland and Sweden, and, in 1977, settled in the United States. He returned in Czechoslovakia in 1989. He teaches documentary filmmaking at FAMU.

2001—*Night Talks with Mother* (director, screenplay, DP, edit, music)
1996 —*Code Name Ruby* (director, screenplay)

1993 — *It Happened in the Fall* (director, screenplay)
1993 — *Americans in Prague* (director, screenplay)
1990 — *In the Heat of Imperial Love* (director, screenplay)
1975 — *Metamorphosis* (director, screenplay)
1975 — *Das Ruckendekollete* (director, screenplay)
1968 — *Oratorio for Prague* (director, screenplay)
1968 — *A Necklaces of Melancholy* (director, screenplay)
1966 — *Report on the Party and the Guests* (director, screenplay)
1966 — *Martyrs of Love* (director, screenplay)
1967 — *Mutter und Sohn* (director, screenplay)
1965 — *Crooks* (director, screenplay)
1964 — *Diamonds of the Night* (director, screenplay)
1960 — *A Loaf of Bread*

Awards

Golden Leopard 2001 in Locarno (*Night Talks With Mother*)
Pesaro Film Festival 1964 (*Diamonds of the Night*)
Venice Film Festival 1964 (*Diamonds of the Night*)
Grand Prix of the Mannheim Film Festival 1964 (*Diamonds of the Night*)
Grand Prize in Oserhausen 1960 (*A Loaf of Bread*)

Saša Gedeon

DIRECTOR

What does New Wave mean to you? Have their films influenced you?

The Czech New Wave. They called the Czech New Wave a "Czechoslovak Film Miracle." It is a very flattering term, so it must leave some imprint on everybody, or at least on all filmmakers. I think that the new generation of filmmakers is not connected with the New Wave. They don't try to rationalize it, analyze why it worked and then build on it. The influence, if any, is on a subconscious level. Film critics saw in my films the influences of Ivan Passer, Miloš Forman or early Jiří Menzel. I never studied or analyzed their films. Somehow I'd sucked it in like a sponge. Like it or not, we are not living in isolation and are not immune to the history. We live in continuity. So, I believe that it is definitely a strong point in the history of Czech cinema from which we all thrive on, even if we don't want to.

Is there any common theme today?

No, I don't believe so. There is no one single theme. The New Wave was united by opposition against the regime, against its ideology and esthetics. The situation today is so fragmented. The direction we are going in is not clear. Nothing is black-and-white and the new generation of filmmakers is actually a bunch of isolated individualists. One wants to make commercial films, the other comedies or drama, somebody wants to be sarcastic. The tendency to analyze social issues is miss-

31

Saša Gedeon (photograph by Robert Buchar).

ing. Actually, I would say, they see the filmmaking more as a playground. Maybe that playfulness is a common theme of young filmmakers today.

How do you select a theme for your film?

My choice of topics comes from some internal reasons. Actually, I don't know where it's coming from. I choose topics that emotionally touch me. Usually they are related to human character: relationships, emotions, the polarity between men and women. These things are more interesting to me then social or political issues.

What is your definition of a "good film"?

Actually, I have a simple answer for it. I believe that film today must be, most of all, entertaining. It should compress time when you sit in the theater to intensify your feelings. Most films are doing that except for the fact that an hour later, after you leave the theater, you've forgotten what the film was about. And I believe that a good film is the one that doesn't bore you when you are watching it and a week later you still think about it because it deeply touched you. In the other words, it was an entertaining and enhancing experience simultaneously. That's what I would call a good film, when these two things are in balance.

What do you think of contemporary cinema?

The role of film in society is constantly evolving and changing. You asked about the 60s. Film then was perceived as a source of ideas. Unfortunately, the situation has changed a lot, and today probably nobody

Return of Idiot, 1999 — Pavel Liška as idiot-František. Saša Gedeon, director, screenwriter; Štěpán Kučera, DP; producer Petr Oukropec; premiere screening February 25, 1999 (photograph courtesy Negativ s.r.o.).

expects cinema to be a source of ideas. Everybody expects film to be a source of entertainment.

I perceive this as a significant and powerful shift. That means cinema is moving more in the direction of show business than in the direction of artistic self-expression. It logically leads to the fact that film is, more or less, a product to market. Even Lenin said that film is the most important art form, and I agree with him on that, but I believe that to try to "think with film" and communicate ideas on film is more and more difficult and strange. Somehow, it's not expected any more.

What can you say about the responsibility of filmmakers for the films they make?
Definitely there is a responsibility but it is hard to define it. I mean in general. I would say it's up to the individual. The responsibility of each individual, with its broad connections, is hard to trace. It's different

for everyone because everybody is different. I would say that the film-maker shouldn't manipulate viewers by putting out disinformation or twisting facts. Also, he probably shouldn't be anti-humanitarian if we are still willing to respect this codex. That shouldn't happen. Then he would become dangerous. This responsibility reaches everyone. But as we all know, film is an interesting phenomenon. Its personality reaches from an ethereal woman to a prostitute. That means it displays all expressions from spirituality to amorality. Film is a deep basket and that's what makes cinema bizarre.

What do you think of contemporary Czech cinema?
    As I see contemporary Czech film, the generation of directors from the 60s is fading out. The middle-aged generation has also lost touch with reality somehow and the new generation of filmmakers, in their thirties and younger, is coming up. They are fresh and energized. It is surprising. It looks like the older generations are out of the game. But the problem with this new generation is that they are like children. Or we are like children. We are suffering from adolescent problems. We have energy. We have talent, but we lack perspective, wisdom. We lack a spiritual and philosophical background. There is no tendency to analyze social issues. The young filmmakers approach filmmaking more as play, I would say. We are in a developing stage and suffering from many adolescent illnesses. We need more time.

Is it difficult to make a film in the Czech Republic today?
    It's strange and it differs from case to case. For someone it can be very difficult while for another one it can be quite easy. As we can see, it is not necessary to be a successful filmmaker to get money. There are two primary sources of the financing here: government grants and public television. Once you manage to secure money from these two sources, then you have a chance to produce your film, even a non-commercial film. Of course you need a good producer, crew and so on, but that's not impossible to find. But if you don't get financial help from the government, and television is not interested, then everything becomes much more difficult. Especially when you want to make a so-called "art film." If you want to make a commercial film, you can probably find investors. That's probably possible but I don't have any experience in that area. I don't think it's a safe way to finance a film anyway.

What is a commercial film?

Deciding if a film is commercial or non-commercial can be subjective or we can apply some criteria, like box office numbers. And even that is not a right parameter. No, it's always subjective. You can clearly see it in my films. Two-thirds of film critics say my films are "art films" suitable only for festivals and the rest of them say that my films are too much audience-oriented. So no two people can agree on this. But for me, what is important — and I said this before — is to make a film that doesn't pretend to be smart. Because some commercial films, like American films for example, are very smart. They are thought-out very well. The structure is brilliant, they are smart but they are not wise. They are cleverly structured to look intelligent, to catch attention, to convince viewers they are not wasting their time watching it. But in reality they don't give you anything. I like films that are wise because the filmmaker invests himself in the story. He takes a risk. You can see it easily. And I believe that this is a European specialty. Of course, this way sometimes you end up with a film nobody cares about. The film is not interesting. That's the danger of author's or non-commercial film.

Return of Idiot, 1999 (Saša Gedeon) — Pavel Liška as idiot-František (photograph courtesy Negativ s.r.o.).

So for me the non-commercial film starts where there is an element of wisdom or self-expression, a subjective view of the world or interpretation of life.

How did you become a filmmaker?
When I was 14 years old my parents told me the story of one of Fellini's[28] films. When they were describing it to me, I was imagining pictures and realized that this must be very different from films I ever saw. I realized that this filmmaker was doing visual poetry, something I believed was not possible or had not being done yet. At that moment I knew I wanted to make films, to make films a different way. Then I went to see another of Fellini's films. That experience touched me deeply and I decided to be a filmmaker. Later, when I came to study film at FAMU, there were other influences. My interest moved from Frederico Fellini to Robert Bresson[29] for his exactness, purity and asceticism. He inspired me a lot. But that's something not exactly popular here in the Czech Republic. From American filmmakers it was Jim Jarmusch[30] who inspired me greatly with his film *Stranger Than Paradise*. It actually somehow corresponds with the Czech New Wave — especially with Miloš Forman and Ivan Passer — the way it digs out the true and deep meanings out of banality. Jim Jarmusch looks like Miloš Forman's brother when you watch this film, *Stranger Than Paradise*. Anyway, it helped me to realize that you can make a film that seems to be about nothing while it's about everything. I found this idea very intriguing and it gave me the strength and energy to make films like that.

What would you say about the present state of democracy in the Czech Republic?
I am not good at politics, but if I compare today with what we had before, then it is democracy. If I compare it with our conception of democracy, then it is not democracy. In the other words, it is a democracy with many disorders, or a democracy where the rules are not working yet. Anyway, I feel a free space. I perceive democracy as freedom in this new state. Democracy as a system has yet to develop. It takes time. Freedom came overnight and it is chaos, which can be very positive and also very negative, depending on how we use it. So, I see this freedom, and it is amazing to me. The information boom is amazing. We have access to all that stuff we couldn't read, hear and freely work with in the past. That creates chaos, of course, but for me as an artist, or just as a

human being that wants to learn and create, this freedom is extremely important. I can excuse the deficiencies of democracy.

What do you think about foreign film influence on Czech cinema?
I don't think this is just a Czech problem. The information boom in all areas, from politics to spiritual issues, is pulling the whole world together creating an information vortex. It creates chaos but also a creative climate as well. All cultures are coming closer together, mixing together, which wasn't possible in the past. I believe that's good. I see that as very positive because it is pulling us from our isolation, from our egocentrism. It's somehow very creative even if it appears to be chaos. There is nothing to do about it. It has to evolve.

Filmography
SAŠA GEDEON (born 1970)

He came to FAMU to study directing in 1988. The short films he shot at school received many awards at international film festivals. He graduated from FAMU in 1995 with his debut *Indian Summer.*

1999 — *Return of Idiot* (director)
1995 — *Indian Summer* (director)
1994 — *Štace* (director, story, screenplay)
1991— *Zavřeno pro rodinný smutek* (director, screenplay)

Awards
Czech Leo Award 1999 for directing (*Return of Idiot*)
Jury Award at IFF in Sao Paulo (*Return of Idiot*)
Prix Europa 1999 (*Return of Idiot*)

Jiří Menzel

Director

Which period was best for you, the most happy, personally?
It was in the 60s when I started. It was such an ideal time, ideal atmosphere, ideal place to make films. On one side, there was an ideological ease and plenty of topics for films, but on the other side there wasn't total freedom, so there was a stimulus for creativity to break the ideological barrier.

On the other hand there was an economical irresponsibility here. Nobody was responsible for anything. That was good for young debuting directors because nobody risked anything. There was a demand for our films. The whole cultural atmosphere was ideal for filmmaking. I was lucky enough to have had an opportunity in filmmaking at that time and was able to make, together with others, a few films. It was a happy time period for me as a filmmaker. For me as a citizen, of course, a happy time is today. It is much better today than it was during the time of the Bolsheviks.

What were the consequences of the Soviet Invasion in 1968 on Czech cinema?
The consequences of the Russian invasion? Big changes took place, even moral changes. Many people gave up and realized — like myself — that the world was not as ideal as we thought it was. That people were not as good as we believed. I was raised in a bourgeois family, in comfort,

without any conflicts or stress. I lived my life believing that there is something good inside of every human being. And then I discovered that this was not true! I suddenly realized that some people are purely evil. It was a bitter discovery for me. Also, many people were fired from jobs.

Simply put, Communists did what the Nazis didn't dare. They let people with bad professional skills be their servants. Nazis never made an alliance with Member of the Flag and people of the lowest social order. Here, Communists and bad professionals caught the opportunity and used politics to advance their careers. It wasn't only in the film industry. It was in literature, in all areas.

Suddenly anyone could point a finger at you and say, "You are against the new regime. Get out of here!" And you were out. Even if you were, for example, a good engineer, you were fired and your job went to a poor, adaptable engineer loyal to the new regime. And that's what brought this regime finally down: because they put unqualified and morally repugnant people in all the top positions. And this happened in the film industry. Films degraded esthetically and technically as well. They stopped shooting sync sound and used lip sync instead. They started shooting faster to make more money. Not to mention the fact that they started shooting bad films. People didn't believe in the quality of their work any more. The decline in the quality of films (and filmmakers as well) happened very quickly.

Decisions about what films would be shot at Barrandov Studios were then made by the chief dramaturg, Ludvík Toman.

Not just Ludvík Toman. Toman was only a puppet, a very willing puppet in the hands of our colleagues. Because directors Jiří Sequenc, Jaroslav Balík, Václav Matějka, and Jaroslav Vorlíček, were fully aware that they had no chance when compared with the New Wave. They would have to live in the shadow. Their first objective was to bury all those who were successful, and Toman did that for them with pleasure because he was a failed filmmaker himself.

This didn't happen just in film. A bad actor became the director of the National Theater. He always played supporting roles and, of course, he didn't want any good actors to act with him. A third grade writer became the Chairman of the Writers' Association. They couldn't stand someone like Bohumil Hrabal,[31] Arnost Lustig[32] or Milan Kundera[33] in that position. Simply put, the first action of these people was to get rid of the competitors, their better-qualified, more talented colleagues. And

they had a great, very efficient weapon in their hands to do it — the new regime, the Bolsheviks' regime, in which those who didn't quickly show their loyalty to the Russian occupation were unable to work any more. I would call it a "Biafra of intellect."

And what about those who joined the Communist party and the militia, like Karel Smyczek for example, just to be able shoot films?

Watch out! Karel Smyczek and Dušan Klein are respectable people. They are clean-handed.

Jiří Menzel (photograph by Robert Buchar).

They had to do it. I don't know about Klein, but Smyczek joined the Communist party. But they wouldn't have been allowed to make films without it.

This is a different matter. This is about Vorlíček and his like who were in the Communist party for a long time and did everything possible to stop non-members from making films. It's like Karel Capek[34] said in his novel *From the Life of Insect.* Two slugs there are saying, "What's important is to have a lot of cabbage for just a few slugs." And this was the motto dominating the 70s.

Are you saying that joining the Communist party for the purpose of making good films was okay?

If you want to make a good film and there is no other way, then you have the right to join the Communist party if that film is worth it. To join the party and make films just for money is low. It's not worth it. But I know that if Vojtěch Jasný wasn't in the Communist party, he wouldn't have made the nice films he did. It is the same as blaming someone who immigrated. If Miloš Forman hadn't immigrated, he never would have made all those nice films he did in America. Excuse me for putting

Closely Watched Trains, 1966 — Václav Neckář as Miloš Hrma (right) and Josef Somr as train dispatcher Hubička in the adaptation of Bohumil Hrabel's novel. Jiři Menzel, director; Jaromír Šofr, DP; premiere screening November 18, 1966; produced by Filmové Studio Barrandov (courtesy National Film Archive Prague, photograph by Jiři Stach).

it in the same bag, but conditions are never ideal. In those days, there was this condition to be a member of the Communist party, and maybe I have more respect for those who swallowed it and worked than for those who didn't overcome their pride, didn't join the Communist party and didn't make the good films they could.

It's hard to make a judgment. But I definitely wouldn't look down on someone who was in the Communist party and didn't take advantage of it for himself, and helped others.

How would you compare that period with today?
It was a period of innocence. People, because they lived in isolation, also lived in a kind of innocence. We knew what was bad, what was wrong with the system. The Bolsheviks' propaganda was hopelessly toothless.

Larks on a String, 1969 — Václav Neckář as Pavel Hvězdář in the adaptation of Bohumil Hrabal's short story *An Ad for the House Where I Don't Want to Live.* Jiří Menzel, director; Jaromír Šofr, DP; premiere screening January 1, 1990; produced by Filmové Studio Barrandov (courtesy National Film Archive Prague, photograph by Josef Janoušek).

It was ridiculous. Everybody knew it was stupid. But that's why people were out looking for quality. Like the films of Ingmar Bergman or Frederico Fellini. Books were selling very well and quickly. There were many good books, good literature.

To be involved in culture was a sort of protest, a type of resistance. Everybody wished for it a little. Now, of course, there is nothing to resist and we were flooded with propaganda from the other side, which is much more sophisticated. This is the propaganda of a free individual who can do whatever he wants, who can break anything he wants. He can kill any time he wants. This is a destructive idea, which is very attractive to many artists and viewers alike. And morality suffers. And it's not just in the movies. It is on TV, in literature, music, everywhere. That shift away from humanity is not purposeful, but is simply profitable. People prefer evil to good. Good is boring, unfortunately, and artists are not aware of the fact that they are contributing to the dehumanization of people. This is probably the first time this has happened in human history, because throughout the history of the arts, from the Greeks and Egyptians, the arts always cultivated humans, educated, guided them to some spiritual values. Including so called "cheap art." It had a purpose. Today, it's different.

It's not because of a lost of creativity. This is the way of minimal resistance. First of all, it's much easier to do evil things, and secondly it's more attractive. People want it more. It sells better. And even if there is an anti-violence film, you can see that the creators are actually impressed with the violence. They enjoy it. Even as they pretend they are against it. Like for example Oliver Stone or David Lynch. These are people, how would I put it, with some kind of defect: psychological or maybe physical. Lately I've seen many films in film festivals made by young filmmakers and they all have, I hate to use that world "decadence." There is a lot of perversion in these films. Things which are against harmony, against humanity, against… They are films without any compassion. And compassion pertains to art.

Are you saying that the new generation of filmmakers is different?
They are trained that way, raised that way. When I ask them what they are interested in, they are not sure. They are interested in attractiveness.

When a student brings me a script with the action happening in a public rest room and that place has nothing to do with the story, when I see what environment he is attracted to I am bewildered. But the world is full of stories, very hearty stories. Things which would strike our hearts, make an impact on us. Because man has been given compassion, a feeling of togetherness with each other. But the new philosophical trend in the world is that man is an individual who should care only for himself. And that's a tragedy.

So, what can we expect in the future?
I will tell you something. I am glad I have no children. Because if I had any, I would be terrified of what's ahead for them. If you compare what was in the past and what is here today, you can pretty much imagine what will come tomorrow when we will be gone. It's not a pretty pic-

Larks on a String, 1969 — Jiří Menzel on the set with his friend and actor Rudolf Hrušínský in his lap (photograph by Josef Janoušek).

ture. Because I don't see any turning point where things could get better. The point where people would come to their senses, or at least a little bit, and would turn back to real values of humanity–to help each other. It is, it always was, in our genes but it's fading out from generation to generation. Generations of our ancestors were always reinforcing this, the awareness of a moral code in each individual. From books, the Bible and social life people were confirming what was good and what was bad. It's not happening today. It's inside us, the awareness of what is moral and what is conscientious. It's fading out from our children and in their children... I don't want even think about it.

This is the breaking point where people are starting to think differently. People had something common to talk about when they had the Bible or the Koran. The source of the information was the same for everyone. Today everybody reads only a few paperbacks and because of that the same words have different meanings for different people. Then people don't understand each other any more; they don't have the same upbringing, the same education. The era of a New Babylon will come. Not a linguistic Babylon, but a conceptual Babylon, a confusion of thoughts. Jesus Christ, I am so glad I have no children!

If you look back to the year 1965 and compare it with how you looked at the world then and how you see it today...

Until 1968 I strongly believed that everything bad was doomed. I believed that as human knowledge and intellect progressed people would become more educated and because of that also better. When I reached my thirties, I started to doubt it. I studied the history better. I had my own experience with the Soviet invasion, and I learned how people could change their characters under changed conditions. It was a great educational experience for me. I lost my faith that people would one day become better. And I believe that the films today are so brutal because the young generation today, compared to our generation, doesn't believe that people will become better. They know there will be no better times, that it is all about grabbing as much as you can now to enjoy your life, and not to think about the future. This is the normal philosophical

The Life and Extraordinary Adventures of Private Ivan Chonkin, 1993 — Jiří Menzel (behind the camera) on the set of his last film *Private Chonkin* with cinematographer Jaromír Šofr (right). Producers: Eric Abraham and Katya Krausová (photograph courtesy Jaromír Šofr).

approach of, not all, but the majority of young people today. Then there are people, who try to change this, and I hold them in high regard, but the methods they use are somehow toothless. They may be attractive, but they are worthless, because demonstrations, revolutions and violence won't change anything. The only chance for change will come from patiently hammering at people's awareness of an absolute moral code. That's the foundation. A moral person can't be racist, can't be an asshole and can't be a fascist. A moral person can't be politically, or in any other way, bad. He can be black, white or whatever color, but he can't do bad things if he's got morals. And there are not many people like that.

How difficult was it in the totalitarian regime to push a script through?

Actually it was easier than it is today. Now you have to beg potential investors and talk to many people. You waste a lot of time if you don't persuade them. The process was simple during the Bolshevik era. You had to know what stories were be approved and adjust to it. And if the story didn't get approved, you just didn't make that film. That was a standard procedure and it functioned quite well. You knew how far you could go and sometimes try to push the envelope a little bit further. Which later became possible. This experience, that the door of the censors could be gradually opened, came from the 50s and early 60s. Once in a while the door slammed in your face, but then it opened again. But you knew the rules of the game and realized that if you respected those rules you could make, within those boundaries, decent films. Now it is different. You can have a great idea but you must have the ability to convince investors that you are the only one who can make this great film and make a lot of money. If you don't have this ability, you can't make a film. And because I never learned to talk about myself as the best, I can't imagine myself walking from one bank to the other, talking to powerful people saying, "Look, I have a great idea. Give me money and I will make a great film!"

What is the situation in Czech cinema today?

I think that Czech film is doing okay. A bunch of good films have been shot, to my surprise. I am very optimistic. Unfortunately, there are some films nobody will miss but that's the same everywhere around the world. You never know ahead of time if the film will be good or bad. My only complaint about Czech film is that it doesn't have its foundation at Barrandov Studios any more. Films have to be made by makeshift means. It's sad because it hurts the films' quality.

What happened at the Film Academy? Why did you resign from the position of the Directing Program Chair?
They kicked me out, quite unfairly, too. There was a revolutionary atmosphere in the school at that time and students felt they could pull it off. They went on a strike. I wanted to bring order to the school. There was no discipline there. Filmmaking is a collaborative profession. You can't let an individual keep a camera indefinitely while others are waiting. You must establish strict deadlines for scripts, etc. Even FAMU is an art school, you can't let students come only when they feel like it. That wouldn't be a school. On the other hand, I didn't like how the school became excessively fat — too many administrative people, too many teachers, too expensive. The films they made were too expensive. I wanted to establish some order there. Some people didn't like what I was trying to do and found some silly excuse to get me out. For example, they said that I was neglecting my work at school, which was not true. They orchestrated a coup against my administrative assistant and they insisted I fire her. I refused and they went on strike. Later they apologized to me but I had to leave. I have quite bitter feelings 'til today. I told myself I would never walk in that building again.

It was also an issue of generational dissonance. Young people don't like those who are established and successful. Maybe it's an issue of envy. I got pissed off. I didn't need anything from anybody. I was cool knowing that their buzzing was ridiculous and I didn't hide my attitude from them. I feel sorry about that. I think this was much worse than what the Bolsheviks did to me.

How did the Academy Award for your film, Closely Watched Trains, *affect your career?*
It didn't at all, because Russian tanks rolled in a couple months after I received the Academy Award. After that, everything was different. Well, I got a raise at Barrandov Studios but after the Oscar I shot just one more film, not so good, and then came the period of diminution. It didn't make any difference.

I have one funny story about the Academy Award. Regardless of my Oscar, nobody talked to me any more. I was blacklisted. When Miloš Forman received his first Oscar in the U.S. it didn't get in any media. Writing about it wasn't allowed. However, the Vice President of Barrandov Studios called me in and told me that something has to be done about that provocation [meaning Forman's Academy Award]. He said I must make a film that would get an Academy Award again. He thought I was a saboteur when I tried explaining to him that it's not so simple. He believed that I purposefully didn't want make a film that would get an Oscar. He was an alcoholic. But that shows what kind of people were there. He was a poet and a drunk. Otherwise a nice guy... he was Slovak, but I can't remember his name.

Which of your films do you like the most?
Some films didn't come out very well, some films failed and I would prefer not to talk about it. I put it this way — some films came out not so bad and some came out more bad.

Is film today still art or just an entertainment?
A question is, what is art? Are Steven Spielberg's films art? Or Francis Ford Coppola's? Or just Andy Warhol? I believe that what is important is what people walk out of the theater with. In that case I prefer Steven Spielberg against Andy Warhol regardless that for most snobs and intellectuals Andy Warhol is the bigger artist. I don't care. Steven Spielberg speaks in a positive way to more people and that's what I see as important. And as long as filmmakers like Spielberg or Woody Allen are around, the situation is not so bad.

Would you still like to make a film?
Sure, you know, I still have a hope to shoot *The King of England*. I would like to do it, but... I am afraid to talk about it.

How did you feel when you were beating your producer Sirotek[35] with the whip at the Karlovy Vary Film Festival?
It was a nice moment. I had the whip ready and I wanted to beat him in the lobby. But that fool came to me in the auditorium. It ended in the courtroom and I have to pay some money to charity now. Everybody envies me this moment.

Filmography
JIŘÍ MENZEL (born 1938)

He is the youngest of the Czech New Wave directors. He studied at FAMU in 1958–62 and graduated in 1965 with his thesis film *Our Mr.*

Foester's Died. He received an Academy Award for Best Foreign Film in 1967 for his film *Closely Watched Trains.* His next film *Larks on a String* ended up, after the Soviet invasion, in the vault for next 20 years, but he managed to come back to Barrandov Studios in 1974 and continue shooting film. He is also an actor — he acted in 22 feature films and he directs in theaters. He directed over 20 stage plays at home and 16 abroad. During 1990–92 he was a Chair of the Directing Department at FAMU. Since January 2000 he is the Artistic Director of Vinohrady Theatre in Prague.

1993 — *The Life and Extraordinary Adventures of Private Ivan Chonkin* (director)
1991— *The Beggars' Opera* (director, screenplay)
1989 — *The End of the Old Times* (director, screenplay)
1985 — *My Sweet Little Village* (director)
1983 — *Snowdrop Festival* (director, screenplay)
1980 — *Cutting It Short* (director, screenplay)
1976 — *Seclusion Near the Forest* (director)
1974 — *Who Seeks a Handful of Gold* (director)
1969 — *Larks on a String* (director, screenplay)
1968 — *The Crime at the Cabaret* (director)
1967 — *Capricious Summer* (director, screenplay)
1966 — *Closely Watched Trains* (director, screenplay)
1965 — *Crime at the Girls' School* (director)
1965 — *Pearls on the Bottom—* The Death of Mr. Baltisberger (director)
1963 — *Our Mr. Foester's Died* (director)

Awards

European Gold Medal 2000—Award of Italian Association of Film and
  Theatre Artists (UNUPANEC)
State Honour—Merit Medal 1996 from president Václav Havel
Czech Leo Award 1996—for artistic contributions to Czech cinema
Ennio Flaian Award 1996—for a life time achievement in film, in Pesaro
Audience Award and Jury Award at IFF in Vevey 1994 (*The Life and
  Extraordinary Adventures of Private Ivan Chonkin*)
Golden Medal of the President of Italian Senate at IFF in Venice 1994
  (*The Life and Extraordinary Adventures of Private Ivan Chonkin*)

Akira Kurosawa Award for Lifetime Achievement at IFF in San Francisco
   1990
Grand Prize at IFF in West Berlin 1990 (*Larks on a String*)
Best Film and Best Director Awards, IFF in Los Angeles 1990 (*The End
   of the Old Times*)
Emblem of Officer of the Order of Art and Literature from the Govern-
   ment of the French Republic, 1989
Directing Award at IFF in Montreal 1989 (*The End of the Old Times*)
Directing Award at IFF in Las Vegas 1989 (*The End of the Old Times*)
Golden Eagle Award at IFF at Rueil Malmaison 1989 (*The End of the Old
   Times*)
Jury Award at IFF in Montreal 1986 (*My Sweet Little Village*)
Audience Award at IFF in Valladoid 1986 (*My Sweet Little Village*)
The Golden Cane Award at IFF in Vevey 1982 (*Cutting It Short*)
Special Honorary Mention at IFF in Venice 1981 (*Cutting It Short*)
C.I. Caward at IFF in San Sebastian 1976 (*Seclusion Near the Forest*)
Golden Hugo Award at IFF in Chicago 1976 (*Seclusion Near the Forest*)
FIPRESCI Honorary Mention at IFF in Mannheim 1976 (*Seclusion Near
   the Forest*)
Grand Prix at IFF in Karlovy Vary 1968 (*Capricious Summer*)
Grand Prix at IFF in Mannheim 1967 (*Closely Watched Trains*)
Academy Award for Best Foreign Film 1966 (*Closely Watched Trains*)

Věra Chytilová

DIRECTOR

How is Czech film doing now?

Overall it's hard to say. I believe that a concept is missing. The same way the course of culture in general is totally missing. Because today, actually immediately after the fall of Communism, people were afraid to use the term "cultural politics" because it was used so much in the past. So, after the revolution, everybody did an about-face. They turned around 180°. An infantile turn. Anything goes but something from the past. If Lenin said that film was the most important art, then let's kick film in the ass, let's kick culture in the ass. Simply put it, film and culture are not trendy now.

I expected that after that period of enforced materialism we would have a spiritual period, and spiritual problems would become a priority. No! Today we have materialism, that is more materialistic than Marxism ever was. Now it's simply a fight for money. Before we had an ideology of propaganda, today we have an ideology of money. That's it. Something like a "mission" doesn't exist any more. That's what we had [back then]. We were willing to make films for free, if necessary, just to have a chance to say something, to express our opinion. Surprisingly, plenty of films are still being made under our present unfavorable condition — no financial support, no state grants (with the exception of the National Film Foundation,[36] which was mugged anyway because all kinds of cheating happened). Probably some dirty money was involved in the begin-

51

The Ceiling, 1961 — Věra Chytilová and director of photography Jaromír Šofr on the set of *The Ceiling* in 1961 (photograph courtesy Jaromír Šofr).

ning to finance filmmaking because people thought they could make a profit there. But later investors realized that there was no way to make money in film here because the Czech Republic is such a small nation. The whole of Europe is facing this problem because the English language market rules. [The English language market] is the biggest and producers and distributors are only interested in big money. Small money simply doesn't attract them.

So, do you see the situation as critical?

I am a member of the European Film Academy. We meet every year, and every year we discuss how to save European cinema. But we can do nothing because we have no control over distribution. The bottom line is that if the distributor wants an American hit movie, he must take the whole package, a shitload of other bad films, and they fill their theaters.

And the new generation is spoiled. They are voyeurs. We used to have a very sophisticated audience, an audience we could communicate with through film. When film had a mission, it had a cultural impact on society. It was a historical reflection of the society. Filmmaking has no dramaturgy today because anybody can make films. There are no creative teams any more that would know they could make, for example, five films. In the past, every team had 20–25,000,000 crowns and when films were made for 5,000,000 each, they knew they could make five films every year. They could systematically work on the development of scripts. They were employing a bunch of authors who worked on story ideas. Simply, it was known what was coming. And there was diversity in films,

Věra Chytilová (photograph by Robert Buchar).

diversity of ideas. Now anything can be in the film. If they are hunting an investor for a film, they put into the story anything he likes. If he thinks there must be sex, murder and all these audience-pulling stereotypes, then the film will look ... You know how.

I think regardless of the fact that we are so small a nation, we are still making a lot of movies because we have a great tradition in filmmaking. I believe around 20 films again this year. The quality is not too good, but once a while something okay comes out.

Is the problem in story ideas and scripts?
First of all, in the 60s writers who couldn't publish were hiding inside production groups. Good quality writers who knew how to write a script. When we filmmakers made our debut, when we came out of FAMU, the studio saw potential new talents and pushed us to generate new scripts. They were hunting us! I was shooting one film and they wanted to know what the next one would be about. I told them, I can't work on two films at the same time. I have to finish one, take a breath and look around and then slowly think about the next film. I can't work simultaneously.... And we wanted to make "auteur" films only. It had to

be "my film." Or in the worst scenario, if it was someone else material, we adapted it.

One always reflected one's own vision on the problems of that period. Topics always had a moral component. Topics based on ethical issues are always modern. But they don't want to hear about morality today. They don't want to hear about it, but I believe it's the bottom line of all human problems. That is the reason for everything that goes on here. The entire depressive atmosphere, the cheating–people have no reason to live. There is no enlightenment to live for a noble belief. The difference between now and then is that today the cultural front has completely broken apart. In the past, there was an active artistic community. Writers, artists, all communicated with each other. Writers had their clubs and filmmakers had their clubs where they met together. Today there is no platform whatsoever where we could meet. Do you know what the only platform we have today is? It is a funeral. When someone dies, we all get together and realize we are still alive!

That's because everything is spread around. There are many small production groups and special interest groups and so on, and we don't know about each other. Only a few people are keeping in touch. For example, I meet some people because I teach at the Film Academy. Or I keep in touch with my editor who is editing a film with somebody else. That's how I get information. But it's not like in the past when you stopped in once or twice a week at the Film Club where everybody was hanging around and you could talk to them. Every week there was a screening of new films and we talked about them. There was no jealousy, no spite or envy. No one put anyone or their projects down. It's horrible now! Shooting commercials has changed people's attitudes. The focus now is on making a lot of money. Also, everything has become very expensive. Actors want a lot of money. Or the lip-sync guys. Lip-sync became a gold mine! It is fine to make the money, I suppose, but at the same time these people must realize that they are wasting their productive lives as artists.

Was it a change for the worst?
    I have lived quite a long time and I went through many changes.... Every change brings damage, a deep loss. I don't know how many years every change takes. Now ten years have passed and there is still no consolidation in sight. I believe it must come from the top. The next government must enact some moral principles. Law must enforce it, but they

say no, no, it's against freedom. But freedom starts and ends with the freedom of others. It doesn't come by itself. There must be some rules, but they don't want any rules because there are some people.... Just look at how dirty the Parliament is! Parliament is dirty because so many of the deputies are businessmen and they shouldn't be doing business because there is a conflict of interest. And they don't pass any laws that would limit them. Take television law, for example. We wanted one crown from each videotape rental to go to the Cinema Fund. No! Not because they wouldn't like to charge an extra crown, but because it would bring tax control to their system. That kind of bullshit!

And they take a vote on it. They are not ashamed. They are not ashamed to give themselves a raise when the whole nation is down. They are not ashamed. I told them this at city hall when I got accidentally elected as a district representative to the city government. I thought I

Daisies, 1966 — Jiřina Cerhová and Ivana Karbanová (in the background) as Mary 1 and Mary 2. Script by Ester Krumpachová and Věra Chytilová; Věra Chytilová, director; Jaroslav Kučera, DP, premiere screening December 30, 1966; produced by Filmové Studio Barrandov (courtesy National Film Archive Prague, photograph by Pavel Dias).

could function there with my plain mind. But then I realized how many intrigues are involved in politics. You have to be a good lawyer and economist to achieve anything there. Because politics, and all politicians, revolve around money: around swindle and around money. All the tricks.... It's a chess game and you must be 20 moves ahead, to read their intentions, what they are after, where they are going. It's not enough to make indignant, primitive protests. They ridicule you. You would look like a great fool who knows nothing. Then you realize that you really know nothing. For example, I saw that after the revolution nobody was building any new houses. They completely stopped all housing development. And I protested. There was an apartment shortage in the past when we were building huge apartment complexes. If we stop now building low income housing, what will happen? Every month, every year of delay is a huge loss. No! Nobody listened. Then three years later they woke up. But three years were lost, creating a huge backlog. And so on. You can see these kinds of things everywhere around here.

So, what now? Give up?

I believe that a responsible person never gives up. You can't give up. You give up only when you are totally finished. But an active person who likes life and wants to be involved in the community can't give up. There are some people who say no, I am not interested and I will not read any newspaper. Bullshit! You see the same stuff on TV over and over gain, nothing new. And the truth about everything in the world you have to find somewhere else on your own. But I believe it is important to keep pushing. It's like a pressure cooker and it will blow one day. Like now, the political parties are in big trouble because the Communist party's influence is on the rise.[37] This is a clear result of bad politics by right-wing parties. They are responsible for it. It's not a failure of the social democrats — they are somehow mushy, slow and so on, but I don't believe they are responsible for the rising popularity of Communists. Well, they [social democrats] had some stupid ideas, but you can't judge them after one year. We should give them four years, but the social democrats are trapped now, they are cornered. Conservatives, because of the trends of a Communist comeback, have surrounded them. And that's actually good. I believe it's good. They can see their own mistakes now and they can wake up. But those same individuals who made those mistakes in the past will never wake up.

People who are immoral and don't hold any ethical values, these people will never become better. They have to leave. I think that Vaclav Klaus is a big obstacle. He must go away. People still support him regardless of how many scandals he goes through. That gives you an idea of how many dumb people we have here.

Look at Austria now. People don't like to see extremists gaining popularity. They are surprised where it's coming from. But those extremists are people who live with them every day. And that comes back to the issue of morality. It comes from the most primitive people, "Foreigners, you see, they look strange." Any time they see something new they are against it. They want to get rid of it. They are idiots! It's like in the village where I grew up. I couldn't wear different shoes because when I did, everybody pointed fingers at me, "Look at her shoes! She has different shoes!" That is why I moved to the city, to avoid living with imbeciles. And now you can see that the whole nation has no manners. They act like fools because they don't know anything. This riddle has roots somewhere in the beginning.

What happened when the first national budget was put together? Our representatives, those representing the cultural affairs, didn't even open their mouth. And when we asked them, "Why didn't you say anything? Why didn't you ask for any money?" They replied, "There was not enough money for education, not enough money for health care, and we were ashamed to ask for money for culture." But they didn't give any money to education and health care anyway! You see? When they are dying because there will be no doctors to help them, that will be another story. And because the way they are rising the new generation we will have to deal with the consequences one day. Then we will have to start again from scratch. I always believed that a continuity of knowledge would prevail, that we would get rid of bad things and to continue building up good things. It didn't cross my mind that we would turn back and do the same stupid things over again. But that's exactly what's happened. People are stupid and that's it.

What was the situation after the Soviet invasion in 1968?
It was horrible! At first we thought we would not communicate with them, but then came the urge to work, to say something, or at least to be in opposition, aloud not just silently. At first we pulled back, we thought, "This is the end." No further communication. But then when an opportunity arose to make films — to continue, and to be in opposition — making films then became a mission. We didn't leave. We didn't

immigrate. We stayed here. We were members of a nation that was help-
less, but it was necessary to speak up. It was necessary to be aware that
we were not alone. It was necessary to realize that we could somehow
speak up.

The Communists were hypocrites. They were proclaiming a morality and intellectuals around the world took the bait. It was an altruistic
morality — solidarity, no egocentrism, etc. And people seeing all the social
injustice around agreed with them. They wanted there to be social justice, to get rid of poverty.

I felt this was my duty. So I don't believe I was unfaithful in any
way. I definitely didn't collaborate with them. I was tricking them. They
were saying to me, "How can you criticize us when we are paying you?"

I replied. "My critique is in the context of the moral principles you
preach, isn't it? A critical reflection is necessary. People have to keep bet-
tering. You talk about responsibility and I am drumming up the issue of
responsibility. People should be aware of it. I agree that morality is important. You say that your ideology advocates morality, but you don't comply with it. We are just pointing out that there is lack of compliance."

So there was room to do something. One has to realize that within
that ideology everything was turned upside down. One thing was declared
and something else was done. We were calling attention to that. What
is proclaimed should also be done. They felt very uncomfortable with it
because it was exactly what they didn't want to hear about.

How did you live through it?

I must say, I was a special case. I think I am one of a few female
directors worldwide who raised a family and was intensively making films
at the same time. Usually, they have kids first, or no kids at all, or later
on. This situation actually helped me going. My husband was a cinematographer and we had several contracts signed up to make films abroad.
We bought a piece of land in the beginning of 1968 and started building our house. Then everything collapsed and we just continued to build
the house. We had plenty of troubles to deal with. I was banned from
making films and we had a huge debt to pay. So I focused on the
house–which we were building with our own hands with the money my
films were making abroad. We built this house for 300,000 crowns. Then
I started to make commercials. But because I couldn't work under my
name I was shooting using my husband's name, Kučera.[38] I was doing
that for quite a while until the clients got fed up with my experiments.

I was playing with the material, letting the sound stutter and so on. So they fired me.

But then came 1976. There was a crisis, people weren't going to see any movies. They offered me a chance to make the film *The Apple Game*, but they didn't want to approve the script. I still wasn't certified as politically reliable and they put me in Short Film Studios. The director at Short Film Studios was in a fight with the director of Barrandov Studios and he wanted to prove that I could be manipulated, that he knew how to handle me. And immediately when I came to him, he said, "You can put everything that they took out back in your script." So I put everything back.

Sometimes it came down to elementary things. For example, they always moralized [the stories]. The main character couldn't be a lover of this woman because she was his friend's wife. He couldn't betray his friend. They opposed these basic aspects of drama. How can you build a drama when the character — like the state employee, the soldier, in *Calamity*— can't play cards while avoiding a rescue mission. They interfered with everything.

I saw that everything they did during what they called "normalization" was what they wanted the rest of the world to believe–that nothing wrong was going on here. They wanted everything to be done quietly. And I understood that it would irritate them if I screamed loudly. So I scandalized everything anyway I could. I loudly passed everything to the newspapers or called abroad.

I got, for example, a phone call from the United States. They were organizing a Year of Women festival and they wanted to open with my film *Daisies*. They wanted me to come for the opening. I said, first of all, they will not give you the film here. Second of all, they will not let me go. But prints are in Brussels and in the Cinemateque in Paris and you can get it from there. So they got it from there and wrote a petition to the Czech Embassy in Washington requesting an explanation as to why I was not allowed to attend, why I couldn't make films and so on.

The positive reception my films received abroad in the 60s helped me, they couldn't fire me. And I kept bugging them. If they didn't approved one script, then I came with another and another and I fought over each sentence. They knew that to deal with me meant an argument. But that type of argument where ... I was physically fighting with them. I beat them. I realized that each of them had a hysterical wife at home, that those wives didn't make their life easy and that all men have a basic

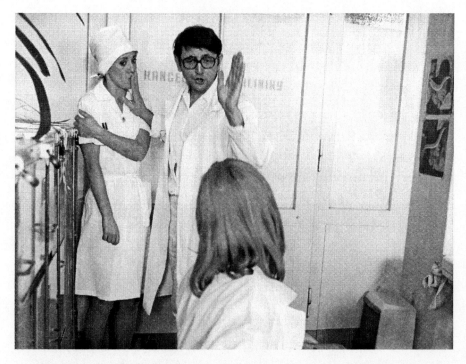

The Apple Game, 1976—Jiří Menzel as Dr. Josef John. Věra Chytilová, director; František Vlček, DP; premiere screening February 1, 1978; produced by Krátký Film Praha (courtesy National Film Archive Prague, photograph by Pavel Štecha).

fear of hysterical women. That was my strategy. I was playing this game always saying, "Don't say anything to me. I will tell everyone anything you say!" And I confronted them all together.

How was it with your film The Apple Game?

There was a period at Barrandov Studios when naked women were not allowed in film. You couldn't show naked breasts. Actually, you could show only one naked breast, not both. In my film *The Apple Game*, actress Dáša Bláhová sits by the fire and takes off everything. Her breasts are very small and I used it in connection with her line, "It's interesting how little you need to be happy." That's what she says when she reveals her breasts. It had a secondary meaning. This scene raised hell. They said it was pornography and tried to ban the film. My colleagues started the whole nonsense, of course, because—why should I be allowed to show two breasts when they can't? Then the film was shown at the Karlovy Vary

Film Festival. I was not invited but I went there on my own anyway, just to make a scandal. I went to a party, pulled out the General Manager Jiří Purš[39] and some other guy and asked him, "What jerk came up with an idea that only one breast can be shown on the screen?" And Purš said, "That was my idea." He confessed. It was a funny situation and he was ashamed.

It was a difficult time and there are many stories about it. But that's how I was fighting them. And then there was all that spite between Barrandov Studios and Short Film. They were passing me around like a hot potato and I was a sort of catalyst in the middle. I knew that the Communists, even though they had power in their hands, didn't trust each other. If one of them screwed up, they kicked him out. And I was the one who could make fun of them. One time, I was invited to a meeting for a screening. They tried to offer me something other than directing jobs and I refused to take them. I kept interrupting them and they said, "Don't let her speak! She must not speak without permission!"

I said, "Why should I ask for permission to speak when you talk such nonsense?"

They replied, "There are moments when the party can do anything!"

And I said, "Are you threatening me? Are you saying you can kill me? Do you want to kill me?"

"We didn't say that, take her out of here!"

I said, "I will not leave and all of you are witnesses that this man here, this comrade, threatened to kill me or put me in jail! I insist that this be recorded in writing! The fact is that at these screenings you are threatening to kill people!"

Later I wrote down all the questions and answers from the meeting in a letter and mailed it to the Ministry of Culture, the Politburo, a General Manager of the Film Industry, etc. Everybody could read who said what. Everything was written there, precisely who said what. Incredible bullshit! The chairman of the committee refused to do any more screenings! He didn't want to do his job because everyone was laughing at him. He was stupid. It was the best way to deal with them. Unfortunately I don't have that letter, but this was the best tactic. After that, they were afraid to say anything to me. And if somebody tried to tell me, "You know, just between you and me, I am not...." I would say, "Don't say anything to me, I will tell everybody anything you say to me!" I got the reputation of making everything public, making a scandal out of everything. So they let me work.

One day I went to see the top vagabond in the Politburo — comrade Müller in the Ministry of Culture. I went to see him in a spa to ask why he stopped my film *The Apple Game*. I wanted to know why they banned *The Apple Game* again shortly after they let it go. Because we had contacted youth organizations, the Ministry of Education and the Ministry of Health emphasizing the importance of educating young people about responsible parenting in an effort to get it released after the first ban. Then they banned it again. My colleagues, when they found out that the Soviets had bought up all Czech films except my *Apple Game*, wrote a memorandum to the Soviet Embassy saying that Věra Chytilová had made a film which the Soviets couldn't afford to buy. The Soviets replied that they didn't buy the film because it's heavy-duty stuff— for their men to see a woman give childbirth. So, they bounced the complaint like a hot potato to the President's Office. They sent it to General Manager Jiří Purš and he got scared and banned it again. Then he sent me to Müller to straighten it out with him.

I went to see him in SANOPS where he was in rehab. He was an alcoholic. I went to him and said that it's me, Chytilová, and I came to ask him why my film was pulled from theaters shortly after release.

And he said, "Oh, Věra is that you? You are a dissident and I am a bloody executioner! Mary, Mary," he called some woman, "Mary, come here! This is that famous director! What do you want?"

I said that I came to talk to him about my film.

"If you wouldn't have come, you would have no chance to work again."

And I asked, "Is it enough just to come and we all can work again?"

"I like you, you are not afraid of me!"

I said, "Why should I be afraid of you? Some people say you drink too much, that you are an alcoholic.... "

"I really like you, what can I do for you?"

I said, "I came to ask you to release my film again. Since the film was originally released, let it play in theaters."

"I can't do that! Do you think I am God?"

I said, "If you are not God, then I will go find the real God! Just tell me where the real God is and I will go talk to him. If God is in the Soviet Union, I will go to the Soviet Union!"

"No, come on, it's not like that. You must write a letter to the President of Czechoslovakia."

I said, "What should I write to the President? I already did! I wrote letters to everybody. It didn't help!"

"No, you will write a new letter to the President. He will send it to me and then I will call you and we will take care of it. But it would be better if you forget *The Apple Game*. Forget about it. You will make other films."

I said, "No, I shot this film, it cost some money and I want this film to be released! I don't believe you will let me shoot other films. What's the big deal about shooting other films? I make films to be seen, otherwise it doesn't make sense!"

He said, "Do you think I am such a rascal? Do you think I am a rascal and I wouldn't keep my word?"

I said, "It doesn't matter. I will believe you when you release my film! That's the only way you can convince me."

I went to write the letter to the President, but then I realized I had nothing new to write in this letter. I couldn't write the same letter again, and what else could I write about? So I went back to him and said, "Excuse me, I.... "

"Are you still here?"

I said, "No, I am here again. I don't know what I should write to the President. You must draft this letter for me!" He was also upset about how I was dressed. I was wearing blue jeans. He was like, what is it? Is it from America? I told him it's not from America. You can buy it here in Prague. He gave me the first sentence. I said, "No way, I would never say that!"

"Well, how would you say it?"

We wrote the whole letter this way, discussing every single sentence, and really, two weeks later I received an invitation to come to comrade Müller's office in the Politburo. He was back from rehab. And it went on and on.

And the next film was Calamity.

Yes, the next film was *Calamity*. All those phone calls about the script.

"Věrka, what did you put in the script? You'll complain I am censoring you again."

I said, "Well, yes you are censoring me if you call me about the script. You said you wouldn't censor me, but you do! What do you want me to do now?"

The producers were afraid to hold the telephone receiver because it was a call from the Politburo.

"You are using that word, you know? I don't want to censor your writing but that word, condom, you can't use it."

I said: "It's a normal word and I need it there. The character is a virgin and she is afraid of getting pregnant. She is just asking her partner if he has a condom."

He said, "Can't you use a different word? Can't you say a rubber?"

I said, "Absolutely not! That's so vulgar. I would never say that! Never repeat that word again to me. I didn't know you were so vulgar!"

He said, "Well, can we.... "

I said, "Okay, you know what? If you don't like that the character is a virgin and she asks about a condom, I'll change it. I will make her older and she never experiences.... She doesn't know what libido is. Would you prefer it this way?"

He was silent for a moment; he didn't know what libido was. Then he said, "Okay, you can do it this way. But you will not use the word condom, right?"

I said, "No I will not. But the question about libido will be there. Do you agree?"

He said, "All right."

That's how they censored everything. They asked, for example, "What will the film *Calamity* be about?"

I replied, "You gave me that script! Why did you give it to me?"

Any time they turned down my own script I told them that I was employed as a director and they were obligated to give me scripts. So they gave me a script for *Calamity*. I looked at the script wondering why they gave me that title *Calamity*.

"Why are you giving me this story? You fight with me about every single word and now this title *Calamity*. Why?"

He said, "Because it's a winter film."

I said, "I know, but why?"

He said, "Nobody wants to shoot during the winter, it's too cold."

They gave it to me because nobody wanted to shoot the film in the winter. After I read the script, I asked him, "Excuse me, can you tell me what this story is about? What is it about philosophically? I know there is a train stuck in the snow but...." This was the chief dramaturg,[40] a big shot, Ludvík Toman was his name. He'd read a story in the paper about how an avalanche crushed a train in America. And he said that it could happen in Czechoslovakia, too. Why just in America? They were pulling survivors out with helicopters, but because the Soviet Army came in 1968 in helicopters they didn't want any copters in the film. Helicopters were out of the question because it was too similar. The analogy between the film and the Soviet invasion in 1968 was too obvious. You couldn't say "occupation," of course, it was "help." And when I started work on *Calamity* I asked, "What do you want this film to be about?"

And he said, "You know, I haven't read the script for a long time. I don't remember what it is about."

"If you don't remember what it is about, just tell me what do you want it to be about, philosophically."

He said, "I must read it again. We will meet next week to talk about it."

We met the next week in the Film Club and I asked him, "Do you know what the film should be about now?"

He said, "No, I will leave it to you."

I said, "Let me tell you what I want this film to be about. I want this film to be about a vertical calamity and a horizontal calamity, and how these two calamities converge, overlap. Do you agree with this concept?"

"Yes." He didn't ask anything else.

Well, that's how I had to make my films. It was really a tedious, uphill battle.

A story goes around that once, when you couldn't work, you tried to jump out of a window.

When those so-called political screenings began (I am not sure where this fits in), then supposedly only Jiří Menzel "crawled through the chimney." I didn't! I went to the administration office and turned it upside down. There is another story that general manager Jiří Purš jammed me between the doors. It wasn't like that. The opposite is true. I was opening drawers looking for Ludvík Toman. I was looking for Toman in Purš' office desk, making a hysterical scene, pretending that he was hiding from me. They all hid from me, in rest rooms and so on, because I kicked doors and opened windows threatening to jump out. At the same time there was a meeting of Slovak filmmakers and I told them, "If you are meeting here, you must be discussing problems of cinema. And I am the problem here. Let's talk about me!" Then I left and had the car accident somewhere in the countryside. I fell asleep at the wheel and ran off the road, in the snow. I woke up there the next morning. Somebody pulled my car out with a pair of cows. Since I didn't come home, my husband called the police and they were looking for me. They found out that I was last seen with Ludvik Toman. So they interrogated him. That scared the hell out of them, and they let me work. That's how I "crawled through the chimney" together with Jiří Menzel! And Bohumil Hrabal said to us then, "Just watch out you don't get dirty!"

That's how I survived, doing these kinds of [things]. But it was really seizures of rage, seizures where I didn't care about anything. I was screaming at them, "There is nothing you can do to me! I am willing to lick a floor! You can do nothing to me! And if you decide to execute me, I will take you with me!"

I threatened them and I saw they were scared. That gave me satisfaction. And there were rumors going around, "She has something going on with Müller! She must...."

Any time I needed something, I went to the Politburo building and waited for Müller to come in. Comrades Lenárt,[41] Kapek[42] and others all passed by me. I was between the doors. They were passing two feet in front of me. And finally Müller came along. I stepped in his way and said, "Comrade Müller, I don't know, everybody is at work and you are late!"

He said, "Are you questioning me? I am coming from the Ministry."

"Okay, excuse accepted," I said.

He asked what happened and I said that those motherfuckers banned my film *Prague*. He said that it was his decision.

"I didn't think you were such a motherfucker. Why did you do that? I glorified Prague, didn't I? Why did you ban the film?"

"You know very well, you know very well what you did!"

"What did I do? I glorified Prague."

"You know very well!"

It was because I manipulated the end of the film using the footage from Spartakiads. Well, it was like this from one film to the other, fight, fight, fight. It was an interesting struggle.

And what now?

We always start from ground zero here. I mentioned this before. During the First Republic and then during World War II — the same. There was always something. The whole family was executed because someone was not registered. It was a constant danger. Then we were able to take a breath for a moment and immediately were punished for that in 1948. There was always a reason for punishment. Somebody defected to the West and you ended up in the prison just because you knew him. The 50s were the worst. At first they were killing themselves, then their enemies, and then the possible enemies: never ending, perpetual liquidations. Václav Havel probably didn't want another liquidation of liquidators. That's why it was the Velvet Revolution. But he should bring up punishment. There should be convictions. They should bring up rigorous laws and moral austerity. No, moral principles were not established and that was the mistake. And we will deal with it forever, running in a circle, and talking about it like imbeciles. If they had brought up the issue of morality, truly, not just hypocritically, to make the leaders responsible as well, to get rid of people who were irresponsible, selfish and crooked — things would be different today. But to go back to the commandments for a moment (which they renounced because it was religious). If this had been a priority, as it was during Masaryk's[43] era, then there would be a chance. All the dirt floated to the top first. It will be very difficult now to put everything in order, to enforce the rules. It's idiotic to start over and over again. Today everything depends on charity. Charities are helping but there is no grand conception of what they are to do. There is no worldwide concept to deal with poverty and hunger.

The Communists were promising to fix these problems but in reality they wanted just the power, the dictatorship. But people knew that they must not publicly admit they are sons of bitches, that they are rascals. They knew that they must not acknowledge they want everything for themselves. But now it's official, now they can. It is the trend now — snatch whatever you can, knock out whom ever you want, kill.... Just to stick a foot in the door. Like the Russians, like the Soviets did. Anywhere they put their foot down, nobody could push them out. So, there is no morality at all. It doesn't exist any more. Our leaders are probably brainless. There is no political message. Politics as a civic duty is absent from their thinking. And if there is no morality in politics, there will be no morality at all. The politicians must become role models first.

When I was in the city council, I told them that the mayor can't be getting rich while the city is going broke. It's not right. He must be as rich as his city is. If the city goes down, he must go down. He can't put city in debt for 20–30 thirty years when he will only be in the office four years! But they allowed him to do it! It's incredible, stupid. Everything seems to me absolutely stupid. That's the same stupidity that I criticized during the socialist era, the same stupidity that was celebrated after the

Calamity, 1981 — Věra Chytilová, director; Ivan Šlapeta, DP; premiere screening January 1, 1982; produced by Filmové Studio Barrandov (courtesy National Film Archive Prague, photograph by Zdeněk Dukát).

Velvet Revolution. At the end of Communist rule, they weren't murderers any more, they were idiots. They were funny — it was a great, grotesque show. The economy collapsed, everything disintegrated. But the stupidity survived and it continues. There is no other model here and people are the same.

Does this time period have a specific theme?
    Every period has one major theme and that is morality. It's a subject of conflicts, everywhere and always. Every human behavior has a moral aspect. Everything. There is no behavior without a moral aspect, and that must constantly be scrutinized because it's often controversial. Explore it. Reveal it.
    What is missing is any kind of reevaluation. We are working with junk all the time because somebody in the past once said so. Or we can't do this now because we were doing this in the past. Nobody thinks.

Nobody thinks about it again. There is no reevaluation. We are just spouting phrases because we are used to talking like that. We keep doing that and we don't even know what are we talking about. What is important is to be authentic all the time. What do I think right now, from this point of view. And when someone says, "But you were saying something else a year ago." Yes, but a year ago I had a different opinion about it. You can't hold on to your opinions no matter what and not think. It is important to think!

I always deal with moral issues. Maybe it's because I was fostered in a monastery. I am from a Catholic family. I left that basic, personified faith, but those moral codes are inside me. I don't understand the complete absence of compassion. Where is it coming from? I don't get it. Or the ability to kill. How much effort it must take and how messy you get with all that blood. How can people do it? They just go and stab someone. They have the capacity to do it! They have the nerves to do it. Where do these people get the ability to do it?

I am working on such a script now–a reflection on who we are. If I can raise the money for it, because who would be interested in a film like this[44]?

Young filmmakers are complaining that it's difficult to find a theme today.

No! There are so many topics on every corner. They are the topic themselves right now if they don't know it. Everything is a theme. They complain because they have no interest in anything. I see it in the Film Academy. They just improvise, or they want to imitate something. They want to do it like Tarantino, but they have nothing to say! They don't know anything. They don't read a newspaper, they are not interested in anything, they don't see. My students get upset when I ask them to keep a diary because they have to pay an attention to what's going on around them. Then I ask them how to make that particular situation into a comedy, and how to make it into a tragedy. And what would a black comedy would look like? They have no idea! Or somebody brings an interesting idea but doesn't see its potential! He mixes storylines together but is unable to do an analysis of the situation, to find out more about the relationship of his characters. They don't know. They can't describe relationships in their own families! When I ask them to analyze their own family situation, they don't know. They don't think. They are dumb.

They submitted some interesting work to get in the school, they have knowledge, but they are unable to take a stand. I don't know if this is a problem from high school where they don't show them how to think, or have an opinion, or how to be self-conscious. What is my opinion about this? Do I agree or disagree? If I disagree, then why do I disagree? And how would I like to change it? They don't know! They just want to make money and enjoy the ride.

Somebody also said that film today is expected to be an entertainment and not a source of ideas.
    But I don't see why an idea shouldn't be entertaining. Why is this a contradiction? It is not. I know that thinking is painful but I can get to it through entertainment. What dummy told you that? He was a human. And a human is *cogito ergo sum*. Isn't it? In that case, he can't be a human. If he is such a fool, it's his problem. Who told you that?

Saša Gedeon said that.
    But ... he thinks ... oh my God.... Why is something art? Because it has an audience? An audience is not a condition of Art. What is he babbling about? He looks at it from a box office point of view and maybe he is pissed off that his audience is small. But that's not the point. He must have desire, and if he doesn't have desire then he can go to Hell. He must have a desire to say something, to spit something out! If there is nothing inside him, and his priority is to be an artist, then he is fucked up! Because it's not about us being artists.

Do you have any pleasant or unpleasant memories of the past years?
    Bad memories I have only from realms beyond my ability to recall. When I forgot to explain to some people my relationship because I was stupid and didn't realize soon enough that there is nothing to do about it. Those are the bitter memories.
    And good memories? Everything was fine. There are plenty of good memories. When I feel badly, I have plenty of other interests to help me feel better. I go to my garden and plant something. There are plenty of things to do and never enough time to do everything I would like to. I am horrified by the fact that I can't read all the books I bought! That I will not have enough time to learn many things. We don't have enough time to do what we'd like to accomplish.... I don't know how to say it.... Once I left my dog on the street and he got lost. I have a vivid memory of him looking around when I was holding him. He didn't know where he was. He was disoriented and I thought he would find the way back

home. He didn't make it home. I get cramps in my guts when I think about it because I left him there alone. That's just one example. These things are so destructive to me.... Or children, when they have to face a misunderstanding or some brutality of this world.... The world seems to be brutal. Very brutal.

Do you agree with Jiří Menzel's belief that the young generation today knows that world will not be better?
     I think they are cynical but they don't believe that the world will not get better. They can't believe in that. Because to believe in it, they would have to try give it a shot first. And they didn't try anything yet, so what. They just say it because it's convenient. They have to realize that it is in their hands: the hope, the expectations. But to know that the world will not be better is nonsense. It's just doomsday rubbish. I think ... everything is constantly changing. The worst thing is that we are exhausting our resources. There is a danger of some kind of environmental end.
     Well, you see, you got what you wanted and we must go now. I have to go.

Filmography
VĚRA CHYTILOVÁ (born 1929)

     She is from Olomouc. She studied architecture and then worked as a technical drafter and later as a continuity girl at Barrandov Studios. In 1957 she decided to study film at FAMU and in the 60s she became a prominent director of Czech New Wave. After the Soviet invasion in 1968, she was unable to make any films until 1976, when she was allowed to shoot a narrative film at Short Film Prague. Then she continued shooting feature films and documentaries until the revolution in 1989. She teaches directing at FAMU.

2001—*Exile from Paradise* (director, story, screenplay, music)
2000—*Flights and Falls* (director, story, screenplay)
1998 —*Trap Trap, Little Trap* (director, story)
1992 —*The Inheritance or Fuckoffguysgoodbye* (director, screenplay)
1991—*My Citizens of Prague Understand Me* (director, story)
1990—*Tomás Garrigue Masaryk a liberator* (director)
1988 —*Tainted Horseplay* (director, screenplay)

1987 — *The Jester and the Queen* (director, screenplay)
1986 — *Wolf's Cabin* (director, story, screenplay)
1984 — *Prague: The Troubled Heart of Europe* (director, story, screenplay)
1983 — *The Very Late Afternoon of the Faun* (director, screenplay)
1981 — *Calamity* (director, screenplay)
1979 — *Pretas Story* (director, story, screenplay)
1978 — *Inexorable Time* (director)
1976 — *The Apple Game* (director, story, screenplay)
1969 — *The Fruit of Paradise* (director, screenplay)
1966 — *Daisies* (director, story, screenplay)
1965 — *Automat World* (director)
1963 — *Something Different* (director)
1962 — *A Bagful of Flies* (director)
1961 — *The Ceiling* (director)

Awards

Grand Premio at IFF in San Remo 1980 (*Pretas Story*)
Exceptional Artistic Contribution to the World Cinema Award, IFF
    Karlovy Vary 2000
Elvira Notari Prize in Venice FF 1998 (*Trap, Trap, Little Trap*)
Silver Hugo in Chicago IFF 1977 (*The Apple Game*)
Grand prix in Bergamo FF 1967 (*Daisies*)

Jiří Krejčík

DIRECTOR

When you look back at your career, what comes to mind?

I worked at Barrandov Studios for 40 years and shot 18 feature films during that period. Well, it's not so many. But at least 20 years out of those 40 were wasted. It's unbelievable. Those years were wasted by all kind of obstacles — injunctions to work, bans. They put me on trial here once as well and sentenced me in a staged people's court. These are unpleasant memories. But what was worse, they didn't let me make the films I really wanted to shoot. Only three or four films out of those 18 were made the way I really wanted. Most of the time they demanded films from me that conformed to the regime — distorting reality and lying. They blackmailed me, saying that if I didn't make those films for them, I would not work at all. That's how it worked then.

Which period was the worst and which was the best?

All periods in the past were quite bad. Some were a little better, some a little worse. It was overwhelming after World War II. In 1945 all the biggest crooks and all the collaborators with the Germans, the Gestapo informers, became zealous Communists all at once. They joined the Communist party and became the most dedicated Communists. Those were bad times, hard times. I was disgusted. At that time I worked for Short Film as a director, but I couldn't stand it. I had to leave. I quit. But these people always seem to creep up during bad times, and with their Com-

Jiři Krejčík (photograh by Robert Buchar).

munist party, how would I put it, brown-nosing, that is the right expression, brown-nosing their way along. And these were people who didn't know shit. That's interesting. Those who knew the least were the most zealous Communists. And fighting with them was tragic. One lucky period for young directors was around 1966. A whole series of interesting films were created: the socalled Czech New Wave. Then after 1968, after the Soviet Invasion, that was probably the worst period of all. Many people were terminated. They were not permitted to work any more. Like my colleague director Ladislav Helge or cinematographer Stanislav Milota. They were expelled from Barrandov Studios with no place to go. Ladislav Helge then ended up working at a post office and Stanislav Milota, a great cinematographer, didn't work at all. Unscrupulous people took power into their hands. Awful films were put into production but I wasn't allowed to shoot anything then.

Why was that?

A talented author is necessary to create a work of art. But talent alone is not enough. It is necessary to know how enforce it, make the most of it. Then it becomes irrelevant if the talent is big or not so big. And, of course, those with lesser talent or without any talent got a green light here. The political interference was the worst part of it, and the corruption, the bribery... You didn't have a chance to make a film without paying off the official in charge. The promiscuity was ruining all honest creativity.

Once a director of the motion picture studio told me, during the time when I couldn't work and I came to ask for work, "Well, you are difficult, you don't want to give anything."

I asked what he meant by "give anything."

"Well, to give something under the table to the chief dramaturg."

"To the dramaturg, you say?"

"All your colleagues are paying. You would be surprised. You don't know that? Some of them pay up to 50 percent of their gross income! Whoever wants to shoot must pay."

I didn't pay anything to anybody, ever.

What was the situation at Barrandov Studios like during the period of Normalization?

An StB agent once came to visit me at home and said, "We would like you to work for us, giving us information about your friends, about people close to you."

"What's on your mind?"

"Well, we would fix your problems at Barrandov Studios and your children at school…"

To become an informant would give me an opportunity to work again?

Once I was invited to the office of the personnel manager at Barrandov Studios. He was the man who performed political evaluations of everybody and that was crucial in the deciding who would be allowed to shoot and who wouldn't. And he asked me, "Do you think we have enough directors?"

I replied, "Yes, you have enough directors, but the question is how many of them are good."

"Well, we all know you are good, so shut up!"

I didn't understand, why shut up? But I got it later! Informers had tipped him off. They didn't want to fire me and I was a problem for him. Then we learned, after the revolution, that almost every other person here was an informer! A newspaper, *Red Cow*,[45] published a list of all the informers, everybody who collaborated with the secret police. I was stunned by how many co-workers, how many friends, were on that list. Even the editor of my last movie was an informer. It was horrifying.

What happened to Barrandov Studios after the "Revolution"?

In 1993, they started to prepare for the privatization of Barrandov Studios. A man emerged, nobody knew where he came from, but his name was Vaclav Marhoul.[46] He, with others, started CINEPONT corporation and came up with the so-called "privatization project." Approx-

imately ten people were involved in this, including cinematographer
Miroslav Ondříček,[47] Miloš Forman and other memorable filmmakers,
but they were not involved in the Czech film industry any more. They
only worked abroad. The great costume designer, Mr. Theodor Pištěk,
was also one of them. They presented the CINEPONT Privatization Project[48] and we suspected that if this were to happen it would be a disaster. There were some negotiations going on… At that time I made my
objections clear to Prime Minister Pithart,[49] I told him it was illegal. And
the Prime Minister said to me that if it was as I said, the privatization
project wouldn't be approved. Of course, the next day the Cabinet
approved it under the chairmanship of Vice Premier Lukeš. And the wife
of Lukeš was the secretary of those totalitarian directors of Barrandov
Studios before the revolution and it was in their interest. Minister of
Culture Uhde assured us that there was a "golden share" for the nomi-
nal amount of 5,000 KC and this "golden share" had a major influence
that, without it, other shares couldn't be sold, that the company couldn't
be sold. The whole thing was sold for 500,000,000 KC [$13.5 million],
a minimal amount at that time, nothing, and look at it today. Today it
is a dead city, a dead factory. Czech films are not made here any more.
All the specialists and craftsmen were fired. They are gone. Where is it
all going? The whole company is slowly sinking and one day it will
definitely hit the bottom.

How would you characterize the present state of Czech film?
    Well, I see the situation as gloomy and very depressing. It has reached
a critical moment. Maybe it's only my subjective feeling because I can't
work any more, because I can't push through projects I want to do. I can't
make it happen. I don't know. Maybe I am too old. They say, "The old
man, what more does he want? He is old, he's made enough movies
already."
    They also say, "You made so many beautiful films. You should write
your memoirs." But I don't want write my memoirs!
    What kind of films are being made today? They make films that are
shallow and cheap, which of course don't make any money. They only
lose money.
    There is a grant to help filmmakers. Czech Television is broadcast-
ing old Czech films, those made after 1965, and these films are making
a lot of money. One hundred million crowns a year. This money goes —
after the deduction of royalties and other fees — to the National Fund for

Cinema and this grant supports a few films a year. But Czech films today can't make money. They can't break even, because the production costs are high and the box office in the Czech Republic can't bring it back. They can make some money only if they're distributed abroad or sold to foreign broadcasting companies. That's the only way to make a profit. But what are the topics, what are the stories people abroad would like to watch? There is no dramaturgy of any kind here and that's why everything is the way it is.

Why are there so few good films made today?
I believe that a dramaturg who reads a script must be a sort of fortuneteller. He must guess how valuable the idea is and what the potential commercial value of it is as well. Of course, there are some themes

Wedding Under Supervision, 1967 — Ivan Janžurová (left) as Hanička, Jan Vostrčil (center) as an older policeman, and Vladimír Pucholt as a young policeman. Jiří Krejčik, director; Josef Střecha, DP; premiere screening June 1, 1967; produced by Filmové Studio Barrandov (Courtesy National Film Archive Prague, photograph by Jaroslav Trousil).

that can't make any money. It's interesting that mere entertainment and superficial stories make more money while those more valuable themes usually lose money. But people who could distinguish a good script from the bad script are not here any more. They don't exist.

And there is corruption in addition to this. The corruption in the past led to terrible consequences. Incredibly stupid films were shot here. What a waste of money that was. One couldn't believe it! No private investor would ever put money in that. It was possible only because the government financed film production. Any stupid script could be made into a film because of the system of bribery. I didn't pay anything to anybody. Not a dime. But later I realized that I was part of that system of corruption anyway. It worked like this: An author wrote an interesting story but the script was not very good. It needed some additional work. He bribed somebody to push it through the system and I got that script to rewrite it, to make it work. I was the one paid to get it into a form that could be shot. That was how the system worked. There were directors here in the past who were shooting year after year so-called "unnecessary films" that nobody was interested in. Detective stories with a murder for example. We called them "substitute themes," because these topics substituted for stories we would like to do but were not allowed to shoot. They were taboo. And how does it work today? I don't think it's too much different.

I had problems with every single film I made. I always had bad luck. You can't have this. You can't have that. One producer told me once, "You are always complaining about something. You always want something you can't have! You should realize that you will never get what you want! And we don't need directors who can't shoot a film with what they don't have. Do you understand?" I believe that this mentality is still here. The corruption did not disappear in November 1989 after the political coup. Unfortunately it didn't. People who got used to bribes are still around. The production of a film has to be based on common interests. But I am amazed that in our new capitalistic system that the same stupid ideas can be materialized while good ideas can't. Why is that? I believe that people who make decisions have bad judgment, they are unable to evaluate quality. Of course, it's not so simple. And, of course, sometimes you can sell a very stupid idea for a lot of money while nobody gives a damn about a good one. Film now has become a way to profit merchandise from merchandising and nobody is willing to admit that it also has artistic, cultural values. These values can be very important for the society and can rise with the times.

Did you ever think of emigration?

Emigration? Sure, the option to emigrate came up in 1968 when the situation here got unbearable. Incidentally, I was in Italy with the whole family when the Red Army invaded Czechoslovakia in August 1968. We were staying in Florence driving a car with a Czech license plate and people were screaming at us, "Czechoslovakia salute." We had no idea what was it all about. We didn't know what was happening in Prague. Later on we learned the tragic news that the Soviet Army occupied Czechoslovakia. Just the thought that we could never go back to Prague was horrible. I was politically involved during the so-called "Prague Spring." I signed the petition "Two Thousand Words" and it was clear to me that I would be arrested when I came back. So, the pressure to emigrate was very strong. We spent a couple of horrible weeks in Italy.

But I wasn't born to emigrate. I couldn't imagine myself living somewhere else. We had our relatives in the United States who would give us a hand, but I didn't speak English anyway. But I couldn't imagine myself living somewhere other than in Prague... So I thought if they didn't throw me in jail I could still walk in Petřín Grove and look at Prague, but only if they didn't put me in jail. We came to Prague, packed our stuff and went to Vienna with our children, but we couldn't take it any more and returned to Prague. I shot two more films but suddenly in 1972 the chief dramaturg, Ludvík Toman, that criminal asshole, that agent of the Soviet Union, that KGB agent, wrote in my personal files, "He demonstrated his anti-socialist attitude at Masaryk's grave in Lány." And I was finished for the next six years. Six years I couldn't work.

I was ready to become a bellboy in a hotel in Holešovice but then, in 1979, I got an opportunity to make the film *Divine Emma* about the actress Emma Destinová.[50] I was 60 years old then. The film was a great success, especially with our domestic audience. People in theaters stood up and applauded after the screenings. It was unbelievable. I had never seen anything like that before. And here is the question, if I had emigrated I would never have made this film.... And I would probably never become successful in America anyway.

But that asshole, the chief dramaturg of Barrandov Studios and the agent KGB, Ludvik Toman, took the film to the Soviet Embassy. The ambassador got upset, saying the film raised undesired patriotic, nationalistic feelings and should be banned. It was terrible, only the Soviet Union could have patriotic feelings! So after a while the film was pulled out of the theaters. But there was one screening in honor of Emma Destinová at the Metropolitan Opera in New York City. And as I said, this film would not exist if I had immigrated to America and I couldn't make any films there anyway. I am not made for the life in America and now I am not made for a life here either.

So T.G. Masaryk's grave in Lány became an important point in your life.

There was one funny moment, but it is almost impossible to describe. Years passed. It was all about disclaiming the past or not, but by then nobody actually wanted me to disclaim anything. It is interesting. And time passed and I was called in...

The General Manager of Czech Film, Jiří Purš, once in a while, every month, called these "temporarily wretched" people to his office. Evald Schorm, Věra Chytilová, Jiří Menzel, they all came every Friday afternoon to his office and he asked, "So, what's new?" And nobody knew why. I figured out later that it was because we were still his employees and as the general manager he was responsible for our actions — if somebody would say something against the government or to the foreign press...

Věra Chytilová wanted to jump from his window once because she was banned from making films. I don't know if it is true or what happened, but the fact is that later they let Chytilová shoot a feature film in Kamil Pixa's Short Film Studios. Maybe two films. Jiří Menzel probably put his signature on something. I don't know who signed something or not. I didn't want anything. And then one day Jiří Purš called me into his office and asked me, "Well, that grave in Lány, was it Masaryk or T.G.?"

And I said, "Well it was March 7 [the anniversary of Masaryk's death], so it was T.G."[51]

And then he smiled and said to me, "Excellent! You know what? You will write me a special letter. Do you know how to write this kind of letter?"

I said I don't know, and hesitated for what would come next. He said okay, and do you know so and so. He named some people and I said I don't know this one, and I don't like that one. No problem, but then he said what about this one, and that was a longtime friend of mine, and I suddenly froze. He has to help me write this letter. It must be some kind of brown-nosing letter, something dreadful!

"He will meet with you, I will call him, and he will take care of it," Purš said.

We met in a hotel. My friend was silent, didn't want to talk.

I said, "What are we going to do about that letter? How is that you are so trusted to do such a thing?"

He was still quiet, didn't want to talk and then he shouted, "Please don't tell anybody that I was in Lány, too. But I was in the back by the wall and you were up front laying down the wreath. Please just don't tell anybody anything!"

And then you shot the film Divine Emma.

When I was casting Emma, my first choice was the actress Mrs. Hlaváčová, but she declined the offer. My second choice was Mrs. Turzonová and we went to Bratislava to see her. In Barrandov Studios, everything was ready to kill my project and my producer had instructions to check the situation and announce that this film couldn't be shot. So I was driving to Bratislava with the Deputy Director of Barrandov Studios, Comrade Hájek. He was a former army officer, womanizer and alcoholic. When he was talking over the phone, it was like this, "What are you saying? Shit! Fuck you! What do you have? Fuck off!" That was how he was running his business. And this man was going with me to Bratislava to see if the actress Mrs. Turzonová will accept the leading role in my film. And as I said, if she didn't, the film would be off because I couldn't find a lead actress. I was sitting next to the driver and Hájek was sleeping in the back seat of the car. When we got out of Prague he woke up and said to me, "Hey you, director, you son of a bitch, why are you so stubborn? Why do you insist on making a good film? Nothing will happen if you make a piece of shit! Others make shitty films, so why can't you? Don't be nuts, times are different now!"

The whole system worked like this. Here was Jiří Purš, and he was backed by Ludvík Štrougal[52] [Prime Minister], and Toman was backed by Müller, the head of the department in the Central Committee KSČ, that asshole, that criminal, and he was tied up with Vasil Bilak.[53] Those two, Štrougal and Bilak, were in the Central Committee and they fought each other for control and sometimes one had more influence, sometimes the other and that trickled down. So one day I ran into Jiří Purš and told him that I had sent him a letter and hadn't received any answer from him. He said to me, "I don't give a damn any more. I don't care about anything." So I said, "Thank you, Mr. General Manager, for not giving a damn about me." He said, "It's not about you personally, but I don't care." But this was at a time when he was going to be fired. Then when

Štrougal resigned, he was cut off immediately. So you were in the hands of who knows who, and you had no idea who supported you, who was against you or what was really going on. You never knew. It is like being in the middle of a storm, a tornado, you don't know and when it's all over you just look around at what happened. If you can see what just happened. Sometimes you can't see immediately what happened. So it was crazy.

Don't you want sometimes to say, "Fuck it all, I don't need this any more?"

Well, fuck it all, that's like if they dump you in the water and you are going down. What will you do? Will you give up? Of course not. You try to stay alive. You try to swim. Maybe somebody gives you a hand, maybe not, or you somehow manage to make it on your own. But you

Divine Emma, 1979 — Božidara Turzonová as Emma Destinová and Juraj Kukura as Viktor. Jiří Krejčík, director; Miroslav Ondříček, DP; premiere screening December 1, 1979; produced by Filmové Studio Barrandov (courtesy National Film Archive Prague, photograph by Karel Ješátko).

can't just say fuck it, lower your arms and go to the bottom. You have a family, kids, and they depend on you!

Today I could say fuck it all, but I can't. If you have the energy, you can't let it go! I still have to wrestle with it and I don't feel like I am 81 years old. Sure, my joints are weaker and I prefer to sit down than to stand, but here, in my head, it hasn't switch off yet! Maybe I am an idiot... And this is a human comedy, because we are all here, more or less, as cogs in some kind of a nonsense machine.

If you had the opportunity to be 25 years old again, what you would do differently?

If I could be 25 years old? That's the question of Faust. But to be like Faust means you sell your spirit to the Devil. Only the Devil can give you back your youth, like Faust... And you know what? I wouldn't want it. On the contrary. I have children and grandchildren and when I look at young people today I am deeply troubled about their future. I fear what they will inherit from us.

It's impossible to think like a 25-year-old at the age of 81. That's absurd. And to be physically 25 and think like an 81-year-old is absurd as well. Only the Devil can do that as he did to Faust. And it didn't work out for him anyway. It was an agony. It's impossible. I tell you if I were to have this choice, I wouldn't go for it. Because here we have a philosophical question about the meaning of life and its length — how long the meaningful life should be. For some people, life doesn't have any meaning any more after they reach 40. It's different to push a creative person out of work, somebody who has many ideas and plans for projects to do, compared to somebody who worked his entire life in a nine-to-five job and grew vegetables in his backyard on weekends. I personally don't have any backyard with vegetables. But I know one thing. I get extremely tired if I am stuck at home and can't do anything. That's that mental fatigue, weariness for nothing from passing time waiting to die, wondering if the death will be unpleasant, painful or quick. When Jan Pucholt came here last time he told me: "Don't worry about suffering. You will drop dead without any warning."

I have outlived others by six years now. František Vláčil died at 75, Geier at 75, and the one who invented Kinoautomat, Radok, also at 75. I am wasting my time here six additional years ... and one is in the hands of absolutely irresponsible people here, and they control our destiny... They are ruthless.

What do you do when you don't make films?

I am hammering through public issues now. I fight with government authorities. It's not about my personal issues. It's in the public interest. When I encounter a stupidity, I go after it. But in reality, what can I accomplish? Nobody wants talk to me anyway. I shot 16 hours of footage about the absurdities of everyday life but nobody wants to deal with it. Last time I shot a segment for the television series *Black Sheep*. It was about how dogs are shitting all around the Memorial of our World War II pilots. I got great shoots. A Duke of Edinburgh salutes, soldiers bring wreaths, veterans who survived the war were there, and 548 names of those who gave their lives for our freedom carved in the marble. And now dogs are shitting all over the place. And in the commentary I said that the memorial was build just for a visit from British Queen Elizabeth II, giving the Duke of Edinburgh a place to salute and lay down a wreath. That's why the memorial was built so fast. They built the whole thing in a few days! Now the memorial is decaying because it was so poorly built.

And then I quote from a documentary film about a British air raid on Germany. The planes are taking off from England flying over La Marche and the commentator says, "You can see the seashore of England below. There is nothing extraordinary about it. But when we come back, believe me, it will be the most beautiful sight in the world. And these men, whose names are carved in the marble here, never got to see it." It's an emotional commentary and the television producer told me that they need the piece 40 seconds shorter and that I should cut this part out! It's not necessary and it doesn't fit there anyway. And I said that that's what this piece is all about.

I saw [a Hollywood movie] 50 years ago and I still remember it. It was shot by the great American director William Wyler, and Jiří Voskovec was reading the commentary. A beautiful film. There are great shots of planes landing. People are waiting, looking at the sky to see who is coming back. Planes are shooting flares announcing they have wounded on board, ambulances are coming. Every plane has a name. One flying fortress was Memphis Belle, the other Bill. And the voiceover says, "The landing gear is gone, part of tail is gone, but Bill is back!" Then the wounded are getting blood transfusions and the voiceover continues: "Who knows whose blood is it? Maybe from a farmer in Oklahoma, or a student from Ohio or maybe from an actress from Hollywood? Whoever donated it, thank you!"

I get excited every time I listen to it. It is a classic commentary, which elevates reality to the level of art. Those people sacrificed their lives so we could live better! They sacrificed their health, many of them were wounded, and many of them didn't survive the war! And we are fucking up everything here. We are destroying everything. It's shameful... And this is what I would like to make a film about.

Filmography

JIŘÍ KREJČÍK (born 1918)

After his graduation from high school, Krejčík studied at the Technical College in Prague. When Czech schools closed during the German occupation, he worked as an extra at Barrandov Studios. He became interested in film and shot a couple of short films. After the war he worked at Short Film Prague making documentary films. He left Short Film after, as he says, "untalented Communists took over." He debuted in 1947 with the feature film *A Week in a Quiet House*. He shot 16 features at Barrandov Studios. Most of them received awards film festivals both home and abroad. During his career he was banned from work many times. During the Normalization period he managed to shoot only two films. He also directed many classic dramatic plays for television and once a while he directs stage plays in theaters.

2000 — *A Graduation in November* (documentary)
1984 — *A Salesman of Humor*
1979 — *Divine Emma*
1972 — *Suspicious*
1971 — *Deluding Love Games*
1967 — *Wedding Under Supervision*
1967 — *Boarding House for Bachelors*
1964 — *Cintamans and a Con Man*
1962 — *Midnight Mass*
1961 — *Labyrinth of the Heart*
1960 — *A Higher Principle*
1959 — *Awakening*
1958 — *Morale of Mrs. Dulská*
1958 — *Gloria*
1954 — *Frona*

1953 —*A Dawn Above Us*
1948 —*A Village on the Border*
1948 —*Conscience*
1947 —*A Week in a Quiet House*

Awards

Award of the Czechoslovakia 1948 (*A Village on the Border*)
State Honor Award in 1953 (*A Dawn Above Us*)
Award at IFF Karlovy Vary 1954 (*Frona*)
Second Prize at IFF in Locarno 1959 (*Gloria*)
Award at IFF in Mar del Plata 1959 (*Gloria*)
Grand Prize at IFF Karlovy Vary 1960 (*A Higher Principle*)
FIPRESCI Award 1960 (*A Higher Principle*)
Silver Sale Award at IFF in Locarno 1960 (*A Higher Principle*)
President's Medal at IFF in Venice 1960 (*A Higher Principle*)
Medaile Festivalu na MFF Karlovy Vary 1962 (*Midnight Mass*)
Fighters Against Fascism Award 1962 (*Midnight Mass*)
TRILOBIT Award 1967 (*Wedding Under Supervision*)
Múza Erato 1968 (*Wedding Under Supervision*)

Jaroslav Bouček

PRODUCER

I haven't seen you for over 20 years. What did you do all that time?
I worked at Barrandov Studios for the last 20 years. I was a co-founder of AB Barrandov and since 1993 I've worked as an independent producer. I started a bunch of production companies: BucFilm, BullFilm, Simply Cinema and ABJ Film. I specialize in feature films, TV series and co-productions with foreign producers.

How would you describe the situation in contemporary Czech cinema?
It's not good because the government doesn't support filmmaking. Our government pumps only 50—60,000,000 crowns into film production through a Grant Committee at the Ministry of Culture. But actually this is not the government's money. This money comes from the royalties of old Czech films produced between 1964 and 1990. The government's financial support is zero. I am also a member of NAP, which is the Association of Independent Producers in Czech Republic, and the European Forum in Strassburg invited director Vladimír Michálek and myself to the European Parliament to report on the situation in Czech Republic. We told them it's tragic because there is no government support for film production and we are 90 percent dependent on private investors. Thank God Czech Public Television is the biggest co-producer of theatrical films in Czech Republic. Without the financial support from television, Czech cinema would not exist at all. That is how it is. It doesn't look good at all. It's almost tragic.[54]

But films are made regardless of all that.

Yes, a relatively large number of films are being made. On the average, 15 to 20 films a year. For the size of our country, it's plenty. I don't know exact numbers, but as far as I remember some 100 or 150 feature films were shot in the last ten years after the revolution. Only four of those films made any money back. Financial resources are drying out now.

Jaroslav Bouček (photograph by Robert Buchar).

So where does the money come from?

It comes from Czech Television and private investors. The private investors invest only until they find out it's a total loss. In the post-revolution euphoria, all the big entrepreneurs and the first *nouveaux riches* started to pump money into film. A lot of money. Well, I don't do this, but many producers approached big banks and corporations lying to them. They promised, for example, a profit of 50,000,000 on a 10,000,000 investment. It can't be true. It's a lie, it's nonsense. It doesn't fit the reality. So the private investors willing to put money in films are dropping off and with other companies going bankrupt, investment for Czech films is fading out. Without the government's intervention, the consequences for Czech cinema could be quite catastrophic.

What about international co-productions?

I believe there is a way to do it now. Times have changed. It is a question of a good script and money. It's my dream, the dream of any Czech producer — to find an American script, an American director, American stars, and produce that film. The question is where does the money come from? For example, Martin Dejdar[55] just shot a film here staring Peter O'Toole.[56] I don't know how the film played abroad but, in

Czech Republic, it was a box office disaster. But I think even in America there are only a few commercially successful films out of so many that are shot every year. We see here only those hits that make hundreds of millions of dollars, but there must be many more bad films out there.

Why do you produce films if they lose so such money?
Normally I wouldn't do it. Film, as an investment, is a risky business in the Czech Republic. But I am a playful being — I like to gamble. Producing films is like gambling to me. But I don't try to tell my co-producers or myself that if I invest 10,000,000 in a film I will get 100,000,000 back. That's nonsense. The reality is that we will be lucky to get back 1,000,000. But there are ways to stay in the business. It's very complicated and it differs from project to project. You don't get rich by producing Czech films, no way!

So, what happened with Czech cinema?
In the past, there was Central Management of the Film Industry. They were managing Barrandov Studios, Short Film Studios, Army Film Production and some other subsidiaries. Cinema was considered to be a strong propaganda vehicle for the government's ideology and the Communist regime fully supported film production. In those days, Barrandov Studios produced 30 feature films a year. Of course, after the fall of Communism they pronounced the Central Management to be undesirable and tore it down. That brought the government's support to an end. Minister Václav Klaus is saying that filmmakers brought it on themselves but I don't believe that. That's nonsense. The privatization of Barrandov Studios or Short Film Studios didn't affect this issue. I don't have to shoot my film at Barrandov Studios, I can shoot anywhere I want to. If I need lights or a camera, I can rent it from Germany. That's not a problem. It is a problem for foreign productions coming here to shoot their films because we have big studios here. But for Czech filmmakers making Czech films, it doesn't make a difference. Czech cinema needs financial support and the only place to get it is from the government.

What is the solution here?
Fortunately for us, the Czech Republic wants to join the European Union. Countries of the Union have quotas. Denmark, for example, is a country of the same size as we are and they spent an equivalent of three billion crowns on supporting their national cinema! It's a huge amount

of money. We don't want so much. I know, the economy is not so good, but why should culture be the last in the line? When the government is supporting health and education, it should support culture as well. Anyway, we wrote a letter to our Minister of Culture in which we suggested the government should invest in Czech cinema around 500,000,000 crowns a year. That is equal to $15,000,000 dollars. It's not too much money after all. If they can pump 70,000,000 into the National Theater, why not into film? Our film is equally part of the nation's cultural heritage as our theater is. Czech film school, Film Academy and Czech filmmakers have a good worldwide reputation. The quality of work at Barrandov Studios was always high. But the government's help is necessary. Our government must declare its affinity to Czech cinema. We don't want to shoot 100 films a year, but we should get enough money to make ten films every year. They said it's private business and let it go. Not one government administration since the fall of Communism has made an effort to help Czech cinema! It's unbelievable.

How do you select the films you want to produce?
    The script is the most important for me. I read scripts all the time. I am not a screenwriter but I pick the scripts, which makes me feel good. If I like a script, I have three or five other people to pass it onto for further evaluation. Then I make my final decision. But the most important criterion for me is my feeling. I don't look for a specific theme. I look for anything — comedy, fairy tale, anything. But it must be a good script first. Then, when I select the script, I start raising money. To find financing for a feature film takes two to four years.

It looks like audiences abroad are not interested in Czech films today.
    Good scripts are extremely rare. We don't have any young screenwriters here. The young generation didn't generate any. No screenwriters, period. Everything starts and ends with a good script and because only average scripts are available, average films are being made. I read every year, well, between 50 to 100 scripts. Out of all those scripts only two or three are okay.

Is there nothing to write about?
    It's strange. Before the revolution, we spent a lot of time in one wine bar where many writers and screenwriters, including our Mr. President, were frequent customers and all of them were saying they are writ-

ing stuff for the time when this regime will be gone. When we asked them after the revolution where are all those scripts, nobody, with exception of Mr. President, who wrote all those great books and plays, had anything to show. [The] genre of comedy completely disappeared. We have a few good screenwriters like Jiří Křižan[57] or Vladimir Kerner but their stories are very depressing. It's a very difficult, very complicated situation. I am sure there are some good authors here, but good quality screenwriters? I don't believe there are any.

A story goes around that you came to the Barrandov Studios shareholders' meeting with a suitcase of cash and paid off all of them. What really happened?

No, it wasn't like that. I bought Barrandov Studios but not with a suitcase full of cash. It was a legal transaction at the bank. I was one of the approximately 20 shareholders of Barrandov, who privatized the studios and we started to fight as Czechs usually do, we couldn't agree on anything. We were divided into a few factions and there was no way to find common ground to make the studio prosper. Simply because there were many different opinions and nothing was working. We all agreed that after a three-month period whoever wanted to could buy out the others' shares to make the management of the studio more efficient, to give Barrandov Studios a chance. During that time I was in Marhoul's faction, we were friends then, and I helped him. The other faction was Michal Kocáb[58] with Peter Frejda, they had already decided to buy, and I simply managed to get the money overnight and I bought the Barrandov Studios for Václav Marhoul. It wasn't a suitcase of cash as commonly happens in Czech Republic, but it was a perfectly legal bank transaction. We bought 70 percent of the shares. The power was accumulated in one set of hands and theoretically everything should have prospered. Unfortunately it didn't happen that way. I believed it could have worked better, but Václav Marhoul couldn't handle it and the studio never become what it should be, and I was disappointed. Somebody succeeds, somebody fails. It was a bad bet, of course. Shit happens in your life. But now Barrandov Studios is actually functioning well and making a profit. There is no capital investment money, but the studios are running fine. The majority owner is Moravia Steel Corp. They bought it to expand their portfolio and get more loans. Now they would like to dump it. It's complicated. But it's the same everywhere you look around in Czech Republic, not just at Barrandov Studios. A big influx of foreign capital investment is necessary to make it work.

Filmography

JAROSLAV BOUČEK (born 1951)

Bouček studied producing at FAMU, where he graduated in 1974. Between 1974–92 he worked at Barrandov Studios. He worked there first as an assistant producer on 20 features and TV series and later as a line producer on another 12 films. In 1991 he was a production director of Barrandov Studios and in 1992 a manager of the Production Center. In 1993 he was one of the co-founders of AB Barrandov, Inc. Since 1993 he is an independent producer. He is a founder and manager of the BUC-FILM, Simplicity Cinema and BULL-FILM production companies and a member of the European Film Academy, Czech Television Academy and Producers Association.

2001—*Sleeping Beauty* (producer)— TV series
2000—*Angel Exit* (producer)
1999 —*Life in the Castle* (producer)— TV series
1988 —*Prosecuted Justice* (producer)— TV series
1998 —*Sekal Has to Die* (producer)
1996 —*Life in the Castle* (producer)— TV series
1995 — *Trip Through the Hell* (producer)
1994 —*Amerika* (line producer)
1992 —*Black Barons* (producer)
1990—*Pějme píseň dokola* (line producer)
1989 —*Go Back in Your Grave* (line producer)
1989 —*Swedish Trip Attractions* (line producer)
1988 — *Tainted Horseplay* (line producer)
1987 —*Birthday of Director Z.K.* (line producer)
1986 —*Octopuses from 2nd Floor* (line producer)
1986 —*Merry Christmas Greetings from Octopuses* (line producer)

Awards

Critique Award at AFI Festival 1998 (*Sekal Has to Die*)
Kristián 98 annual award of Czech critics (*Sekal Has to Die*)
Polska Nagroda Filmova 99 (*Sekal Has to Die*)

Jaroslav Brabec

CINEMATOGRAPHER, DIRECTOR

What is the situation in Czech film now like?
It's actually a stupid question because I am unable to answer it. It can be answered two ways, earnestly or from your own experience. I believe that whoever wants to make films can, and there are many capable people still around. Because film hasn't become, and probably will not become, a commodity here, hence the finances don't pour into film production as they should. To raise money for film is difficult and only the toughest individuals can do it. If you find a good script and a good producer who gets personally invested in the film and helps the director, you can always make it. It all depends on the determination and the will of people who want to make it happen. You can always make a film, or even a relatively good film. I believe those rocky days we had to go through are over and films are again becoming an integral part of our culture, finding its own parallel existence outside of entertainment products. I believe the prognosis that film would go to the Hell were foolish. I believe that Czech cinema will survive.

Often I hear here, in the Czech Republic, that there is no theme to the work, there are no screenwriters.
But that is not just a local problem. That's the problem in general, because to have a good script means to have a good film. Or at least have the foundation for a good film. Years ago many screenwriters were saying

Jaroslav Brabec (photograph by Robert Buchar).

they had great scripts that couldn't be shot because of whatever reasons. Maybe it was their personal judgment of what is good and what is not. Now, when there are no restrictions on what can be shot, the only criterion is artistic quality. On the other hand, it's also about connecting artistic qualities with commercial values. But no one can say any more "I have a great script but I can't get made it into a film." That's nonsense because it can be done. It would definitely get a grant from the Ministry of Culture. There is always a way.

Is there any dominant theme for filmmakers?

I am not sure. I think that topics are being picked up one by one by each filmmaker. To find a good theme, a topic for film, is extremely difficult. It depends on if you want to make a complicated film or a simple film, or a film for entertainment, or some other film... Some directors and producers are specializing in certain topics. I am not aware of any special theme arising from our present situation. And regarding our reaction to our past or the near past, those topics are not here yet. It is probably good that they are not here yet because it would be too soon to deal with them well. That period is still too recent to deal with and nobody is able to analyze it seriously. Maybe it will become a reservoir of ideas a couple of years from now. People are looking for topics all the time. Films of all kinds, in genres are produced here now, from auteur films to comedies. It is good that this period has no dominant theme because then it is still all about the film itself.

So, a specific theme? No, I don't have any. I like to make films as it is, you know what I mean. It's as simple as that. If you don't enjoy doing something, you don't do it. That's it.

Does Czech film need the government's financial support?
This is a valid issue because in Europe you can't make films without financial support from the government. Film can't become merchandise here like it is in America. And definitely not in the Czech Republic. It's a simple thing determined by the size of the market. If you add the numbers together, to find how many people would have to see the film just to pay it off, you realize it's impossible. That's why you can't compare the budgets of two relatively similar films shot here and in the United States. It is a question of the box office. That's why we have to look for different ways of financing by using non-commercial resources. The government's financial support of film production exists in all the civilized nations of Europe. The fact that we are now somehow struggling is partially our own fault. We have to learn filmmaking as a whole. Not just to be able to shoot a film but also to promote it and sell it–to deal with it from the beginning to the end. It has to happen. And once somebody succeeds the others will follow. But the box office issue will probably always be a problem. It means that the government's support is necessary. Actually, it is not necessary but it is very helpful. It gives the other investors a guarantee of investing in a good film.

Have films of the New Wave influenced you?
I don't feel that the Czech New Wave influenced me in any way. Well, except for one man — cinematographer Jaroslav Kučera. We knew each other. We were friends. I was his assistant at FAMU and later I took over his class, which I still teach today. He taught me to look at film from the other side, as it were, from inside of the script. I don't know if he fully succeeded in that, but his influence on my professional career was great, maybe the greatest. It wasn't about learning techniques but about the conceptual approach to film: how we are to look inside the film. But the New Wave itself? No. I believe that those films were good and revealing at the time but they passed away with that period. They became a resource, an inspiration for many people at that time but it didn't go anywhere. It didn't develop into anything. It just ended. Those films were important for Czech cinema, maybe even for European cinema. I don't know if they have any place in world cinema. Anyway, they were important once but it's over now.

Do you feel like you are a director or cinematographer?

I can't tell, but I think I still don't feel like a director. I was always a cinematographer and I love this profession. My directing debut was *Bloody Story* and that was by an accident. I was almost forced into it. At that time I just went through an unpleasant experience with a director and I decided to try to direct myself. *Bloody Story* was a novel sitting on my desk. I was reading it and I thought it could be a great film. At that time I wasn't aware that many directors had previously tried and failed to make it into a film. After I finished *Bloody Story*, I continued to direct. I learned a lot. Now, as I am working on my latest film *Chicken Melancholic*, I can see how important that previous learning experience was for me. I wanted to make this current film really badly. I discovered this novel when I was 16 years old. The story touched me deeply then. Then I forgot all about it and it came back to me again when I was shooting *Bloody Story*. I believed it could be an interesting film. Then I realized it's an extremely sad and depressing story and I wasn't sure if it would make any sense to make a film like that. But I couldn't give it up and wrote eight versions of the script. From total nonsense to a version I did together with the screenwriter Jaromír Kerner. I think the theme itself is really current because it's about human relationships overturned by egoism. I am no way a moralist but I feel it fits our times.

How would you define commercial film?

The question here is if you are asking it as an American, or if I answer it based on my feeling that commercial film can never exist in Czech Republic. What are the defining factors for commercial film? Is it the fact that the film makes a profit within a year? Or are there some other criteria that are harder to define? Commercial film could be, but doesn't have to be, a bad film as well as non-commercial film could be, but doesn't have to be, a bad film. Commercial film is a category that could be a… It is a category. It can be anything. It can co-exist with others. It doesn't have to necessarily be a bad thing. The problem is that commercial film should make money. That's for sure. But there is the issue regarding the government's support. A good film can become a commercial film just because it gets screwed up. And that can happen when the government's money gets involved. What I just said can sound like an excuse and maybe it's an excuse… It is wondering in a circle… We have to look at it from a different angle. It would be great if we could make a commercial film for 5,000,000 crowns, for example. But you can't make it for that amount of money. So, it is impossible. Only as an exception, maybe, and then just by accident. It's complicated.

Why do you make films?
Why do I make films? Because I enjoy doing it. You can sell cucumbers, real estate or make films. You don't do something you don't enjoy! It's simple like that.

Filmography

JAROSLAV BRABEC (born 1954)

Born in Prague, Brabec was an electrician when he studied cinematography at FAMU, where he graduated in 1979. He then worked as a camera operator at Barrandov Studios. In 1983 he shot his first feature film as DP with director Fero Feničr. In 1993 he directed his debut *Bloody Story*. He has taught cinematography at FAMU since 1987.

2001—*Hell of a Luck 2* (DP)
1999—*Chicken Melancholic* (director, screenplay, DP)
1996—*Girls for Love and Death* (director, screenplay, DP)
1995—*GEN a GENUS—B. Sipek, J. Kylián, K. Nepras* (director)
1995—*Last Move* (DP)
1995—*Zdislava* (DP)
1995—*V erbu lvice* (DP)
1993—*Bloody Story* (director, screenplay, DP)
1991—*My Citizens of Prague Understand Me* (DP)
1990—*Time of Testing* (DP)
1990—*Distinctive Beings* (DP)
1989—*Closed Circle* (DP)
1988—*Seven Hungry Men* (screenplay, DP)
1988—*Tainted Horseplay* (DP)
1987—*Why?* (DP)
1987—*Princes Jasnenka and Flying Shoemaker* (DP)
1986—*Who Is Scared, Runs* (DP)
1985—*Experiment Eva* (DP)
1984—*Treasure of Count Chamaré* (DP)
1984—*Džusový román* (DP)

Awards

Czech Leo Award 1993 for cinematography (*Bloody Story*)
Zlatý Ledňáček Award at Finále Plzeň 1993 (*Bloody Story*)
Directing Award at IFF of Sci-fi films at Rome, 1994 (*Bloody Story*)

Jan Svěrák

DIRECTOR

How would you characterize contemporary Czech cinema?

I would say Czech film is like a homeless child. It was thrown out on the street and nobody wants to take care if it. It has no parents. In the past, when the government controlled the film industry, this child was locked in the dormitory, but it was fed regularly and it was taken care of. Somebody was watching to keep it off drugs and to go to bed on time. But there is no scarecrow any more. Today there is no organization to control, or just monitor, what is being shot. Not even mentioning the fact that the government doesn't give a damn about the film industry in general. They don't care if we make any films or not. Their opinion today is that the values of culture are in the past, not in the present. So, culture, for them, is made up of old castles, classical music and literature. But what's happening today is that culture that actually influences the society now doesn't get any support at all.

Ten years after the revolution our government hasn't found a way to support filmmaking. And I believe they don't want to find a way to help. They don't care.

Does the situation at Barrandov Studios affect the production of Czech films?

It's irrelevant. You can shoot an entire film on location. You don't need go to Barrandov Laboratories to process your film. You can go to Czech Television. High speed film stocks today don't require too much light. You don't need studio sets today to make a film.

Jan Svěrák (photograph by Robert Buchar).

What does the Czech New Wave means to you?
It means a lot to me. We are pretty much jealous of the time they lived in, because those times allowed them to jump on the bandwagon and create something (even for those with a modest talent). They inspired each other. It wasn't that ten great directors were born at the same time. It was the time period that allowed them all to bloom. There was a sense of bonding which we don't have. We don't have that today. Maybe we are just idealizing that time period now. Maybe there were rivalries and with time passing we just see it more as an ideal epoch where they all loved each other and worked together. Maybe it wasn't that way. Maybe it was all different.

I often hear that there are no topics. Is there any specific topic today?
I can speak only for myself and I am not a film theoretician. What interests me, and this shows up in my film *Kolya* and the others as well, is a man versus himself. It gets at what an individual may do in a society where everything is allowed. Where are the boundaries? Actually, it is about morality. Establishing boundaries inside of each of us. How far can I go and what is the right thing to do? Because that's the problem in this society. The self-consciousness is missing. We don't believe in a God. Czechs are mostly atheists because they beat it out of us long time ago. We don't have a Czar to love and we don't have any dictator to be afraid of. Suddenly we are on our own and responsible for our behavior. One must be accountable for one's acts. We can't use the excuse "They didn't let me do it" as we did in the past. Now we can do anything and are fully responsible for our own lives. I believe that this is the big theme.

A Ride, 1994 — Anna Geislerová as Aňa (left), Radek Pastrňák as Radek (center), and Jakub Špalek as Franta. Jan Svěrák, director; František A. Brabec, DP; produced by Luxor (photograph by Biograf Jan Svěrák LTD).

What about you, do you have any theme?

I wouldn't put it that way. As I am getting older, I am dealing with my own problems. Things which personally bother me. That's how I pick topics for my films. Looking for films helps me solve my problems, gives me some answers to my questions. You can follow this pattern in my films. *The Accumulator* was such a crazy film — a mosaic of the period after the revolution where everything seemed to be possible. But the film was not about the euphoria of freedom or about the internal strength of a man. It was about a young guy without any strength who lies in a bed thinking he is dying. The film is about how he finds his strength. My second film, *A Ride,* is about two friends driving through the country and trying all kind of things. It's about the limits of our freedom. Where do they cross over to the territory of another person's freedom? And *Kolya* is about responsibility. It's about selfishness and about what it takes to be responsible for somebody else–the fact that responsibility doesn't necessarily keep you back but can enhance your life, make you a better

A Ride, 1994 (Jan Svěrák) — Jakub Špalek as Franta (photograph by Biograf Jan Svěrák LTD).

human. So, in this way I am solving problems I encounter in my life. *Kolya* was a very personal theme for me because I got married very young and have two kids — to stay single and enjoy the life versus taking care of someone.

No, I don't have any specific goal, any theme to follow. I look forward to the future and what else will come out, what problems I will have to deal with, and what my next film will be about.

How has winning an Academy Award for Kolya affected your career?

Actually, it hasn't. Of course, there was a big media circus. I couldn't go anywhere because I was like a rock star. Wherever I went, news people were there asking me questions. I had no private life. When I went to the Karlovy Vary Film Festival, I had to give ten interviews a day. Screw that. I would rather have stayed home. It changed me. My life became more secluded. And if you think it opened doors to me for new financial resources to make another film, you'd be wrong. That didn't happen because there is no money for filmmaking here anyway. Those few resources which are here I already knew because my father is a famous and well-respected filmmaker. I never had a problem going to Czech

Kolya, 1996 — Zdeněk Svěrák (left) as František Louka and Andrej Chalimon
as Kolya. Sctipt by Zdeněk Svěrák; Jan Svěrák, director; Vladimír Smutný, DP;
producers: Jan Svěrák and Eric Abrahám; premiere screening May 15, 1996
(photograph courtesy Biograf Jan Svěrák LTD).

Television and asking for money. So, to win the Oscar didn't help me
here at home. But it helped me abroad. Once you have an Ocsar, doors
are always open. Nobody will refuse talk to you.

*Somebody here said that cinema is no longer expected to be an art form.
Films today have to be entertainment.*
    I don't think so. I would say that learning is a part of human nature.
People were always passing stories, learning where a danger is and how
to deal with it ... how to survive and how to act rightly. That's our perpetual dilemma — how to behave and be true to yourself. Of course, we
expect stories to be entertaining. There is a formula that says that every
film has to have sex, politics and humor. But in addition to this, there
has to be more. A good film must have the addition of wisdom or some
kind of thought. That's what makes it good, I believe. Then it's not just
a pretty box but there must be something good inside of it as well.

Kolya, 1996 (Jan Svěrák) — Zdeněk Svěrák (left) as František Louka and Andrej Chalimon as Kolja (photograph courtesy Biograf Jan Svěrák LTD).

Do filmmakers have any responsibility to society? Are they responsible for the films they make?

I believe that filmmakers have a great responsibility to society. They are the bearers of culture. I don't want to make a bubble of the word "culture" or something.... But because they have direct access to so many people they deeply affect the society. That makes them responsible for their words and actions. It allows them to be very influential.

Every time I talk to any of our politicians, I say, "You should support filmmaking. You spend a lot of money on police, on the revenue service to collect taxes and on health care. If you'd financially support filmmaking just a little bit, then people might change their behavior a few years down the road. And then there might be less crime and people will pay their taxes because they realize it is normal to be responsible to the society, to be a moral person." Maybe I am a naive person but I believe in that.

Is Czech film dead?

I wouldn't say it's dead. I would say it's lost. It's like a homeless person wandering on the street. It doesn't have an identity. It doesn't know

where it is going and what to do. We have a great shortage of good stories. There are no screenwriters here. There are no stories to tell. But there
is a great need within the society for it. Look at the box office numbers.
When a Czech film, which has something to say comes out, masses go to
see it. It always beats any American hit in the box office. At the box office
my film *Accumulator* beat *Four Weddings and a Funeral* (which was a number one hit in Europe). *Kolya* beat *Titanic* as well and *Cozy Dens* did better than *Star Wars* or *Armageddon*. There is a demand for good domestic
films. As long as there is a demand for domestic films, Czech cinema can't
die. And economically speaking, there is a box office issue. Our ticket
prices are still half of what it costs in the rest of Europe. And because
prices of commercial products are equalizing, we can expect that movie
tickets will cost soon 200 KC. And because the numbers of moviegoers
will not change — I believe we've hit bottom — films could potentially
make some money. Czech film will never make a profit from box office,
video release and TV broadcast, but the amount necessary to raise for
the production will be lower, let's say just one-third of the total budget.

Kolya, 1996 — Director Jan Svěrák (left) and Director of Photography Vladimír
Smutný (behind the camera) on the set of *Kolya* (photograph courtesy Biograf
Jan Svěrák LTD).

Everybody is complaining that there are no scripts here, no screenwriters. How is it possible? In America, everybody wants to be a screenwriter!

Well, I don't know. I would say it's because screenwriting is not prestigious work here. A screenwriter here can never become respected or famous. We have maybe one or two like that. And he can't make enough money in screenwriting to survive living in anonymity. Nobody can afford to spend one year working on a feature script. To make a living, screenwriters must work also as dramaturgs on TV series, game shows and short documentaries. They must pick up change everywhere. Then, in their spare time only, they can work on a feature-length script. And that work for television greatly infects you, and you lose the necessary scope for feature films. Great ideas fade out. Everything becomes dull. The same applies to directors who work on commercials. I shot commercials for a long time and I enjoyed it. It paid well, you can come up with any ideas, can rent any special equipment and make amazing shots. But you spend a whole month working on each commercial, it's exhausting, and you don't have time and can't focus on a feature. In addition to that, you become spoiled because you make the same amount of money for each commercial you would make on the feature film! So you have a dilemma — does it make sense to make a feature films after all? Sure, making feature films makes you an "artist," but the bread and butter are in commercials.

The other thing is that if you make commercials for longer periods of time, you start to think like that. That happened, I believe, to many famous directors. Like Ridley Scott, for example. His films are built out of a bunch of great short commercials but it doesn't work together as a whole. It's like if an architect builds just a bunch of beautiful small shrines instead of a vaulted arch for a cathedral.

Is there a "European film"?

I don't think you can talk about European film. European film doesn't exist. It always will be French, Italian, Hungarian or Danish film. Every nation has its specific characteristics. That's what is cute about it. We understand each other. We feel all the nuances, which are actually entertaining. Like Italians are lively while Scandinavians like to drink themselves almost to death and then commit suicide. We understand them, we know why it is like that and we enjoy it. But you can't say that Swedish film is like Czech film. We are, Czechs are, like snakes. We are a hybrid between Russians and Germans. We have that Russian soul, sorrowful about ourselves and everything around us, but at the same time being exactly like Germans. Somewhere inside us is an Austro-Hungarian bookkeeper. Every nation has some specifics of its own. I would like to see a united Europe but I don't believe there will be ever one type of a European.

Filmography
JAN SVĚRÁK (born 1963)

He studied documentary film at FAMU and graduated in 1988 with the film *Ropáci*. He received an Academy Award for the Best Foreign Film in 1996 for *Kolya*.

2001—*Dark Blue World* (director)
1996 —*Kolya* (director, producer)
1994 —*A Ride* (director, screenplay)
1994 —*Accumulator 1* (director, story, screenplay)
1991— *The Elementary School* (director)
1988 —*Ropáci* (director, story, screenplay)

Awards

Academy Award for the best foreign film 1996 (*Kolya*)
Czech Leo Award 1996 for best director (*Kolya*)

Zuzana Zemanová

DIRECTOR

Can we say that under the Communist regime more and better quality films were shot then today?

It's very sad that consequences are not positive for us, because we can do anything now, we have freedom, maybe we have less money, but that's not such a big deal. I think the biggest difficulty is that we don't have a theme, a theme which would attract, or an interesting theme to focus on.

Why is there no theme?

Because all barriers have disappeared. Now, finally, we have freedom. Freedom that is so vast we are dwarfed by it. Actually, there should be plenty of topics but they are somehow unreachable. It is hard to define but maybe it is a global problem. That period of the 60s, the period of reflection and so on, is gone and to find a theme ... it's extremely difficult.

Films and TV programs produced now are our reflections. I think that we can't complain, because what is produced must somehow reflect what is going on inside each of us now. And I am afraid that there is not too much going on inside of us now.

Does New Wave mean something to you?

Of course it does. New Wave films fascinated us when we were in the Film Academy. Most of all, we felt it was the struggle for freedom,

freedom of expression, because at that time we couldn't do anything. For us it was a sign of hope for the future. I admire New Wave and I deeply bow in front of those people.

On the other hand, it is a paradox because they made those films during the period of hard Communism and many of them were banned from distribution. I believe that this is a period in our film history we can always rely on or, at least, admire.

Zuzana Zemanová (photograph by Robert Buchar).

Would you say that democracy has suppressed creativity?

I believe that our spiritual life is minimal. We are in a period when our priorities are focused on how to survive, and how to get more and more money. It is a natural reaction to the flood of merchandise and all that stuff coming at us like an avalanche, and all at the expense of our thinking, self-reflection, and our spiritual life. I think that the spiritual life of people stagnates. What happened in Communism — people were withdrawn because they didn't trust anyone — has its twin today because they are withdrawn again but the reason is not obvious. It has yet to be identified. I have a feeling that people are busy these days and all that is reflected in movies that strive to appeal to the masses, and it's related to the taste and the background of the filmmaker. On the other hand, there is one other important thing — the ability to raise money. There can be many talented people here who have no ability to do that. We were not used to it. We were not used to that vigor to make it on your own. I don't know. I think that if František Vláčil would apply for a grant today to shoot *Markéta Lazarová,* he would never get it. He would never make that film.

So, is money the problem?
    Yes, sure, but also desire. Actually, that desire, that primary thing why one would want to do this work, I don't know if it is the same today as it was in the past. I mean that one wanted to do it because he saw it as a mission, to create something nice, to pass a nice message to people. I am not sure what motivates people today to make films, especially features. Because when you see these new films, you really have to ask why, what is the purpose? And do you know what puzzles me the most? What kind of garbage is being shown on the screen. The censorship is gone, that's great, but I believe that every one of us should retain some sort of self-censorship. And I have a feeling it's not happening.

Well, here we are back to the moral of the individual.
    But what is moral? Morality is hard to define. I believe it's genetically coded in each of us. We are born with it and then, later on, it can be somehow distorted. Everybody has his own moral code. Where are the boundaries if they are not established and enforced? And morality, I am not sure if any exists in our society, when even in the highest places you can't trust anybody. De facto, this is a total loss of morality in this society.

Should everyone have a boundary he cannot cross?
    Sure, everyone should have his own boundary he cannot cross. But this boundary changes sometimes because you push it further and further and you are forced by your internal agenda to cross your imaginary boundary. But we can't move forward without morals.

Do you believe that joining the Communist party to make films was okay?
    I don't think I want to make that judgment. It's difficult. This is actually an issue of the relationship between an author's morality and his artwork. This is a fundamental question because we know from the history that some "bad guys"—amoral people—created great art. I don't think we can make that judgment today. It's too soon for that. History will do that later. Personally, I wouldn't do it. I couldn't sell myself for something I didn't believe in order to fulfill my ambitions. But that's my viewpoint right now. But who knows? If the result would be high-quality artwork—something what would make an imprint in history—then maybe we could forgive the personal debacle of the artist. Because an artist himself is not so important. What is important is the work he leaves

behind. But it would have to be a really good piece of art, something what would overcome all the negative aspects.

From an absolute point of view, if people didn't collaborate through this seemingly harmless way, being a passive member of the communist party, then we wouldn't be where we are now. And that is the bottom line of it, the horde is always innocent.

Filmograhy

ZUZANA ZEMANOVÁ (born 1956)

Zemanová studied directing at FAMU and since 1992 has worked at Czech Television. Her films have received awards at international film festivals.

2001 — *Companion* (director)
1998 — *Three Times Life, Three Times Death* (director)
1995 — *Eine Kleine Jazzmusik* (director)
1994 — *The Sand Castle* (director)
1993 — *In Love* (director)
1989 — *A Story of '88* (director)

Awards

Special Jury Award at Zlín 1996 (*Eine Kleine Jazzmusik*)
Prix Europa 95, Marseille (*The Sand Castle*)
TROIA 95, Portugal (*The Sand Castle*)
Grand Award at Chicago Children Film Festival 1993 (*In Love*)

Alois Fišárek

EDITOR

How would you describe the difference between Czech New Wave films and the contemporary Czech cinema?

In the 60s, all filmmakers, regardless of their style, had one common goal — to fight against the totalitarian regime. That was the foundation of the New Wave. The conditions were fertile for creativity because every filmmaker had to find a way to fool the censors. Because they couldn't express themselves openly, they had to find other ways. Everybody knew it. Even the censors knew it but they couldn't do anything about it because it wasn't in the dialogue.

Filmmakers today don't have to fight for freedom of expression. There are no forces forcing them together, and compared to filmmakers of the New Wave who worked together, they are working alone. Everybody stands just for himself. Back in the 60s they were also fighting the old ways of making films. They left studios' lots and went out to shoot on locations, bringing into the cinema new types of stories.

The fact that today the Barrandov Studios are not available for Czech filmmakers has its negative influence on Czech film. Films are not made exactly in a professional way; television has too much influence over the production. That influence is no good. Television dramaturgy is not feature film dramaturgy.

It's not that there are no talented people here any more, but the production system, which in the past was part of Barrandov, is missing.

What is left is production chaos — most of all in dramaturgy. Film dramaturgy does not exist. Nobody knows what a "film story" is. They don't know what to do and don't know how to do it. They have no idea what will work on the screen. This wasn't a problem in the past. Everybody knew what would work and what would not. Because the common enemy is gone, there is no universal theme, and everybody is wandering around looking for topics.

Alois Fišárek (photograph by Robert Buchar).

Every time after the revolution (well, this wasn't any revolution but let's *say* "revolution"), everybody is looking for a new identity and that is why they have a hard time finding topics.

We are going through a period of a great confusion now.

Filmography

ALOIS FIŠÁREK (born 1943)

He is one of the most prominent contemporary film editors in Czech Republic and a professor at FAMU, where he teaches editing.

2001 — *Dark Blue World*
2000 — *Prophets and Poets*
1999 — *Return of the Lost Paradise*
1999 — *Canary*
1998 — *Virginity*
1998 — *A Dead Beatle*
1997 — *Wonderful Years That Sucks*
1997 — *Road Through Deserted Forest*

1996 — *Kolya*
1996 — *Marian*
1995 — *In the Garden*
1994 — *A Ride*
1994 — *Accumulator 1*
1991 — *My Citizens of Prague Understand Me*
1991 — *The Elementary School*
1990 — *In the Heat of Imperial Love*
1990 — *Butterflies Time*
1987 — *With Love*
1984 — *Prague: The Troubled Heart of Europe*
1983 — *Faun's Very Late Afternoon*
1976 — *The Apple Game*
1970 — *Arch of Madman*
1965 — *The Rain*

Awards

Czech Leo Award 1996 for editing (*Kolya*)
Czech Leo Award 1994 for editing (*Accumulator 1*)

Otakar Vávra

DIRECTOR

You lived almost through the whole history of Czech cinema. How did you start?

Let me make this clear: I didn't go through the whole history of the Czech cinema. I am old but I am not so old. If that was the case, I'd be dead now. I started at the beginning of sound film as a screenwriter. I wrote ten scripts that were shot by other directors. During shooting those films, I was learning the craft. That was my self-education in filmmaking. The eleventh script I directed myself and since then I've directed 49 feature films. I was still writing scripts for other directors and wrote a few scripts that were never shot. After World War II, in 1949, I was invited to FAMU in Prague to teach. There was no directing department yet at that time. Gradually I was released from other appointments. For example, I was a director of Barrandov Studios for some period of time and spent more and more time teaching. In 1954 I took a one-year leave of absence to form a Directing department at the Film Academy. I wrote the curriculum for a five-year directing program, including all my lectures, and started my first directing class in 1955. And this was, by my opinion, the most talented class I ever had. Students in that class were Evald Schorm, Věra Chytilová, Jiří Menzel, Jan Schmidt and … there were five of them. They wanted to use films as a protest against the pressure from the state administration, against the totalitarian regime. Their films rose out of that pressure and that's how the Czech New Wave was

Otakar Vávra (photograph by Robert Buchar).

born. The common theme was alienation, the alienation of man within a society. It was extremely powerful.

Other generations of directors, screenwriters and cinematographers came along and they made together some 60 unbelievable films. Each one better than the other. All that came to be from the pressure they felt. But it wasn't as easy as it sounds. They had to find a new, adequate form of film language. It was really a new cinema. Not just differently made old films. And topics were different as well.... It was a new look at the world. And the vision of Věra Chytilová was different than the vision of Jiří Menzel or Evald Schorm. These were the best years of Czech cinema, when our films reached out in the world.

Actually, it was a paradox. The regime wanted to cultivate directors for their propaganda and everything took a turn in a different direction.

Yes, it turned the other way. FAMU had a strong influence on Czech cinema. Our graduates had a great reputation in the industry worldwide. Orson Welles[59] once said that it is impossible to teach directing except at one place, the Film Academy in Prague.

How would you characterize the situation in Czech film today?

I don't think that it's very good now. To make a film these days costs too much money, much more than the box office can make back. Back in 1935 we already talked about the possibilities of the state supporting film production because it can't live on just the ticket sale because we are such a small nation. In a nation of 10,000,000, film can't make a profit if it costs over 20,000,000 to shoot it. They are trying to make films cheap and the result is predictably poor. The exception can be a film with one adult and one child as the actors, like *Kolya*. That film had great success. But that's not cinema. You can't treat cinema so cheaply because the audience wants to see something in the theater. It's not television.

On television, you can get away with many things, you are fine if your actors perform well. Film in the theater opens the window to the world. Viewers demand to see something. Anyway, back then we were thinking about how government should support filmmaking, about a committee that would evaluate scripts and recommend them for a state grant. I know that France has a system like that, they subsidize their national cinema. European films simply don't have the opportunities American films do. They don't have that large audience, which can recover expenses.

Grants that our government is giving to our filmmakers are too small to make any impact on film production. Let's hope it will change in the future. Hopefully somebody will figure out how to revitalize Czech cinema. I mean to improve conditions. I believe this will happen because Czech film is extremely tough and has survived many bad times. It survived for a hundred years, since the silent era until today.

After the "Velvet Revolution," the film industry was actually dispersed...
Every time a coup comes along, there are radicals who destroy everything from the past. But that's not good. There must be continuity. Everything new should be built on the past. Actually, our regime collapsed because the regime in Russia collapsed, because the Soviet Union collapsed. We knew it would happen one day, but we didn't think it would happen so soon. I thought it would take ten more years.

What period gave you the most creative freedom?
I didn't make any film in this new capitalist system. I shot my last film in 1988. It was shortly before the coup and that time I was quite free to do what I wanted. It wasn't bad. But otherwise it was always hard work to push my projects through. I always chose my own topics, wrote my scripts — sometimes with a co-writer — and directed the film. I never made a film as a job or a film that somebody else ordered me to do. I never made a film I didn't want to make.

What are your happy memories?
The beginning of my career was nice. When I was shooting *Philosophic History* (Filozovská historie) or *Virginity* (Pannenství). Or I like to

Hammer Against Witches, 1969 — Vladimír Šmeral as Boblig (right), Ilja Prachař as magistrate (center) and Josef Kemr as Ignác. Adaptation of a novel by Václav Kaplický, script by ester Krumpachová and Otakar Vávra. Otakar Vávra, director; Josef Illík, DP; premiere screening January 23, 1970, produced by Filmové Studio Barrandov (courtesy National Film Archive Prague, photograph by Jitka Bylinská).

remember the films *Rosina the Foundling* (Rozina Sebranec) or *Mischievous Bachelor* (Nezbedný bakalář) that I shot right after World War II, after the Nazi occupation. Films I like most are *Golden Rennet* (Zlatá Reneta) and *Romance for Trumpet* (Romance pro křídlovku), based on the work of poet František Hrubín. *Golden Rennet* had a complicated structure and wasn't commercially much successful. But everybody liked *Romance for Trumpet* and I believe that this was my best film because it is lyrical and philosophical at the same time. Later I had some problems. It was difficult to push a script through the system. Hussite trilogy for example. Or films about Jan Ámos Komensky[60] or Jan Hus. The Communist censors gave me a hard time there because Jan Hus wasn't revolutionary enough for them. And Jan Ámos was a pacifist, so why to make a film about a pacifist in the first place? They didn't like the fact he was a priest, which was then considered ridiculous. So we had to suppress his priesthood and that hurt the story. But he was really an amazing man.

He is known as a founder of pedagogy but he had many other qualities
that made him immortal. I tried to put all of this in the film but I was
criticized that I gave in to the censors.

What period was the worst?
   The worst for filmmakers? It was in the 70s. The Communist party
tightened the screws in 1971. Many things changed then.[61] New people
came, people who didn't succeed. It's interesting that the Communist
films, with the theme of socialism, didn't succeed. They completely failed.
It didn't catch on. It didn't achieve anything because it was [a] lie. It wasn't
true. It was political propaganda. I still managed to make *Hammer Against
Witches* (Kladivo na Čarodějnice) in 1969, which was a historical para-
phrase of the political monster processes in the 50s. The same thing happened in the seventeenth century in northern Moravia. But I denied any
similarities, insisting that I just made another historical film.

*Everybody is telling me that there is no theme. Nobody is interested in the
present reality.*
   I think there is a theme here today but it would be very difficult to
put it in an art form. I believe it's the theme of two democracies. I remember Masaryk's democracy. I was brought up in the democracy of the 20s
and 30s. That, I believe, was the real democracy. People had to work hard
to make a living, to buy property. People were honest and patriotic. It
had roots in the Austro-Hungarian Empire and was growing for a long
time. When democracy came in 1918, and until 1938, the Republic was
proud. It was a rich state that Germans came to eat up…. I never forget
how in Koruna, at a buffet in Václavské Square in Prague, German soldiers were eating cakes with whipped cream. They were eating full plates
of cakes, the cakes they never saw before. Hungry Germans, Nazis, came
to eat a rich Czechoslovak Republic.
   And now after the Velvet Revolution we have a democratic republic — capitalistic republic — again. But this one has a long way to go to
be called a democracy yet. People are affected by the occupation and by
the long years of the totalitarian system. Their spines are quite crooked
and their perception of life as well. They'd like to get rich quickly without any hard work and so on. Values changed. I believe it will take a long
time, maybe two generations, before we will get back to normal. But I
believe it will come one day because our Czech people are indestructi-
ble.

So, is it the theme of two democracies?
That problem, that theme, is here but to make a film about it — transform it to the screen — is extremely difficult. Because that problem isn't solved yet. That theme needs distance. But it will come.

How did you manage to survive all the periods and changes?
Maybe because I am tough. I am persistent. The most successful films here were usually little comedies, small films easy to shoot. But I always took a big bite. I loved to direct big scenes.

Is there a moral responsibility of the filmmaker to the society? A line which he shouldn't cross?
I would say that filmmakers must not work only for money. When times were politically bad, when the censorship was tough, I was making big films. I shifted from contemporary topics to history. I chose historical topics nobody could attack. But even that wasn't easy. I was fighting ten years for my film about Komenský. They didn't want me to make that film. Many topics took years to push through.

Do you think there is a relationship between censorship and creativity? During the totalitarian regime, everybody was saying they were writing for better times to come and now there are no scripts, no topics.
It was always like that. They were saying the same the same things during the Nazi occupation too. And after War World II ended, nobody had anything. And it's the same now. Because you can write something you know you can't shoot. If you now you can't shoot a film, you just can't write that script.

Is it possible to say that the switch to a market economy affected Czech cinema?
Absolutely. I believe that it totally destroyed Czech cinema. Film industry was when we were making 30 films a year. That's what I would call a film industry. But to make a few film every year, ten films or so, waiting to see if somebody gives you money or not, that is not a film industry. And it will take some time before the government will understand that its help is necessary. We don't have any big corporations, like in America, to support culture. Over here they can support football the most, but they will never give any money for film.

How would you define "a good film"?

What a question! It's hard to give you a simple answer because this is a question of what art is and I would hate to talk about it without giving it more thought.

Well, let me ask you another way. What distinguishes a good film from a bad film?

Truthfulness. The truthfulness is what distinguishes a good film from a bad film. It's a simple answer, one word that says it all.

What is art?

What is art? We discussed this before. Art is when an artist, creator, is reacting to a pressure from the outside world through his own internal emotions, expression, and he is able to share this expression with others. Ancient hunters knew that "share it" when they drew a bison on the wall of the cave. The drawing of the bison didn't just resemble the real bison but he was also running, in motion, very dynamic but at the same time it was like a dream — it was an emotion of the bison representing a God, a demon to man who was watching him and trying to capture him. That's it. All this together — emotions processed by an artist's conscience leading to a form — that's where film becomes art. If it just represents something then it's not art, it's just a craft. That's how it is with film, life, everything.

Do you feel that the idea of a Hollywood film will destroy European film?

I don't believe that will ever happen. The concept of American film is oriented outward — it's about emotions and the creation of tension. American films know perfectly how to create a drama and that's why they are so successful with a broad spectrum of audiences. They know how to build up drama. And that's why they focus on action films, on the motion. René Clair said that motion in a film is poetry. Like when horses run on the screen. That's why all big actors in America wanted to appear in Westerns. Because in Westerns they rode horses and the audience rode along with them. They became 12-year-old boys fascinated with the motion. Riding a horse was a principle of an American man, a man who, with a shotgun, can take care of himself and perhaps his wife. But today because of the commercialism, the principle of brutality is becoming overwhelming. It is catchy as well but the outcome is negative. The European film is different. Because European film, if it is art film, is built on the Mediterranean culture — the oldest western culture.

Mediterranean culture came to Europe from Africa through Crete and Greece and created famous epics — Homer's *Iliad*, and *The Odyssey*,[62] Romanesque legends about King Arthur,[63] and the Scandinavian hymn about Nibelungs.[64] These are the cornerstones of European culture, literature, and film. European culture has a deep foundation. The literature reflects the evolution of our civilization and film should do the same.

Would you like to make another movie?

I have a script written but I can't shoot the film because the rights for the story are in London. That lady, the owner of the story, died and her heirs don't want to make it into a film. Also nobody would pay for it. It's about the murder of Jan Masaryk.[65] Nobody wants to touch it. They are scared because it looks like the KGB murdered him. And you are recording all this... I just don't want to be run over by a car on the street. And the budget is high. It would cost over 100,000,000 crowns ($33,000,000) to make it. It's hard to put together this amount of money if you know that the domestic box office can bring you back only some 10,000,000.

Why are some directors, including those from the New Wave, feeling that the younger audience today doesn't understand them?

From the New Wave? Who said that?

Jiří Menzel, for example, says that the young generation today thinks differently and is interested in very different films.

Well, his last film was actually a Russian film [*Life and Extraordinary Adventures of Private Ivan Chonkin*]. The story was Russian, the actors were Russian, and the only Czech in the film was actually himself.

What was your relationship to your students?

It was nothing personal, but I knew them very well. I spent five years with them, from junior years 'til graduation. They don't do it at FAMU like this any more. Now they have a different instructor every year. But back then, I was teaching them for a full five years and that allowed me to know them very well. I saw their work through their personalities. It's interesting. It was my first class when I started the directing program and it was, at same time, the best class I ever had. And I must say something. Today most of the students want a degree and get out. But back then, they really loved to be there and make their films. They enjoyed themselves. They studied with euphoria, they wanted to learn, to do something. They were helping each other regardless of the fact that they were very different personalities. Jiří Menzel was the youngest one. Věra Chytilová was more thoughtful. It was great. Unfortunately, Evald Schorm was seriously ill all the time. He was exceptionally talented but very ill and I had to watch him die for years.

What would you say to those people criticizing you for making films through all regimes?
    Beg your pardon? Oh, yes, there are some people saying that. Making films is my life. I was shooting films through all regimes, but I saved my face.

Filmography

OTAKAR VÁVRA (born 1911)

Vávra was born in Hradec Králové in 1911. He shot 49 feature films and wrote 80 scripts. He studied architecture in Prague and during studies shot a couple of experimental shorts: *Světlo Proniká Tmou* (1931) and *Žijeme v Praze* (1934). He started writing scripts in 1933 with Hugo Haas and František Langer. He directed his debut *Filozofsá Historie* in 1937. During World War II he directed 12 feature films. After the war he served as general manager of Barrandov Studios and started to teach at FAMU, Film Academy of Fine Arts in Prague. In 1955 he became a founder and Chair of the directing department there with Věra Chytilová, Jiří Menzel, Jan Schmidt and Evald Schorm in his first class. When the dust settled down at FAMU after the reorganization following the Soviet invasion, he was suspended from his position there. He shot ten more films during the Normalization era and in 1997 published his memoirs *Podivný život režiséra* (PROSTOR 1997).

1989 — *Evropa tančila valčík*
1985 — *Veronika*
1984 — *Komedianti*
        Oldřich a Božena
1983 — *Putování Jana Ámose*
1980 — *Temné slunce*
1977 — *Příběh lásky a cti*
1976 — *Osvobození Prahy*

1974 — *Sokolovo*
1973 — *Dny zrady* (*The Days of Treason*)
1969 — *Kladivo na čarodějnice* (*Hammer Against Witches*)
1968 — *Třináctá komnata*
1966 — *Romance pro křídlovku* (*Romance for Trumpet*)
1965 — *Zlatá reneta* (*Golden Rennet*)
1962 — *Horoucí srdce*
1961 — *Noční host*
1960 — *Policejní hodina*
       Srpnová neděle
       Národní umělec Zdeněk Štěpánek
1959 — *První parta*
1958 — *Občan Brych*
1957 — *Proti všem* (*Against All*)
1956 — *Jan Žižka*
1955 — Jan Hus (*John Huss*)
1952 — *Nástup* (*Lining Up*)
1949 — *Němá barikáda* (*The Silent Barricade*)
1948 — *Krakatit*
1947 — *Předtucha* (*Presentiment*)
1946 — *Cesta k barikádám*
       Nezbedný bakalář (*The Mischievous Bachelor*)
1945 — *Rozina sebranec* (*Rosina the Foundling*)
       Vlast vítá
1943 — *Šťastnou cestu* (*Happy Journey*)
1942 — Okouzlená
       Přijdu hned
1941 — *Turbina*
1940 — *Maskovaná milenka*
       Pacientka Dr. Hegla
       Pohádka máje
1939 — *Humoreska*
       Kouzelný dům
       Dívka v modrém
1938 — *Cech panen Kutnohorských*
       (*The Guild of Virgins of Kutna Hora*)
1937 — *Filosofská historie*
       Panenství (*Virginity*)
1936 — *Velbloud uchem jehly*

Drahomíra Vihanová

DIRECTOR

*According to statistics, 80 percent of moviegoers are 20 years old or younger.
Jiří Menzel said he couldn't make commercially successful films any more
because this generation thinks differently.*

He is right. This is the problem of the whole New Wave generation. The reality is that only young people go to see movies today. I am
not sure for what reasons they do that. Maybe they come for other reasons than watching a movie. Their way of thinking is different from ours.
They probably need different kind of films. Something shocking, brutal, or on the other hand absurd, crazy, or … I don't know what. It seems
to me that they don't need what we believed a good film should have —
a message, which should be somehow beautified. I am finishing my new
film and I don't believe young people will go to see it. So, who is this
film for? František Vláčil was always saying it was worth the effort to make
a film only one of your friends would enjoy. This theory was possible
during the Bolsheviks' era only. Today it's not trendy to make a film for
one person or for yourself. But I still do it. I am making this film mostly
for myself. I do it because I feel an urge. I know that this is somehow
masochistic. This attitude is unacceptable today and I am fully aware of
it. My films can never make a Top Ten list and it doesn't bother me. Realistically, I can think of 15 — 20 people who could like it. But I enjoy going
abroad with my films to international film festivals. I realized that people abroad understand my films better than people here at home. For

125

Drahomíra Vihanová (courtesy CINEART TV Prague, photograph by Vlastimil Malaska).

example, my film *The Fortress*. People here didn't get it. They took it as my personal getting even with the Communists. That idea never crossed my mind. People just reflected their own feelings onto it. Viewers abroad understood my film as the central problem of human existence: how to live in this absurd world. The film is about how one day something is allowed and the next day it is forbidden. What is the truth today can turn to a lie tomorrow. I was happy that they didn't apply the story to the Communist regime. In Spain they told me I shot a film about Christ in the Twentieth Century. I believe that my new film will find its audience elsewhere if it doesn't succeed here. I am certain that the audience here will not like it. Just because it sides with the Gypsies or they will not like in order to be politically correct. I am not trying to idealize the Gypsies or something. I am just trying to point out their differences. Differences in values. To show that their values are very important to them, to their community. This is not a simple matter. And Czechs don't like to hear it. Because for Czechs, only their values are good and everything else is not acceptable. You have to be like us, Czechs, or go away!

Do you still feel there are some "restrictions" on what you can do?

No, there are no restrictions. You just can't touch some topics or personalities belonging to the "circle of myth." For example Václav Havel is one of them. You can't dig in his personal life, his marriage. You'd better not try. People are very sensitive about it. For example, if you make a documentary about Lucie Bila[66] that will show her somehow in an unflavored light, people will kill you because the whole nation loves her.

You wouldn't be able to walk on the street any more. Like my documentary film about Eva Olmerová *Metamorphosis of My Friend Eva.* Everybody knew her, people had their own image of her in mind and they refused to accept the reality. You can make a harsh film about an anonymous drug addict. No problem, it doesn't bother anyone. But you must not get personal. People don't want to see and hear it and they are extremely touchy about that.

Your documentary about Eva Olmerová is a great film. I show it to my students in Chicago and they like it a great deal. It's so powerful.
Well, we love myths. Everybody knew that Eva Olmerová had an alcohol problem. And not just that. She had problems with drugs as well but she got out of that and the alcohol problem continued. But nobody talked about it any more. It was forgotten. The fact is she was a great singer and fully enjoyed her life. I didn't mean to hurt her. I wanted to show how she lives and who she is. How she is fully enjoying her life. Maybe she wouldn't be such a great singer without all that. It's all connected. And that's how I approached the film. I moved into her apartment and lived with her for some time. We became friends. Unfortunately, our friendship ended after this film came out. But I just wanted to show where her beautiful singing comes from. If she hadn't lived her life the way she did, including the alcohol and lovers she dumped out of windows, there probably wouldn't be her beautiful singing. The viewers abroad seems to understand that. Rudolf Krejčík was showing the film to his foreign students at the Film Academy and they loved it. When we were shooting the film, we had no idea what would happen from minute to minute. I believe you can feel it there. All that tension, handheld camera, rack focusing and trying to catch what is going on. It feels authentic and her voice is beautiful. But here, in the Czech Republic, the film raised all kinds of hell. I was afraid to walk on the street. The television network received bags of mail after broadcasting the film. Very nasty letters! (Well, I have no illusions about the average TV viewer when I see what people are watching the most.) But the fact is that in the aftermath of all that our friendship was gone. At first she approved the print and she liked it. We had a private screening with her, our crew, and a couple of her friends first. She said "Don't change anything" and approved the film for release. But after the TV broadcast, all the friends around her were telling her, "Eva, you looked like you were coming out of the shower, you shouldn't look like that on TV." Then she started to blame

Dull Sunday, 1969 — Ian Palúch as Armošt (left) and Míla Myslíková as Mary. Story by Jiří Křenek; Drahomíra Vihanová, director; Zdeněk Prchlík and Petr Volf, DPs; premiere screening April 1, 1990; produced by Filmové Studio Barrandov (courtesy National Film Archive prague, photograph by Miloš Schmiedberger).

me for a couple of things. First of all, she accused me of showing her a different film for approval. Second, she said she wasn't aware of when we were shooting and when we weren't. That's nonsense! We were shooting 35mm and you can't hide that. We didn't shoot with a hidden camera. She was aware of the camera all the time and we didn't tell her what to do. What she was doing was entirely up to her. But most of all she accused me of forcing her to drink alcohol (which came out of the fact that without the bottle she wasn't able to communicate). And that boulevard magazine REFLEX jumped on it and printed a big interview with her about my film being a lie. She claimed she was going to sue me for it and if she saw me on the street she'd kill me. The big discussion about the ethics of documentary filmmakers, led by director and critic Rejžek, arose from this — does a filmmaker have the right to shoot a film like that? I say it's rubbish, why make an intellectual bubble out of this? What are you mumbling about? What ethics? She knew we were shooting a film with her and it was up to her to get drunk or not. She knew that whatever she did in front of the camera was up to her, and her only. She knew that if she didn't like my question, she didn't have to answer. There is no ethical issue here and never was. She was completely in charge of her actions. I was aware that the shooting would not be easy. I witnessed much worse situations when I was living with her before the shooting started. I could imagine what the film would look like and I knew I couldn't make a Cinderella out of her. This madness lasted for six months and it was everywhere. In *Film a Doba* magazine they were discussing the ethics of documentary — what a director can and can't do. Director Jan Spata[67] attacked me because he always made those sweet and sentimental documentaries. He used to add Gustav Mahler's music to it and everyone was cunning. His logic was to show only the nice things from life to people in order to help them. Okay, it's his opinion but I can't watch it any more. This is the story of my documentary about Eva Olmerová.

A Report About the Pilgrimage of Students Peter and Jacob, 2000 — Adrian Jastraban as Jakub and Zuzana Stivínová as his bride. Script by Drahomíra Vihanová and Vladimír Vondra; Drahomíra Vihanová, director; Juraj Šajmovič, DP, producer Viktor Schwarcz (courtesy CINEART TV Prague, photograph by Vlastimil Malaska).

What about some good memories?

I was very happy when I was shooting my debut *Dull Sunday*. Unfortunately, because it was my first feature film, the trauma later, when the film was banned from theaters, was equally bad. We still managed to strike a release print. Some other filmmakers, like Milan Jonáš or Balada for example, didn't get so lucky. Studio director Vlastimil Harnach,[68] a great human being, told me to finish the print by December 31, 1969. He knew what was coming on January 1, 1970. We were mixing sound over the Christmas holiday and all the people working on the film were great. There was that wonderful spirit to help, which later during Normalization quickly evaporated. But the year 1969 wasn't so bad yet.

It is a fact that my life took a sharp turn when I shot *Dull Sunday*. No question about it. I didn't have the advantage Věra Chytilová, Evald Schorm or Jan Němec had, for example. They graduated earlier and their films were screened and received recognition abroad. Czech films were very popular then. I basically had nothing and that was disastrous. I was so excited making my first feature film and then it was immediately confiscated and banned. And then void. Seven years of nothing. Then Kamil Pixa offered me an opportunity to shoot a documentary film. *The Last of Kin* was my first short but it was in 1977. I was never inclined to make documentary films. I was never interested in shooting any. But then I said, better than nothing, it is film too. And at least it was some work and there were moments when I enjoyed doing it.

I enjoyed making the film about František Vláčil and the film about Rauch. And I shot a documentary about a crazy woman who was working at a railroad station ticket counter and writing poetry. I must admit that some documentaries gave me a satisfaction. Then some of them started getting awards in film festivals abroad and I wasn't allowed to go. It wasn't 'til 1986 when they let me go to the film festival in Gelbo and I was able to see what was going on in documentary film in the rest of the world. The dramaturgy really loosened in the second half of the 80s. It became possible to push through some interesting topics. Of course, you couldn't say in the film that Jakes was an idiot. But you could squeeze something in. The situation was much better in the Short Film Studios than in the Barrandov Studios. Barrandov was occupied by Balík, Kachlík, Steklý, and other characters like that.

Then I was very happy again when I got the opportunity to shoot my second feature film *The Fortress*. I didn't expect it to happen. I expected ending my life in a retirement home and reading *Rude Pravo*.[69] The

A Report About the Pilgrimage of Students Peter and Jacob—Drahomíra Vihanová on the set (courtesy CINEART TV Prague, photograph by Vlastimil Malaska).

opportunity to shoot a feature again was a resurrection from the ashes for me. Theoretically I should be happy now. The truth is that my life stumbled because I shot *A Dull Sunday*. That's the fact. But how could you know what would happen? Even if the Soviets hadn't have come in 1968, maybe I would have lost my inspiration or gotten ill. Or I could have been run over by a car. Whatever. But professionally my life flopped. No question about it. But what can you do? Unfortunately, I was already too old back in 1968. I was 39 years old. If that would have happened to me when I was 25 — to have my first feature film put in a vault — I would be still be full of energy today. Well, we were switched to a different rail back in 1968.

If you could go back in time when you were 25 years old, what would you do differently?
I can't imagine how would I think if I were 25 years old today. My thinking was shaped the way I was brought up. It has its roots in some cultural and moral background. I was taught that you must not do cer-

tain things. You don't steal, you don't cheat, and you keep your word. With this baggage I am carrying on. Even if I were to be 25 years old again, I would be in the same shithole as I am now. The age doesn't matter. What matters is what is inside of you. I wouldn't be able to adapt to the absolute self-confidence, superficiality and arrogance of young filmmakers today. No question about it! They have no inhibitions. Not all of them are like that. Saša Gedeon, for example, is different. He also carries baggage with him.

Everything that is happening now seems to me so dirty and amoral. Everything is so superficial. Values shifted, what's important and what isn't. And that's why people are refusing to see films that eventually carry a message. I can't adapt to this. Why should I? Why should I watch with an open mouth as somebody is murdering someone on the screen and the blood is splashing everywhere? Or laugh over totally stupid jokes? People today don't want to think. It's an unnecessary burden to them. They feel better without it because if they had to think about what's happening around them, then they would realize what is going on and they would have to hang themselves. That's my opinion. One can't seriously analyze the situation we are in now. It can lead only to two things, a suicide or an insane asylum, bedlam. Or pushing against the wall, which would get you thrown into jail. Maybe that's why people don't go to see films that would force them to think. For example Andrei Tarkovsky's[70] *The Sacrifice*— the empty theater. Or you can find a couple of fans and then you may wonder why they are actually there. But they are an exemption and thank God for that. The reason why they come is not so important. When you think of it, prices are rising all the time; you have to pay your rent while watching others tunneling millions.

Having no family makes me pretty much free. If I had had a family, I would have been forced to make compromises during the Bolsheviks' era. And I am not surprised that some people did that. I didn't have to. I can always self-restrain and my cats don't need too much. So, I am not surprised that people don't want to see Tarkovsky's films. They have to deal with very different problems of their own.

Sometimes I feel happy I am my age because I believe that with my mentality, if I were be young today, I would look like an idiot here. I don't see my age as a handicap. They would kick the shit out of me here anyway regardless of my age. They would laugh at me. To live your own life here according to some moral principles, so you can look at yourself in the mirror in the morning without getting sick, is hardly possible

A Report About the Pilgrimage of Students Peter and Jacob— Drahomíra Vihanová. A scene from the Rom gypsy village (courtesy CINEART TV Prague, photograph by Vlastimil Malaska).

without some conflict with the people around you. Simply because you are different! Like an idiot. First they try to pull you on their side and then, when they realize it's not possible, they beat the hell out of you.

Director Jiří Menzel said he doesn't have any problem with someone who joined the Communist party to make good films. And he probably has more respect for those who did just that than compared with those who refused, pulled back and didn't do anything.

Well, he applies it specifically to film, but anyway.... No, you can't say it like that ... it's a question of morality in general. It's the problem of that play, *Mefisto.*[71] He performs for the Nazis. Because he insists that if he plays Faust, then it will be art and he will have given a good to the people. But the fact that he is supported, paid by Nazis.... That's what we talked about. It's not so simple. That's the question of personal morality. Simple ignorance is no defense. "We didn't know!" They knew, whoever wanted to know knew that Communists were crooks so I'm not gonna hang around with crooks ... just to bring people pearls of wisdom.... That's impossible! I can't collaborate with crooks. That's the

point. So, I don't think … I don't know. I can't join crooks! But, if he
puts it this way, it wasn't necessary. Look, I didn't join any party or organization, ever! I didn't join the Pioneer Youth Organization. I only went
once to a Youth Organization meeting at FAMU when Antonín Máša
was a chairman together with Goldman. There was a meeting and do
you know what was on the agenda? There was a student, a very intelligent guy name Petr Král.[72] He later defected to France and became a
famous surrealist poet. He was in our class studying screenwriting. They
wanted to expel him from the organization because he was different —
instead of a briefcase, he always carried with him an old-fashioned doc-
tor's chest and an umbrella. And because of that he was expelled from
the organization by Máša and Goldman!

I said that I didn't want to be in any organization that can expel
Peter Král because of his briefcase and umbrella and I left. That was my
first and last association with any organization. And as you can see, it
was possible once in a while to shoot a documentary film. So it is not
true that it was necessary to join the Communist party. Yes, whoever
wanted to rake in a fortune joined! Whoever was greedy and wanted to
make a lot of money had to. I didn't want so much. I was happy with
one short film every two years. They could kick me out any time they
wanted. As freelancers we never knew if we would get another film to
shoot or not. That was a disadvantage. But the advantage was they could
never force us to shoot a film we didn't like. They could never say to us,
"You will shoot this!" Or if they did, I could always say, "This topic
doesn't mean anything to me and I will not do it." So there was a way
around. I could always refuse. So it was possible… Very modestly….
Your shield was always dirty because you worked for Communists, of
course, but it wasn't as shitty as the others' were. And as a matter of fact
they never broke me down. They always held the Sword of Damocles over
my neck. I knew they could decapitate me any time they wanted. But I
was never brave enough….

I wasn't brave enough to sign Charta 77. Only after 1989 I signed
everything. But it was possible this way, with relatively less dirt on your
hands than the others. But some people had, relatively, much harder
times–like Stanislav Milota, Antonín Máša, Pavel Juráček.[73] Even Zdeněk
Sirový, for example, his *Mourning Party* was one of the films ending up
in the vault.[74] Beautiful film. He was also blacklisted. But they let him
do lip synch. Of course, they cut him off because he would make beautiful films. He did lip synch, he did it well and they let him live. So they

The Last of Kin, 1977 — Drahomíra Vihanová, director; Robert Buchar, DP (photograph by Robert Buchar).

really did let some people live, some of us were allowed somehow exist, and some people were kissing their ass, no question about it.

I couldn't believe it when some of my colleagues at Short Film Studios were trying to explain to me why they joined the Communist party in 1972. I can understand that choice in 1963. But join the party in 1972 after all that had happened? And do you know how many joined the Communist party at that time? Unbelievable! Why? Because they wanted to shoot films! But for me to join crooks, wolves, just for the opportunity to assert my wolf's voice a little bit? No way, with wolves, never ever.

He said exactly: "If you want to make a good film and there is no other way, you have the right to do it under one condition: the film is worth it."
Well, they were making, let's say, better merchandise. If Bergman didn't make any films I would feel sad. Or Jean Luc Godard. I recently saw Godard's latest film and I said, "Shit, I don't get it, it looks like a film!" But if Karel Smyczek or Dušan Klain hadn't made any films, nobody would notice. Nobody would notice. What's good is very sub-

Last of Kin, 1977 — Logger František Kříž in *Last of Kin*, the first short film Vihanová was allowed to shoot since her feature debut *Dull Sunday* in 1969. Drahomíra Vihanová, director; Robert Buchar, DP; produced by Kráthý Film Praha (photograph by Robert Buchar).

jective. I believe that films are good when they reflect the author's personality. Like the films of František Vláčil. No question about it. Also Jiří Krejčík was a distinctive personality, or Věra Chytilová. But if Klain's films were directed by somebody else instead, nobody would notice! His personality doesn't show up. Or those TV pilots Karel Smyczek was doing! Or Hynek Bočan, he is so fucked! He was also one of the New Wave and look what he is doing now! You know it's his film only from the credits, but any Joe Doe could shoot it. You can't see any difference.

What can you say about contemporary Czech cinema?
    As Mr. Klaus said: "It's not so bad. What are you complaining about? Nineteen films are shot every year. It's not bad at all!" The question is, what kind of films are shot, and under what conditions. The fact is that I am probably spoiled, not by the Communists, but simply by the responsibility taken by the government for developing a culture. And I would really appreciate if the [current] ministry of culture would feel

some that responsibility. I have a feeling they don't. They labeled film as merchandise, which must be financially self-sustaining. That is absolutely impossible. Czech films can eventually make some money if they're sold abroad. But even if they do very well domestically at the box office they can't make a profit. There are no generous patrons. That's related to the tax system — they can't write it off. It's not like when they sponsored Leonardo or Michelangelo. Unfortunately, those kinds of patrons aren't here any more.

We did many things wrong back in 1990. In all the excitement, we didn't realize that people become assholes when the floodgates open, that people will start raking and cheating. We canceled everything! We canceled the central management, we canceled distribution, and we didn't realize that, first of all, when we draft a bill about the film industry it takes a year or two to get it into the legislature and then they kick us out because it's not in the proper legislative form. American B movies flooded our theaters. Why would somebody distribute Czech films any more? Nothing. This void lasted for two years. There is still no law today and in this vacuum all the assholes revealed who they really are. Greed, greed, greed. The support of values, which were unquestionably in Czech cinema before, has now totally evaporated. Today there is no money. Minister Dostál[75] visited us at the Film Academy and said it's his priority to help. But regardless of how hard he might try, nothing can happen without money.

But this is what I think. As the saying goes, the revolution — it wasn't exactly a revolution — but a revolution swallows its children. It really swallowed us. Because in that excitement, we had meetings every week, including Christmas. The Central Committee of FITES[76] was in session constantly to draft the bill. And nothing! It swallowed us completely. Nothing happened. Barrandov Studios, let's get rid of it, it was the government's institution! What was going on in Barrandov, where did all that money go? Jaroslav Bouček must have skimmed some off the top. Mr. Pištěk was involved in the beginning too. They created a corporation then Václav Marhoul transferred something somewhere else, I don't know, some affiliate… Simply, they filched Barrandov, the money disappeared, and what about film? What about film? Václav Klaus also said that the film production should be self-sustained. Director Dejdar should be living proof of that. But he is an exception. I mean the fact he doesn't need any financial support from the government. Maybe that's because he cast Peter O'Toole. Dejdar knows he can eventually pay off his debt.

I would be willing to put my house up as collateral for my film, but I know I would never be able to pay it back.

How was it in the 60s?
      The atmosphere at the Film Academy was always more relaxed. Bolsheviks didn't work so hard there — except for the expulsion of Peter Král because of his umbrella, which was an absurd happening. We didn't feel much pressure. We could do whatever we wanted, and say whatever we wanted. The films we were making actually criticized the regime and nobody tried to stop us. They were getting awards abroad. So we felt great, it was wonderful. And actually the Communists didn't bother us because we were not in their way. So we kept pushing further and further. It was a great feeling of freedom. It never crossed our mind during that period of relative freedom, or we just didn't realize, that the Communists would always give us enough slack to hang ourselves. We didn't think they would pull the rope. But we should have known from history they would. But we believed they wouldn't and enjoyed the ride. And it was a very pleasant feeling.

In the Sign of the Eagle, 1979 — Vihanová (second from left) shooting the documentary. Produced by Krathý Film Praha (photograph by Robert Buchar).

Do you feel that the young generation is different?

Looking at my students today, I believe there is a difference. A substantial difference. Of course, you can't stereotype. You can't say all of them are like that. But what we tried to do, and all our films from the 60s reflected that, we tried to say something. Evald Schorm tried to say something. Pavel Juráček tried to say something, even Hynek Bočan, and everyone else tried to do it their own way. František Vláčil was an exception, he was an object trouvé.[77] And we were also aware of the responsibility that came with making our films. But film students today, I get the feeling ... I don't think they have any of that. They shoot a film but they don't care. They don't care if the film expresses their opinion or not. They just make a film, a fluff. The responsibility to stand behind the film they make, because it's part of them, is missing. Again, not all of them. Saša Gedeon is an exception. Now there is another one in our directing program who seems to be promising.

But it so exhausting raising money that there is no energy left to fight for your personal view. I don't know. But they are definitely different. We were hanging around together, helping each other. Regardless of being different personalities, we were a united group. You can't find that at the Film Academy today. Everyone goes his own way, by himself, alone.

How did you look at the future back then?

My future, back in the 60s? Make films, of course. Make films differently than Kachlík, Steklý, and the other nitwits. We wanted to show them how films should be made and through our films we wanted to express our opinions. I was fully into it. I believed that once I finished my debut, *Dull Sunday*, I would then shoot one film after the other. At that time I didn't think about the society in general. Everything changed for me in 1970 when I realized what the hell, I will end up in a Bolshevik retirement home.

Actually not too many people, I don't know, maybe Standa Milota because he was hanging around different people, but in general only a few people counted on the Communists going to hell. It was such a surprise, such an exciting surprise, and we underestimated the situation and couldn't handle it. And we are paying dearly for those first steps in 1990. I believe it went so far that I don't see how anyone can turn it around, unfortunately. You can't go back under the whip of a totalitarian regime. That's nonsense. But people are like wild animals now. And the present system supports that. Nobody is punished for crimes that are self-evi-

In the Sign of the Eagle, 1979 — Vihanová (right) shooting the documentary.

dent! Everything is swept under the rug. They say they did an audit and didn't find anything. Of course they didn't because they cleaned up the place beforehand. It is impossible to bring human beings up in this. Because if people find out that everything is permitted.... Freedom doesn't mean that everything is permitted. Unfortunately, that was our interpretation. Freedom is, most of all, taking responsibility for oneself and for others as well. We interpreted freedom as "anything goes" and you can see yourself what is happening. So, I don't know. Nobody wants a totalitarian regime back, of course, but on the other hand this system without any rules.... Many people today will tell you, "Fuck your freedom! What good does it do me if I can travel abroad any time I wish? I don't have any money to go anyway. So what? I want to know who tunneled the bank where I had my saving account! Nobody will ever find out and I will never see my money back. That's what I want to know!" But they will never catch anyone, they never will!

So, freedom is not such a big deal any more. The quality of life is not in buying pornography or jerking off at a peep show. It may be pleasant for some, but it's not essential for your life.

What's next?

Right now I see the situation for the young generation as a stalemate. The young people … they all would have to leave first, to go abroad and find out about taking responsibility for your own life — to work hard, not to lie, steal or kill and to constantly improve yourself. Then they would have to come back home and start putting this place in order. But as long as the younger generation doesn't accept these values, we will struggle here forever. We lived in a schizophrenic atmosphere here for a long time; you were in the party, went to meetings, paid your dues and privately believed that Jakeš[78] was an idiot. Of course, you kept it to yourself. Everyday you came home and you said, "Jakeš is an idiot! There is nothing to do about it." We taught our children this schizophrenia, this amorality — because I believe this behavior was amoral. It will take a lot of time to get away from this and then, maybe. Today nobody forces you to go out and say something you don't believe in. In the past, Czechs has been raised in that amoral environment, "Screw the Bolsheviks, it's Friday and I am going to my cabin. The weekend is mine. I will have a beer, pork-dumpling-cabbage and the Bolsheviks can kiss my ass." Then on Monday they came to their meetings and approved anything they were ask to approve and thought about how stupid it all this was.

In the Sign of the Eagle—Vihanová (second from right) on the set with cinematographer Robert Buchar (center).

Whole generations lived like that. Maybe, if I had children, I would also act like an asshole. Fortunately, I didn't have to. Thank God! People, parents lived in that constant schizophrenia and the children were affected. So now it waits for a new generation to take full responsibility for their actions, to resurrect the issue of a personal morality. Nobody takes any responsibility for one's self here. They don't accept the idea of any mutual respect. But some rules have to be reinstated again. On the other hand, young people today are exposed again to all that crookedness... I don't know. I can't live a normal life swimming in a shit. You would have to be crazy. And in the end, you would lose anyway because the majority always wins.

Filmography

DRAHOMÍRA VIHANOVÁ (born, 1930)

Born in Moravský Krumlov, she studied piano at the Brno Conservatory and music at Philosophy Faculty. Later she went to Prague's FAMU to study directing and editing. She graduated FAMU in 1965 with her film *Fugue for a Black Keyboard* which received awards at film festivals at home and abroad. In 1969 she shot her debut *Dull Sunday*. Together with some other films after the Soviet invasion, the film was immediately banned. Its premiere was 20 years later. She was forbidden from making films until 1977, when she was allowed to make documentary films at Short Film Prague. She teaches editing at FAMU.

2000 — *A Report About the Pilgrimage of Students Peter and Jackob* (director, story, screenplay)
1994 — *The Fortress* (director, story, screenplay)
1969 — *Dull Sunday* (director, screenplay)
1965 — *Fugue for a Black Keyboard* (director, screenplay)

DOCUMENTARY films

1994 — *Conversation on 55th Birthday*
1993 — *A Brief Report About George Sorose*
1992 — *Every Day I Stand in Front of You*
1990 — *Rafael Kubelík*
1990 — *Metamorphosis of My Friend Eva*
1989 — *One Day in Annecy*

1989 — *Behind the Window*
1988 — *A Court Hearing in Radotin or Confession of One Player*
1987 — *Dukovany, the Cauldron*
1986 — *Variations on a Search for Shape*
1985 — *Obsession*
1984 — *Také srýle dělají člověka*
1984 — *Questions for Two Women*
1983 — *Conversations*
1982 — *Snake and Scales*
1982 — *Musical Teenagers*
1982 — *A Garden Full of Dippers*
1981 — *A Day of the Chief Engineer*
1980 — *Counted Days*
1980 — *In the Sign of the Eagle*
1979 — *In Our Švábenice*
1979 — *Searching*
1978 — *Dalešice suite*
1977 — *The Last of Kin*

Awards

FIPRESCI Award, San Sebastian 1994 (*The Fortress*)
Prize for Human Rights, Strassbourg 1994 (*The Fortress*)
Grand Prix Bratislava 1991 (*Metamorphosis of My Friend Eva*)
Trilobit 1991 (*Metamorphosis of My Friend Eva*)
Jury Award at IFF in San Remo 1989 (*Dull Sunday*)
First Prize at Bratislava 1990 (*Dull Sunday*)
Prague Literary Fond Award 1990 (*Dull Sunday*)
Honourable Mention, Leipzig 1979 (*Dalešice suite*)
MFFC Award in Oberhausen 1989 (*Behind the Window*)
Montecatini Award 1989 (*Behind the Window*)
Prix Torino 1985 (*Obsession*)
Fist Prize in Cracow 1983 (*Questions for Two Women*)
Special Award in Cracow 1983 (*Conversations*)
Honorable Mention in Bilbao 1980 (*Searching*)
First Prize in Bruxelles 1967 (*Fugue for a Black Keyboard*)
First Prize in Tours 1967 (*Fugue for a Black Keyboard*)
First Prize in Dakar 1966 (*Fugue for a Black Keyboard*)
First Prize in Marseille 1965 (*Fugue for a Black Keyboard*)

Ivan Passer

DIRECTOR

In general, how was it back in the 60s?

When I look back today, it looks like when people coming home from the war usually talk only about funny stuff. And when you listen to them, you get the impression that it must be a lot of fun to be in a war. That's how I see the 60s today. We were young and the future looked bright to us. The Communist regime was running out of steam and new managers, like the general manager of Czech Film Alois Poledňák, were from a new generation, with new ambitions, pretty similar to our own ambitions. It looked like everything was going to be better. It looked like one day everything would be possible. At that time, we had no idea that this period would last only a short time. We didn't know it would last only six, seven years, which is an extremely short period of time for any art and especially for film because it usually takes three years to get a story idea up on the screen. Sometimes I think about what could have happened if we could have had a chance to continue our work as we started. Sometimes I fantasize about what direction our work would have taken and how individual directors would have evolved. What a pity we didn't get that chance.

But we were young then and there was a chance that everything would get better. Today I see it as a great adventure. The overall spirit of those times was like a conspiracy against stupidity. It was exciting. Of course, everybody's career was different, but what was interesting was that every sin-

gle one of us had a distinct
personality. Everybody was
different. We didn't do the
same thing. Our films were
different from each other.
That was very interesting
and I believe quite unique
in the cinema worldwide.
Because when you look at
Hungarian cinema before
1956, or later at Polish and
French cinema, their films
look much more alike than
the films of the Czech New
Wave.

*How did you leave Czecho-
slovakia?*

Ivan Passer (photograph by Morton Zarcoff).

After I finished *Inti-
mate Lighting,* I worked
with Miloš Forman as a screenwriter on *Firemen's Ball.* At that time I had
three finished scripts ready to shoot but Barrandov Studios signed a deal
with Carlo Ponti[79] to produce the next film. The negotiation was drag-
ging out and we couldn't reach a mutual agreement with him. Ponti was
pushing us to do something we didn't know how to do and we didn't
want to do it. We found out later that there was a paragraph in Miloš'
contract stating he couldn't shoot any other film until he finished this
particular project with Carlo Ponti. Miloš got upset and said he'd give
up filmmaking and he wouldn't shoot films any more. He said he'd switch
to the theater and direct stage plays. So, I offered one of my finished
scripts to Carlo Ponti in exchange for releasing Miloš from that contract.
Ponti agreed and invited me to England to rewrite the script in English
and to shoot the film there as well. Then I woke up one morning to find
out that the Soviets had invaded Prague. I returned to Prague and quickly
realized that the situation would not get any better, it could get only
worse. I'd had my own experience with persecution. I was expelled from
high school. I was expelled eight times from different schools including
the Film Academy in Prague.[80] It was clear to me that it wouldn't take
long and I would end up as a laborer for hire again. In the past, I was a

bricklayer, a foundry worker. I dug sewers, and built a dam. I knew how that tasted. I believe that everybody is responsible for his own life. And because I decided I wanted to make films in my life, and the situation after the invasion didn't look like I'd be able to, I left Czechoslovakia.

Was censorship a stimulus for creativity?
    I saw your documentary film *Velvet Hangover*. What Věra Chytilová and Antonín Máša are saying there is absolutely true about why we made our films. It wasn't because we liked to make films. Well, of course, we liked to make films but our ambitions were much higher. We wanted to say something, to express our feelings, our opinions, to show life from our viewpoint. I believe that our films were a reaction to the official aesthetics of social realism, where nothing on the screen reflected the reality as we knew it. We found it exciting to shoot reality the way it really was, to film people who were not actors. To put the band master Vostrčil or Hana Brejchová in front of the camera. We were young. Life was full of secrets to us, and through our films we tried to get some answers. Not as much through the story itself as through the structure of film, through the way of storytelling on film. We tried to grab the reality, to touch it, to find out who we were. This is what made our films so interesting then. Of course, compared to young filmmakers today, we probably had an advantage because we were living under pressure. The political situation was forcing us to take a stand. Orson Welles talks about it in his memoirs, too. He says that enlightened despotism is good for cinema. It forces filmmakers to find a language which the censors don't pick up on immediately and because of that the language becomes ambivalent — it is able to express more than just definitions.

Did you ever think about going back?
    I very much enjoy coming back to the former Czechoslovakia, to Prague and Slovakia, because I have many friends there. And for some other reasons as well. But I don't believe I could move back permanently because I have many friends in America, too, and I have my work there that I like so much. To immigrate once was difficult enough and to immigrate twice, I believe, is almost impossible.

Are the young filmmakers today different?
    Sure, I heard my generation of filmmakers complaining that young filmmakers have nothing to say or their films are not too important. [The new generation is] lucky they don't have to deal with the problems we

had. They can make films just for fun, to play with the camera. And why not? If a situation arose today where they became pushed around, I believe they would stand up to it and it would be reflected in their films as well. And maybe the pressure they are under to make commercial films today is not so different than the political pressure that was pushed us up against the wall. Arguing with an accountant can be more difficult than arguing with a censor. With the accountant, 1 + 1 = 2, but with a politician, 1 + 1 can be 3, 5 or 7. I sympathize with young filmmakers. I know the problems they have to deal with. I know that people who finance films have absurd demands, sometimes as absurd as our politicians had in the past.

Is there a difference between shooting a film in the Czech Republic or in America?

I remember I was constantly very tired when I was shooting my first film in America because during the day I was shooting the film in English

Intimate Lighting, 1965 — Karel Blažek as Bimbas and Zdeněk Bezoušek as Petr. Ivan Passer, director; Zdeněk Střecha and Miroslav Ondříček, DPs; premiere screening April 8, 1965; produced by Filmové Studio Barrandov (courtesy National Film Archive Prague, photograph by Jiří Stach).

and during the night, in my dreams, I was shooting it in Czech again. That was my biggest problem.

Otherwise, filmmaking itself— during those few years of existence since 1898 — developed in an effective universal process which is the same around the world. It doesn't matter where you shoot. It goes so far that, for example, camera operators in the U.S. dress the same way as those in England or France. You come on the set and just from looking at what people are wearing, you can say what their positions are. They behave the same way as those at Barrandov Studios. I realized what good technicians we had in Barrandov Studios when I started work here. What high quality people were working there. I didn't have any problem adapting in England or here, in America.

I had something different on my mind. I meant a difference from the personal point of view-how we felt about filmmaking back home and how Americans do it here.

Well, that's an interesting question. The role of filmmakers in America is seen differently from how we were looking at it back then in Czechoslovakia. Filmmakers in Czechoslovakia were seen as authors creating art. Film art. Filmmakers in America are professionals who know their craft perfectly but they don't consider themselves to be artists. You don't hear very often anybody talking about film as art here. They call it an industry. The film is a product made for a purpose, namely, to be sold. This is a concept that was to us (and to me still, to this very day) somehow unfit. I didn't understand this concept at all back then. Actually, we didn't *want* to understand it when we came to America. But that's how it is.

There are some filmmakers here who make "art films" but they are very few and they do it for very little money. Sometimes they have to finance their films by themselves. Sometimes they make one or two films and that's it. They never get a chance to make another film because they become cursed — their films never make any money back. I believe that with development of new technologies, filmmaking is coming to the point where you can make very professional films on a relatively small budget. This means that filmmakers will have more freedom than in the past because it will cost less to produce a film.

Filmography
IVAN PASSER (born 1933)

A native of Prague, Passer labored as a foundry worker, toolman and clerk and spent one year touring the country with a carousel. He got to FAMU by accident: One day he met on the street in Prague his brother-in-law, who was going to the Film Academy to fill out the application form. He accompanied him and, once there, he applied as well. He was accepted, his brother-in-law wasn't. Ivan studied directing but after he was expelled from school he went to Barrandov Studios and worked as an assistant director. He co-wrote with Miloš Forman and assisted him on films *Black Peter* and *Loves of a Blonde* (nominated for an Academy Award). After the 1968 Soviet invasion, he went to the United States.

1965 — *Boring Afternoon* (director, screenplay)
1965 — *Intimate Lighting* (director)
1965 — *Loves of a Blonde* (story, screenplay)
1967 — *Firemen's Ball* (story, screenplay)
1971 — *Born to Win* (director)
1974 — *Law And Disorder* (director)
1975 — *Crime and Passion* (director)
1978 — *Silver Bears* (director)
1982 — *Cutter's Way* (director)
1985 — *Creator* (director)
1986 — *The Emperor's Nightingale* (director)
1988 — *Hunted Summer* (director)
1990 — *Fourth Story* (director)
1991 — *Pretty Hattie's Baby* (director)
1992 — *Stalin* (director)
1994 — *While Justice Sleeps* (director)
1995 — *Kidnapped* (director)
1999 — *The Wishing Tree* (director)
2000 — *Picnic* (director)

Awards

The Best Narrative Short, Mannheim Film Festival 1965 (*Boring Afternoon*)
Academy Award Nomination 1965 (*Loves of a Blonde*)

Jury Award, San Sebastian Film Festival (*Intimate Lighting*)
Audience Award, Montreal Film Festival (*Intimate Lighting*)
Academy Award Nomination 1967 (*Firemen's Ball*)
New York Film Critics' Award 1971 (*Born to Win*)
Best Film Director 1975, Teheran Film Festival (*Law and Disorder*)
Best Film and Best Director 1981, New York Film Critics' Award (*Cutter's Way*)
Best Film and Best Director 1982, Houston Film Festival (*Cutter's Way*)
Prix de la Critique, Best Film of the Year, Brussels 1982 (*Cutter's Way*)
1992 Emmy Award: Best Film (*Stalin*)

Karel Vachek

DIRECTOR

What would you say about contemporary Czech film?
You must understand.... I am not so bright today. There is Czech film, but I don't see it anywhere. It is in the students at the Film Academy and it hangs in the minds of students for a while after they graduate until television and production groups destroy their talents. Because what represents Czech film today is Jan Svěrák, Jiří Menzel and some other attractions like that–commercial films. The center of the commercialism and adaptability here has always been television, and television has now become the only source of financing. With the exception of the grant committee, television has a major influence over production and this power is devastating. All managements consist of the same people who worked there before 1989 or they had already trained their children for this "performance" and have all the necessary connections. That created a great illusion about managers who pay themselves very well and who want to make good money as quickly as possible. In business, it's done by dividing a company into small portions and then selling those pieces individually. Companies don't worry about creating any technical background to improve the quality of their products. They only care about immediate success today, this week, this month, and they actually only worry about their accounts. It is the same situation in film. Filmmakers don't care about the social climate, about the system I just described — about the surviving political nomenclature sitting here like a frog in a

151

Karel Vachek (photograph by Bob Barnes).

pond. They only care about their wellbeing and that's why we have commercial film here. And when you ask about the Czech New Wave, the New Wave had its commercial side, too, represented by certain names, like Jiří Menzel, for example. Nobody was taking Menzel seriously at that time because everybody knew it was a deal built on good literature. And today, with that commercial thinking, Jiří Menzel actually stands out again.

Jiří Menzel was the one who reached into America, and his work attracted people with commercial thinking. And I don't know how much of "real" film is in America.... He fits between Greenwich Village and Woody Allen. These are the people living on the borderline between commercial and non-commercial film. They have their own problems, related to problems in America, but they have nothing in common with the commercial part of Czech New Wave. And then, there was a group of filmmakers in that time and films as well, which were not commercial at all.

Are you saying that the situation in contemporary Czech film isn't good?
I don't have any experience from that "wholesale" point of view of the art. I can answer it this dumb way. I shot my first film in 1963. After that, I was not allowed to shoot for five years. The next film I shot in 1968 and after that I was not allowed to shoot anything for the next 20 years. Now, after 1989 I shot two films, each three hours long, and I am shooting a third one as we speak. This is an extremely lucky period for

me now. But I work and live off government grants. If I didn't have the respect based on my ordeal and my previous work, I wouldn't be able to do it. But I believe that I am the only one here like that. I want to say that I wouldn't like to be in place of young filmmakers today who don't have this "safety net" I have, and who must struggle with these forces.

How did you survive "Normalization"?

Look, in 1969 I finished my feature documentary *Elective Affinities.* I had shot all the footage for another feature film about the occupation but all that footage "got lost." I started to shoot a movie with the phenomenal actor, Oldřich Nový and production was stopped. Then I spent four years offering them my scripts and they were pushing me to shoot other films that I refused to do. Then I was fired, worked five years at an incinerator, and went abroad to France and the U.S.A. After I had tried everything possible to make a film and didn't shoot a foot, my wife became seriously ill, so we returned to Czechoslovakia and I worked five years as a deliveryman. After that, I was selling books in a bookstore and then the revolution came. So what was for me a kind of entertaining escapade, for many others was 20 years of filmmaking. But definitely not in my case.

Elective Affinities, 1968 — Karel Vachek, director (courtesy National Film Archive Prague).

On the other hand, I believe I have a great respect for film. You can't expect me to take a book and transform it into moving images. I don't do that!

Director Jiří Menzel said he maybe has more respect for those people who made a tough decision and joined the Communist party, to have a chance at making good films, than for those who, for their selfish pride, refused join the party and didn't create anything.

But this is nonsense, isn't it? Because if people think like that, they must be born mentally ill and if they make any film, it must be only a bad film. I heard him on radio some time ago. He was talking about his problem with obesity. He was advising people on what to do to lose some weight. I have the same problems, but I talk about it only here, in my editing room.

What is a good film?

Good film? There must be a revolution in expression, because without it, the audience uses all of their stereotypes to interpret the film

Bohemia Docta, 2000— Director Karel Vachek (left) with Jaroslav Foglar in the documentary feature *Bohemia Docta*. Produced by Short Film Prague and Czech TV; Producer Jan Šibrava (courtesy Kráthý Film Praha).

images, and actually don't see the film. Viewers only see their interpretations, which were pre-conditioned for them by others. It means you must create a new image. They must see different things than what they are used to. You must kick them away from their prefabricated interpretations of film. That's one thing. Secondly, the film must care about people's social life. If new currents are rising in the society and people are still weak, then film must support them! And simultaneously with this social issue, a filmmaker has to make sure there is also a philosophical base for what is being told. That means a filmmaker must be aware that existence has a metaphysical dimension and that this dimension is reflected back in our existence. It's not enough to only distinguish between good and evil, if good and evil are both partially fate and partially creative. This means that suddenly a deep schizophrenia occurs in the minds of great artists like Dante or Goethe who were able to understand the creativity existing in evil, which is horrifying, and who also were able to understand a stupidity and non-creativity that exists within good, between so-called nice people. And a filmmaker must use all this knowledge when he makes a film. Because films, after all, are about nothing else than the philosophical awakening of the people who make them and those who watch them. Otherwise, it's not worth doing.

Is there any primary theme for filmmakers today?

Look, there is one great topic for the last couple of hundred years and that is a theme of equality. You can never convince Czechs that they must be subordinate to some authority. It doesn't matter if it is the authority of money or a political power, or any other kind of joke. This is simply a society without levels. And this is what Czech art and Czech society brings to humanity. A stoker from an incinerator has something to talk about with the President and the President is not surprised, even if he's pretending now that it's not appropriate any more. But that's a different matter. The bottom line is that nobody is surprised because there is a collective thinking here. In the U.S.A, some people don't think about certain things because they belong to people from a different level. Here, everybody thinks about everything. The fact that their opinion is often stupid is another matter. The fact that they are rascals and rogues is another matter. But all levels of thinking belong to them, and they keep discussing everything from philosophy and politics, to social problems. They keep doing it. And if they lose this, they will lose their own identity.

But this is not reflected in contemporary Czech film.

Look ... what is film all about? Film is only a space to absorb the thoughts of the people living in a specific time and place, in our case, the Czech Republic. The question is what are people thinking about today. I believe that the majority of people in Czech Republic today are thinking about their dissatisfaction with how this society is reshaping. They are not happy at all with the strong utilitarianism of some individuals grasping property and power instead of creating a society, which has no analogy in Europe or in the world. Strong nations create societies, which have no analogy in the world. The U.S.A. has no analogy in the world. France has no analogy in the world. It is evident and Czechs have to find a way to create a society without levels again, within a new political and economic context. They would like to do it, but so far, Czechs are controlled by forces unaware of this urgency.

So, maybe in the future?

But of course... Look, definitely there is a bright future ahead. Because I still run into intelligent people in this country who tell me ratio-

Director Karel Vachek discussing his films with film students at Columbia College Chicago in March 2002 (photograph by Robert Buchar).

nal things. Any activity anywhere in the world can't happen without the most intelligent people. And because I was unable to work for so many years, I can appreciate what is called transpersonal communication. It means as long as people here, at least some of them, have intelligent and nice thoughts, it definitely spreads into the consciousness of all people, even if it is absent in the media. It's not on TV and not even in books, but it gets into people's brains. I am an optimist. For example, I just filmed a man who was beaten twice by the police and he didn't like it. He didn't do anything. He was just a nice guy, sitting with a gypsy. And now he is not happy. And the people around him feel the same and he talks beautifully about it. This is a great hope for the future, refusing to be beaten up, the fact that somebody still thinks like that is simply beautiful.

Well, what has to be done to put Czech film back on track?

Look, do you want talk about it? Look at what is important. From the First Republic there are Jaroslav Vančura,[81] Karel Čapek, and Jaroslav Hašek.[82] Hašek is the key. The fact he is the key I didn't yet know in the 60s. Then the other wave came after World War II. Josef Škvorecký,[83] Milan Kundera, Bohumil Hrabal, and Páral. The most important of all was Bohumil Hrabal. But he also got a bunch of things wrong. His characters, which he loves, have internal voices because they are alive. But many times he doesn't realize that the internal voice is not working — it's only an imitation of that internal voice, and because of that his characters are even not funny any more, they are just bizarre. He didn't fully realize that and his work is inconsistent. But he's got some thoughts that are absolutely genuine. On the other hand, there is Jaroslav Hašek from the First Republic period and his work is absolutely flawless.

And it is interesting that Hrabal was always saying he would like to be like Hašek. He never became "like Hašek" because he was unable to handle certain things. And it is interesting that these things he couldn't fully handle were picked up by many people who then filmed that "bizarre" Hrabal, that "strange" Hrabal, that "philosophical" Hrabal. For example, Jiří Menzel's Hrabal — it's funny, I don't know why I am picking up on him all the time — but Menzel's Hrabal is that "castrated" Hrabal. It's full of fun and bizarre things but without any depth. And there is nothing to do about it. Then everybody around the world interprets these films this way, which has nothing to do with Hrabal's literature. He never wrote anything like this. And this way we are living permanently in an illusion. We talk about the United States as a democratic society but we have no idea what it means. We know nothing about all those non-democratic forms of human existence they had, and still have, to deal with and fight to have a democracy. Do you understand all they have to go through to be even able to talk about a democracy? Just start talk about it? And we have here in the Czech Republic face a similar situation. If we don't look back at what our foundation is, at what is really important ("Who was Jan Ámos Komenský? Who was Karel Hašek?"), and instead we look at imitations representing us like Milan Kundera, Bohumil Hrabal and some others even worse.... If we don't look at it, if we don't look at the difference, then we can't start do anything genuine. That means, if we don't realize what the difference is between all those — now I have to repeat everything again–like Jan Svěrák, Jiří Menzel ... and I don't know who else, and the real literature and images, like those of Ladislav Klíma, for example, if we don't look at this then we will see nothing!

Filmography

KAREL VACHEK (born 1940)

He studied directing at FAMU under Elmar Klos in 1958–66. During that period he shot the films *The Havens and the Road, Kamil Lhoták* and *Mr. Pelíšek*. He was expelled from the Film Academy for his last project, a film about the secret police during World War II. Later he returned to school and graduated with his film *Moravian Hellas*. The film was awarded at Karlovy Vary Film Festival and was immediately banned by the president of Czechoslovakia Antonín Novotný and thus not screened for another 25 years. He wrote the feature film scripts *Who Will Guard the Guard?* (about art, army and politics), *Romany* (the history of the nations of Gypsies) and *The Czech Regurgitation* (about ants, physics and politics. None of these films was shot. In 1975 he shot a 40-minute documentary *A New Apartment* (about the post-invasion consumer society). The film never got distributed. He worked as a boiler room worker between 1975–79. In 1979 he emigrated to France and the U.S. When his wife got seriously ill, they returned to Czechoslovakia in 1984. He then worked as a delivery truck driver. In 1990 he started work on his tetralogy *Little Capitalist* (consisting of the films *New Hyperion, What Is to Be Done?, Bohemia Docta* and *Who Will Guard the Guard?*). Since 2002 he is chair of the Documentary Film Department at FAMU.

2002 — *Who Will Watch the Watchdogs?* (director, story, screenplay)
2000 — *Bohemia Docta* (director, story, screenplay)
1996 — *What Is to Be Done?* (director, story, screenplay)
1992 — *New Hyperion* (director, story, screenplay)
1968 — *Elective Affinities* (director, story, screenplay)
1966 — *Moravian Hellas* (director, story, screenplay)

Awards

Grand Prize at IFF Oberhausen 1969 (*Elective Affinities*)
Grand Prize at IFF Karlovy Vary 1969 (*Elective Affinities*)
Trilobite 1969, FITES (*Elective Affinities*)
Golden Berlin Camera 1990 (*Elective Affinities*)
First Prize at IF of Documentary Films Jihlava 2000 (*Bohemia Docta*)
Best Czech Documentary at IFF Jihlava 2002

Stanislav Milota

CINEMATOGRAPHER

Tell us something about your cinematography career.

I didn't study at the Film Academy, I started work in Barrandov's film lab, but at the age of 17 I was already working as a focus puller and camera operator and later became a director of photography. Because I only went to grammar school, I am basically uneducated. I tried to catch up as much as I could. I dedicated my life to it. I didn't even have time to have children. That's life. You just focus on something and don't let go. So, until 1968 I was completely focused on my profession. I was burning 24 hours a day and it was wonderful. We were shooting all day long and in the evening, at the Palace Club, we talked about films again. But suddenly there was a cut. And, like a severed umbilical cord, everything was cut off and this... happened.

It's actually ironic. Because I was from a working class family and had the privilege of working in Barrandov Studios — I didn't have to join Communist party. Once in a while they tried to recruit me saying, "You should join the party."

And I replied, "No, as long as Otakar Vávra is in the Communist party I will not do that!"

They argued, "We wouldn't need people like Otakar Vávra if you were there."

So this way I didn't join the Communist party or even the youth organization, but I got in this mess.

Your life changed because you filmed the Soviet invasion in August 1968.
It wasn't just me. I was one out of many. It happened by chance because I live here behind the National Museum building and every time history goes by, it always knocks on our door. I was shooting the movie *The Cremator* so I had the camera, film stock and everything. What's true is that in 1968 I was also pulled into society, into political life as a citizen because of what I did. I took the camera

Stanislav Milota (photograph by Robert Buchar).

and went out to shoot what "director" Brezhnev[84] had arranged. The consequences of that in my life were permanent.

What happened after the invasion?
I was the first one invited to the political screenings at Barrandov in 1968 after Gustav Husak[85] took over the government. The people sitting in on those screenings were the same people who were telling me, every time I came to look at dailies from the August invasion, "Standa, keep shooting, it's great stuff!" and were shipping prints abroad.

There was a new general manager at the Studio and he asked me where I was raised and where was all the film I had shot. And then he said, "You sound like an agent of some western intelligence agency."

And I replied to him, "Unlike all of you sitting here, I am the only one who is not affiliated with any intelligence agency!"

I walked out, slammed the door and at same time I closed the door on my professional life, which ended at that moment.

In 1969 I was still finishing a German feature film in Israel and that was the end. That was my last film. I must say it's still painful today. I am aware that my train is gone but the fact is that after the revolution

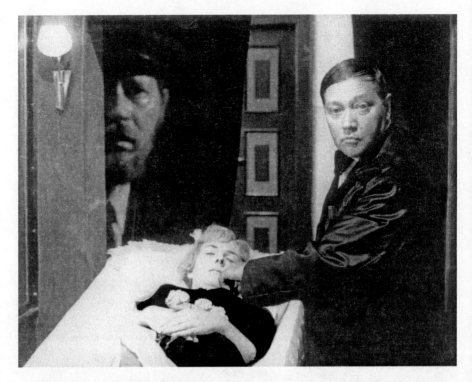

The Cremator, 1968 — Rudolf Hrušínský (right) as Mr. Kopffringl. Juraj Herz, director; Stanislav Milota, DP; premiere screening March 14, 1969; produced by Filmové Studio Barrandov (courtesy National Film Archive Prague, photograph by Karel Ješátko).

in 1989 nobody offered me a film. Of course, I can see only in one eye as a result of three seizures I've had. But nobody even asked. I don't think I was an exceptionally great cinematographer. I just loved my job, the filmmaking. But this is what I wanted to say. Because I was forcibly removed from work I had done all my life and loved so much, I have dreams about it 'til today. I am shooting films in my dreams. And in every single dream I am doing a bad job, I screw up something. I never had a dream where I did a good job. My wife Vlasta [Chramostová] had the same dreams when she was banned from the theater. When she got back to her work, the dreams suddenly ended. That's interesting. In her dreams she always forgot her lines. In my dreams I have a problem with exposure. Most of the time my rushes are underexposed and only rarely overexposed. It's funny.

So the end came when I was at the top of my career and that marked my turn from cinematography into a different direction. But I must say it wasn't unintentional. It wasn't bravery or anything. Simply, the time was up. What I saw so far was enough, and what I knew was also enough for me to quit, even if at that time I naively believed it would not last for that long.

How did you live through the period of "Normalization"?
The pressure at that time was so great and it was the group of people I knew long before 1968. Actually, we were all expelled in 1968 and pulled together like a herd. Suddenly philosophers, politicians and all these types got together and started to write articles and so forth. And that's how it started. After I was fired from Barrandov Studios, I didn't communicate with anybody. For example, I was prohibited from coming to Barrandov. My picture sat on the reception desk so security guards could recognize me. So this was how my wife and I, with the help of Václav Havel and Pavel Kohout,[86] were moving closer and closer to this center.

But there was no way to turn around and go back. Every time I was interrogated they told me, "Well, your wife, if you let her go everything could be different." Then they would say to her, "Well, that husband of yours..." So there was no way out and after all Charta was a sort of umbrella. It was a fact that people who signed Charta, or at least those of us in Prague, were somehow protected. For example, I was never beaten like some younger guys, Třešňák or Václav Malý for example. They beat the hell out of them. They never beat Havel or Benda, or Kohout either. But that pressure of the secret police sneaking behind doors or watching you outside, cars following you and so on it was stressful.... But to go back to why I did it. It didn't matter to me. It didn't make my situation worse or better. I realized that it's better to belong to this group than to be alone. Even if there was no hope, it made the situation better at the time.

You have to realize when Charta was signed. It happened after the Helsinki Conference because Helsinki was an impulse, a chance for change. It was the only way to materialize the spirit of the Helsinki Conference. That's what I thought.

So then everything ended and 1976 came. Shows like *The Anniversary of Mr. Seifrt* were organized, Charta started and I was shooting proclamations in basements. All kinds of people — Hájek, Hejdánek, Havel, anybody — and everything was smuggled to the West. We were sending all that stuff to Jan Kavan[87] who was running Palach Press in London. At

Dissidents Stanislav Milota and Václav Havel in 1977 (photograph by Oldřich Škácha).

that time I filmed, here in this apartment, two shows. It was in 1978–79 and it was extremely hard to get anything. I was buying film stock in the grocery stores by individual 100' spools, we couldn't find sound mixing equipment, etc. We didn't have a camera so they sent it to us from abroad. Also, I had to shoot hand-held because we didn't have a tripod. And when we hung up five microphones from the ceiling and turned the power on, the Soviet national anthem came on — we had created an antenna and got Moscow radio. So we had to pause and fix it. But in the end we made it.

Unfortunately in those days we didn't have video cameras, which would have made it possible to shoot the audience. All those people sitting here, who would normally never meet, one was Communist and the other a national democrat.... They all met here because of something totally different. Those evenings were enchanting because the secret police were down on the street and here something was happening. This apartment is not so large and the hallway is small and there was always a huge pile of shoes because there was no place to put them. When people were leaving, everybody had to find his own shoes.

But we have some records. My wife is now finishing her biography

[*Vlasta Chramostová*, Doplněk Publishing, Brno 1999]. All the documents including police records will be in that book. But it's impossible to film a stage play anyway. Because if you sit in the audience, you have your wide shot, you smell the perfume of a woman next to you, and you zoom in on a closeup any time you want. Watching a stage play is very different from watching a film. It's about the atmosphere in the auditorium. Anyway, there was Macbeth with Pavel Kohout and Pavel Landovský. And when they both emigrated, Vlasta did one more show about Božena Němcová and that was it. That was the end. After that I didn't shoot anything.

There is no respect for dissidents in the Czech Republic today.
It makes sense. First of all, people didn't know too much about dissidents. We were such a small elite group. They noticed only after Charta came out. Second of all, not many people ever read Charta. It only affected the arts community which was forced to sign an anti–Charta[88] proclamation... but the fact that there is no respect for Charta today is understandable because the reality that somebody stood up would contrast with the majority of the nation. The majority is always right. And now when we have democracy and the majority is right again–they don't care. "What did they do? For who? He is in the Castle now, and is a millionaire, the others as well. Look, they knew how to take care of themselves." But Šimečka died for it or Venda Benda who is such a problematic man today ... but he was also in prison while the others were not. Because, of course, everybody was making a relatively good living.

Now there is Dr. Macek from ODS who is today the biggest critic of Václav Havel. He is so rude it's ridiculous. But when you repeat lies over and over again, people start to believe in it. Dr. Macek came, like many others, from who knows where, and he became visible throughout the corrupted world of media.

And actually, that casting of doubt on the Chartists is similar to the Air Force pilots who came back from England in 1945. What happened to them? They were immediately arrested because the whole nation was practically working for Hitler at the time. The Communists couldn't stand it at all! Like Heidrich's assassination,[89] one of the biggest deeds, 'til today, 40 years after, it's still being said it shouldn't have happened. It is not convenient. It is not convenient to the majority, which is actually silent and has no need for it. Here is the problem, here is a man, freely living in the neighborhood, who was sentencing people to death 'til today....

For example, there is a lawsuit going on with a policeman who beat Vašek Malý. The policeman lives around the corner here, he searched our apartment a couple of times and once he came to arrest my wife. And this policeman said in the court, "I didn't beat him." And the judge has to believe him because there was no evidence. Or I was a witness in Vlasta Třešňák's trial because he came to my apartment once after the interrogation, showing me his burned hands. The judge asked me how could I prove that policemen burned his hands. I said, "Well, when he came to me, he had three fresh cigarette burns on his hand."

And the judge replied, "Well, but he could do it to himself before he came to your apartment, couldn't he?"

"That's it," I said, "You are right, your honor. He did it to himself!"

And that's the problem of democracy in general. And that's the problem of democracy itself. And I even understand it. For most judges, it's a convenient solution. They don't send too many people to prison and, most of all, they are scared. They are under pressure. They receive threats! All former Communists, who in the past were well connected in business circles, are arising again. And that's reflected also in the judiciary system. Maybe now it's getting finally slightly better but it took ten years! Look, those pilots from World War II, or people who suffered in the Communists' concentration camps in the 50s, they are still at odds with the government about their compensation. At the same time, the government is wasting money — creating and feeding new billionaires — instead of helping people who really suffered under the Communist regime.

There is a problem. Today I am a member on the Committee for Radio and Television Broadcasting. The Public Television Station ČT1 broadcasted the communist propaganda film *A King of Sumava*. The film is based on a real story. One hundred twenty-seven people were electrocuted or killed some other way while crossing the border. Hundreds or thousands of people were sentenced to jail for attempting to cross the boarder. The film goes on the air on Public Television. We told them, "You can't broadcast a film like that without any commentary. Why don't you bring somebody who served five to fifteen years in prison for an attempt to cross the border? Let him tell how it really was then." No, they didn't do it because here is Mr. Železný with his TV station NOVA who broadcasts the worst trash you can find around the world and they have to compete with his ratings. Actors from that film, and they are distinguished Czech actors, they say, "We have nothing to be ashamed of." Sure, their sons, brothers or cousins were never in jail or didn't try to defect. Actress Jiřina Štěpničková tried and today there are still rumors about it—what, how, when and so on. Her house was confiscated and today, ten years after the revolution, her son still hasn't gotten the house back. Some former Communist is living there. That's how it is and there is so much of this.

And what's left of Charta today? Jiří Suchý sings in one of his songs, "Our brave company became a slaughterhouse." And that is exactly what happened to us. Our group of dissidents changed after November 1989. Many new people came in and the spirit that held us together dried out. The way of thinking, the ideology, all that changed. Suddenly, democracy was offering everything to the whole political spectrum from the left to the far right. Everybody walked out in different directions and joined different political parties.[90] Today there is nothing to hold us together. We have very different opinions on many issues from Kosovo to the restitution of church property. This pushes us apart and there is nothing to pull us together any more. It's logical. That's how it should be.

How do you feel about all this today?

You know what it is ... when you stayed here in the middle of it as I did, you don't have to communicate with it, just let it go. But it gets bad when you hear people defending their past — talking about character, a right for personal opinion, integrity, etc. You can hear it all the time now. I can look at myself in the mirror every day. But this happens here every time the political system changes. And the emigres... They irritate me too, starting with Pavel Tigrid[91]— to be gone for so long and now coming back to tell us what we should do! That tells you something about their intellect. They should stay out of this and shut up. They don't understand that they must not do this. Leave us, we will take care of it on our own. Because you can't just tell people what to do... Because today freedom and democracy freed people from their fear. In the past, they shut up and were friendly with anybody and they did whatever they were told to do. Today everybody has a right to express his opinion and everybody does that. Ten years is a short time to change the whole society. When this generation was growing up, their parents constantly reminded them, "You can't say this in public, we can talk like this only at home." Today they have children of their own, and that generation which lived the most productive period of their lives under the Communist regime, it is impossible for them to say... As Jan Werich[92] once said, "The pickle that is in the barrel together with other pickles can't scream 'I am not sour!' It's impossible." Every one here is somehow tainted. They have left a footprint somewhere, or hidden a skeleton. It's not so simple.

It is important that we don't act like we know everything, that we can judge everybody. It's interesting when you look at young people today. There was a street party some time ago and they demolished everything. I don't think they are much different than the "flower children" were, but they are more aggressive than young generations were in the past. If you realize that during World War I, a word of honor was respected between officers. In World War II, there was no word of honor any more, the opposite was true — it was all about cheating, how to mislead the other side.

How did the "Velvet Revolution" happen?

It all started spontaneously and, because nobody wanted to claim leadership, a specific group of people took over. We were almost the last — Eastern Germany already went down and only Romania succumbed after us. Anything could happen then. A few thousand militiamen were ready in Pakula to move on Prague, but they didn't.

It all began in the Magic Lantern Theater. I was doing what the cameraman always does. He is always somewhere in the background. In the old days, when the camera operator had to look through the film emulsion, nobody really knew what was in the frame. When the operator pulled his face from under the blanket, everybody was looking at him waiting for what he would say — if there was a microphone tracks, or a light in the shot. So from this profession I have this ability to organize, to make quick decisions and so on. That's what I was doing there, sort of.

Dissidents started to put everything together. Other people were coming because, for example, Václav [Havel] said, "Who is going to run the economy?"

I said, "Well, Valeš, he was in jail with you. Okay, call him!"

We called Valeš in and he said, "What about Komárek[93]?"

"Komárek, Okay, who else works for Komárek?"

"Well, somebody name Klaus works there."

So these people kept coming in and Klaus came, "Good day..." and so on. And some people were leaving and I thought — but it's hard to describe, it's all hypothetical... Different things happened and I started to realize that this democracy would be somehow twisted. When it came to the point as to who would go to the Castle and form the government, I was one of two or three people telling Václav not to go, because hardwood floors are slippery and he should go later. He didn't listen and I didn't go with him.

And when Václav went to the Castle and the other became Premier, people dispersed and the OF[94] was left alone with people like Klaus. They felt they were incompatible with the dissidents' movement, and established new political parties and started liberal politics. Don't forget they were not economists as I see it. I believe they were all bank clerks who read about it somewhere and moved on… And those in the Cabinet who were governing, constantly signing piles of documents while a new party was born [ODS], and all along Václav was the President…

Then, I don't know, January 1 or 2, 1990, Václav called me asking me to work for him. He said two things, did I want a big retirement benefit or did I want to help him? I told him, "This is the question that is typical of you because you know that…" I should have said I want to help you and I want the big retirement benefit too. Because today, June 1999, my retirement benefit is still below the average. All Secret Police agents, informants, policemen, they all got high retirement benefits. Whatever. So I started to work there in January and he wanted me act in opposition, as a critique of the situation because all employees from the past regime were still there. From the laundry attendants and limousine drivers to secret service agents, nobody was fired! That was a slow process and it took a long time. For example, the head of the president's security service from the past regime, he is there 'til today.

The first opinions of what should be done … I said, for example, "Starting from Gustáv Husák [a former President] all the way down, let's confiscate all their property, give them 1,300 KC monthly, and a one-bedroom apartment." Not to liquidate them, not to shoot them, but do it like this.

"No, it's not possible, it is against the law!"

"What law? We don't have any yet."

"It's not democratic!"

"What democracy? We will do this today and tomorrow we can have democracy."

"No, we can't do that."

So it didn't happen. They were still discussing if Husák should get a private driver and so on and Vacek was in charge of that bullshit. And to keep eye on it?

"No, it's not necessary. It's a Communist' attitude."

And they came up with libertarianism, violins, here we go, everything will be beautiful! Everybody can take care of himself! Because they knew if I was up here in the government I would take care of myself. They got things going in a big way. Boys like Viktor Koženy[95] came in and found all the loopholes. No problem, we will fix it later... When somebody brought up the idea to create some sort of controlling authority, no, it's not necessary, later...

Today nobody can control anything. You can investigate, sure, but look, there are people who took hundreds of millions in loans and they didn't return a penny to the government. If you don't pay your rent, you would be evicted! But of course, then at that time, Václav changed. It would be impossible for him not to change. It happens to everyone who becomes a tool or a puppet in the hands of the media, and actually the people who worship him... All those grandmothers on their knees, kissing and so on... It must affect him and it is still affecting him today. There is no other way could be, everybody would be affected. But regardless of that, I was, or today still I am, such a primitive idealist because I believed that this nation after 40 years of Communism needed to set some example, something to aspire to. It was impossible, of course, because of this or that. And it went on and on.

Then they started buying limousines and nobody was listening to my naive ideas. And it goes on still today. We have a huge parliament, huge senate, huge administrative staff like we were governing the Republic of China. Nobody cared about the social changes that would come, like unemployment and other things. They were dabbling with it and ten years latter they still keep dabbling.

So I came in January and by June I left. I said, "No, not with you guys, I don't need this and I don't want to." Not just because of how Václav and the advisors he chose saw it but also because, first of all, I don't speak any languages. I believe my idea was that government should be formed out of well-educated people and that these people should be the best we have to represent our nation. It hasn't happened yet. The middle class isn't born yet and the best of the nation were never invited to the feast of conquerors. And that is the problem, or at least for me, and it eventually drove me to leave. After that I only kept in contact with Olga [Havel] because she was a great human being with high moral principles. She was never affected by becoming the First Lady. I pulled back and today I am still not interested and don't go to the Castle. I am not interested in that bullshit, "Hi, how are you?" No, thank you, I don't need that.

How is Czech film doing today?
I think is getting better and better. It is generationally diverse. There are some new young filmmakers like Saša Gedeon who seem to be interesting. Or Jan Svěrák who shot *Kolya*. Or Vladimír Michálek with his film *Who Will Kill Sekal*. Their films have really high professional qualities, which was missing here lately. The older generation is saying that this is the end of post-modern era but I don't agree.

But there is a problem. Compared to France or other European nations, the Czech government doesn't have any money in its budget to support filmmaking. We are a small country and film costs a lot. It is difficult to get financing.

I used to be a member of the Council for Advancement of Czech Cinema. It still exists and the Ministry of Culture runs it. There will be a new media legislation coming out soon and according to that — in compliance with EU requirements — television stations should contribute to a film production fund. In France, for example, they contribute four percent or ten percent. They do it because television stations are unable to produce good quality films. They are not filmmakers. When they produce a feature film, it doesn't look like a film. Anyway, that fund will help free filmmakers from their dependency on private investors. I don't believe they should shoot whatever they want. The grant should support films with focus on important issues in the society, to help our society get back to normal. That is what we need most. We don't need to make 40 films a year. We can make 15. But there has to be good financial support because it can take another five years for a director to make another film. It's not like it was during the Communist era when those guys were shooting non-stop one film after another. Today they are supplementing their incomes by shooting commercials. But I am optimistic.

Let's talk about the privatization of Barrandov Studios.
Oh, that's a problem. A white horse name Václav Marhoul was born there. But he is really a white horse. And I would also blame Václav Havel, Miloš Forman and Miroslav Ondříček for it. Because to get rid of Barrandov Studios like that... Actually, nobody profited from it and the film industry was lost — all the supporting crafts for filmmaking. And

today it's all in the hands of some steel corporation. They simply huck-
ster it away. The Minister of Culture Uhde was, "Sure, sure..." And
everybody else, "Sure, sure, don't worry..." And then they dropped the
ball and sucked away millions, somewhere. They created a board of
trustees but they still haven't paid a dime back to the Fund of National
Property for Barrandov. They have 20 or 30 years to do it.

I don't know what else to say about it but the fact is that the Cabinet of Petr Pithart bartered it off. I was in that session. This issue came
to the floor 20 minutes before noon. Literally 20 minutes before noon
and at noon this Cabinet was going to expire. And Václav Klaus was waiting outside to take over with his new Cabinet. I said to Petr Pithart, "You
can't do that!" And everybody was like, "Don't worry...." And a minister named Ježek[96] was in charge of that. He had a motto, "Run ahead of
lawyers," that's what they called their economic strategy then. In other
words, do everything before the law steps in. So they were running ahead
of lawyers and they ran away with Barrandov Studios too. And I saw when
minister Ježek came out and walked up to Václav Marhoul waiting in
the hallway and said, "It's all yours, you owe me a bottle of French
cognac!"

How do you look at the filmmaking today?

I missed the train, especially in technology. Once in a while I go to
watch filmmakers on location and when I see how they are shooting
now... They have a TV monitor on the set and everybody from the
makeup artists to drivers is watching. The stress of waiting for rushes
two or ten days — what if something went wrong — is gone.

Today I ask myself if I ever did all that. Some time ago I saw my
film *The Cremator*, it doesn't look familiar to me. I watch it and I don't
feel anything... It's like if your child leaves, or your parents, after a while
you somehow forget. But on the other hand, I must say I get excited
when I see a nice film. I remember the same feeling I had when I was
shooting myself. It's like you get, excuse my language, pissed off, when
you see that somebody has shot a great film because you think you could
do it better. So if I see a nice film today, it still brings warm feelings in
my heart. For example, I saw Stopard's *Shakespeare in Love*. Great film.
Great professionalism from the script and director to the actors. You just
sit in the theater and feel great. Or *Breaking Waves*. These types of films
I like to watch. It helps me fell like it was in the old days when I was
making films.

What moment was the most difficult for you?
It's definitely that pivot point when I was fired from Barrandov Studios. I mentioned it before. They gave me the notice in writing. It says: "…You are fired because you acted as a leading participant in the August 1968 events and the footage you shot was sent abroad and used as an anti-government propaganda against the Czechoslovak Socialist Republic." And there was an addendum in that letter saying, "You can't be employed anywhere in the Czechoslovak Republic." Nothing like that happened even during the political cleansing in the 50s. Then they would send you probably to an editing room for a couple of years. At that time, I was on the top of my professional career and many people were telling me to emigrate. People I worked with before in England and France were offering me work. But I decided not to leave. I had my reasons. It wasn't because, like Pavel Kohout once said, you have to have courage to emigrate. I strongly believe that I would have become successful if I had immigrated.

Anyway it was a shock for me. I worked in Barrandov Studios since I was 15 years old. It would be 50 years now if I weren't fired. Back then I thought that the situation would change and they'd take me back. But the situation was worsening and the secret police started to follow me. And here comes that most difficult part of it. I am from a pure working class family and I have no college education. My mother was very proud of me because I made it to a film studio and became a director of photography. I didn't tell her for three years I was fired! And then when I finally told her, I saw how disappointed she was… There is a second part to that disappointment. When I was working in politics after November 1989 and later in the Castle with Václav [Havel], my mother was proud of me again. Arnošt Lustig called me from New York: "Hi dude, I saw you on TV! It's great." I became visible in the media. And our neighbors in Žižkov were like, "Mrs. Milota, your son Standa, he is running the new government!" She was excited because everybody was asking her what was going on, what would happen next and so on. Actually, it is horrible how the media can make you a personality overnight regardless of who you really are. I started wearing a tuxedo to work. And then I suddenly left! When my mother found out that I quit, she stopped talking to me. She cut off all communication with me 'til she died. That really hit me hard. She couldn't understand why I let her down like this.

"You betrayed the President!" she told me.

"No," I told her, "First of all, I didn't betray my upbringing, what I believe in."

"No, you betrayed the President! Your father would never forgive you for that!"

So when you asked me about the most difficult moment, this is it. Still today, any time I think of my mother or my parents, I can see her dying lonely and deeply wounded because I "betrayed the President." But I just had to leave.

What about happy memories?

There was a lot of fun. There are many stories because of that fear which put us together. We went through many exciting and funny situations. The union of these people in critical situations was the most beautiful thing. It's like your memories from the army service. You mostly remember the good stories. That's exactly the same here.

Best of all was the filmmaking, which I loved so much. That was the happiest period of my life. Actually, I didn't enjoy it to the fullest because it was like if you break your spinal cord and then you have to focus just on the wheelchair. Or something like that.

During the Prague uprising in 1945 at the end of World War II, I was 12 years old and my mother had to lock me in the cellar because I

President Václav Havel (left) and Stanislav Milota as his adviser in the president's office in 1989 (photograph by Oldřich Škácha).

wanted to go out and "do the revolution." And when we were playing theater in our apartment, it was the same excitement as when I was a boy. I had to light the scene and the secret police was waiting outside. It was a great feeling.

For example, one night they were watching the entrance at Václav's [Havel] house in Dejvice. I climbed through the back inside his first floor apartment and he said, "What are you doing here?"

I said, "I came to see you."

"Well, you know, I am expecting a cameramen from England. They want to shoot an interview with me, for the BBC."

And I said, "That's me!"

"Really? You?"

And these were those beautiful things because it was like a conspiracy but then we leaked everything out over the phone anyway... But it had all these juicy moments.

When you look back, do you have any regrets? Would you do something differently?

I regret the fact we couldn't videotape all that. If we would have had a video camera like you have today, we could better document the history — all the debates and fights we had. The video recordings would be much more powerful than texts. I would love to do that.

Can you imagine that? It would be interesting now to go back in time and watch it. Maybe we could find out what we screwed up and what was wrong with our thinking. But even Václav, he is defined by his presidency and driven in an opposite direction, to different people. It is a big play he is actually acting in today. He plays the President and he acts, speaks, and thinks like one. But I believe that in a moment he would free himself from that, and I haven't seen him for a long time and I don't need to because it pushed him in another dimension. But I believe that in a moment he wouldn't be a Chief of Staff of this state's army any more and if he were to call a mobilization, I think I would go with him, together with some other people I admire, to fix things.

How do you see the present situation?

There is a new generation here. Dentists came here in this state, people like Mr. Macek, who want to be politicians. Today they want to teach us about morality. And as much as I have reservations today against Václav Veškrna [maiden name of Havel's present wife Dagmar], as I call

Mr. President, and actually I had them from the beginning, and stayed in the Castle for only half a year. Because when I saw the appetite to govern like in China, all those cars and so on… And today again everybody wants some perks. I don't like that. I refuse it.

I think when you see the results after ten years… The primitive idealist thought that everything would be superb. And today when you see those quick-fermented billionaires like the general manager of TV NOVA, Mr. Železný[97]…. The government gave him a broadcasting license and he became a billionaire in five years and acts like he can do whatever he wants. Everybody is scared of him. He is well educated. No, he is sly. He bought a thousand-part TV series *Arabela* from Mexico. Now the whole nation is watching that trash and eating popcorn like in America because they don't need to think: "What happened? What was her name? Did they get married? What happened last week?" So the audience which used to be on a decent cultural level is getting dumb with the help of popcorn and Coca-Cola. It's a big disappointment for me. We have the ČT2 channel here that is really good, a world-class quality. But only four percent of the audience is watching. That's the problem. The consequences of the brainwashing done by Russians are long lasting. The holes in the brain must be filled with Coca-Cola and popcorn first 'til people start screaming: "I don't want popcorn any more, it makes me sick! The Coca-Cola is poisoned!" I believe it will come slowly.

A new generation of politicians is necessary. A completely different breed must come. Not recruited from dissidents. I don't think that would be a good idea. Because today "dissident" is a dirty word. I am on that TV Committee and I hear it all the time: You dissidents, you see it differently! It's not about seeing differently. What we learned was to speak truthfully face to face and that is not popular today. But the new generation will not come overnight.

I was a 15-year-old boy when I started working at Barrandov Studios. And in 1948 suddenly the Communists emerged. Filmmakers from the first republic were wearing bows and scarves and cinematographers leather gloves. One day the working class called in a great set designer Karel Škvor, who was always perfectly dressed. They called him to the steering committee meeting and told him, "Comrade, you can't dress like this on the set. Our workers don't like it." Next day he came in with patches on the jacket to comply with their request.

I say this because of that jump into Communism, the way people crawled into the Communist party. How Vávra immediately became a

Communist and others as well. Everybody kissed their asses. And the same thing has happened here now but in the opposite way. Suddenly all artists became conservatives. And they pissed me off so much... Just because they are all conservatives. I told them, "How can you make any films if you are so right-oriented? Can you have any human beings in your films, somebody with a problem?" But that's my provocation. I am known for it and I am pissing them off by promoting the social democrats rather than the rightists who in the past were obedient servants to Communists and today they... As I say, somebody gets a pimple and somebody become rightists, but overnight!

Most of the artists, at least in the twentieth century, tried to distinguish themselves from the establishment. Today they are kissing the establishment's ass. Today at all the parties and celebrations it's Hollywood all the way. I must say I don't like it. I usually don't go and if I go, I don't wear any tie.

They believed that the transition of economy could happen without any control. Somebody would take care of it later on. Well, nobody did. Nobody has been able to fix it yet today and Zeman's program "Clean Hands," nobody wants to get involved in it, including the police. Because they are scared they might accidentally uncover something and then somebody might come knocking on his door or leave a broken pencil in his mailbox. That goes on here. We have a Mafia here. A broken pencil means they will cut your throat. There are boys here from Ukraine, Afghanistan, Russia–real killers. And those who got involved in dirty business, not just in banking or trade, are smart guys in their thirties who figured it out perfectly. The whole state was larcenously robbed by crooks who knew exactly what to do. That's how it still works today.

Everything is in pieces, socially divided. An impulse within the society would have to arise, like Communism — which is not impossible–an element that would pull people together again. But I think it would have to come from a new generation.

What about the future?
The second half of this century is drifting in a different direction. Another World War is not necessary because it's continually going on today. Not in Kosovo, but it's happening on a different level, a social level. It's twisted. And this is where, I believe, the media should come to help instead of entertaining. The tendency today is that media must entertain. Starting with magazines. People don't read anything. They read

only stuff like "she got her first period at the age of 12" and stupidities like that. Because I am on that Broadcasting Committee, I have to watch television a lot. We have some 15 channels here now. The decline in quality is amazing. Including Czech actors. They all became entertainers. They tell funny stories from the shoot, or what happened to them when they were kids — how they didn't like oatmeal for breakfast — or the other day they cooked something for a change. You know, it's moving somewhere else, to certain insensibility, a passiveness that can be easily abused.

I don't know why I am telling you all this nonsense but I believe that our media, including the actors and directors who jumped into show business... Nietzsche once said that man at the end of this century will become a "Schauspieler" and he didn't mean an actor but an individual who likes to show off... We have NOVA TV run by a quick-fermented billionaire, Železný, who is saying, "We don't have enough entertainers! What will we do when digital television comes with 50 channels? Who will entertain the people?"

And I asked, "Excuse me, what are you expecting? Half of the nation will be performing every Monday and the other half on Tuesday?"

For example, they have those TV shows when they bus people in from all over the place. And everybody waves in the camera: "Hi, Mom, hi, Dad!" And the politicians do the same. They ask him a question on camera and he, instead of looking at the camera looks at the monitor next to it. He is not interested in the question, he wants to see himself on TV. And it's spreading all over the world. We all are becoming "Schauspielers." We all are acting, and we are all part of a play. So, it all sucks and I would end with that.

Filmography

STANISLAV MILOTA (born 1932)

Born into a working class family, Milota came to Barrandov Studios in 1948 to work at the laboratories. In 1950 he started work as a focus puller on the films *Posel úsvitu, Mikoláš Aleš, Plavecký mariáš, Měsíc nad řekou a Cirkus bude.*

Since 1954 he worked as a camera operator on the films *Grandfather Automobile, Citizen Brych* and ten others. In 1963 he became a director of photography and he photographed four feature films and 15 shorts for Czechoslovak Television, German Television, BBC and Israel. In September 1968, he shot some 10,000 feet of documentary footage of the Soviet invasion in Prague. Because of this he was later "fired forever" from Czechoslovak film industry. His career as a filmmaker ended in 1969 with the short documentary film about Jan Palach, a student who set himself on fire in protest of the Soviet Occupation of Czechoslovakia. In 1977 he signed Charta 77 and until 1984 he was secretly filming proclamations of Czech dissidents (Hájek, Havel, Hejdánek, etc.) which were then smuggled abroad. During that time he also filmed performances of the "Apartment Theatre" of Vlasta Chramostová like *Play Macbath* (broadcast on ORF television in 1978) and *Report on Burial in Bohemia* (broadcast on ORF Television in 1983). In January 1990 he became the chief of the first administration office of President Václav Havel but in June of the same year he quit. He was the founder of Masaryk's Democratic Movement in 1990, a member of the Council for Development of Czech Cinema in 1994–97 and a member of Council for Radio and Television Broadcasting in 1994–97. He withdrew from the last position because "the council became politically manipulated."

1968 — *The Cremator* (DP)
1967 — *Picnic* (DP)
1965 — *Angel of Blissful Death* (DP)
1963 — *On the Rope* (DP)

Awards

Trilobit Award 1968 for cinematography (*The Cremator*)
František Kriegl Award 2001— for exemplary carriage of citizenship
Lifetime Achievement Award 2001 in cinematography (Association of
    Czech Cinematographers)

The Velvet Revolution
and Beyond
THE FALL OF COMMUNISM

*"Communism is a fascinating phenomenon, which nobody
in the West ever experienced."*

Martin Ondreját

The Velvet Revolution in Czechoslovakia on November 17, 1989, wasn't
any anti–Communist takeover, but a privatization coup of the reforming
fraction of the KGB with the goal to change the present nomenclature–Communists leaders, secret police agents and militiamen — into law-
abiding entrepreneurs and leaders accepted by the civilized world. They
succeeded not just in Czechoslovakia but in the whole of Eastern Europe.

Analysts at Soviet intelligence agencies at the end of the 60s came
to the conclusion that the Communist system was gravely ill and can't be
fixed. The best brains, designated by the chairmen of the KGB Juri
Andropov,[98] who later became the leader of the Soviet Union, started
secretly developing a strategy of how to save the Soviet Union as a superpower. They were willing to sacrifice the Communist party and its senile
leadership. *Perestroika* and *Glasnost* were not born in the Kremlin but in
the KGB. The goal wasn't democracy but to save the Soviet Union as a
world superpower. Human rights, freedom of the press and a market
economy was a price to be paid.

"The concept of deep reforms in Russia was born here," says Andrej Cernenko, spokesman of FSB, the successor of the former KGB. "Our reforms went much deeper than what politics was able to do."

Many western sources support this version:

- In 1991, Mikhail Gorbachev[99] appointed reformer politician Vadim Bakatim,[100] a construction engineer, to the position of KGB director. He immediately dissolved five divisions of heavily armed special forces of the KGB, transferred the command of the secret service (including a special commando Alfa) to the President and transformed almost a quarter of a million special border KGB units under Red Army command. But before he could finish the job, he was fired by Boris Yeltsin.[101] But in December 1991, Yeltsin signed the bill, which unified all secret organizations in Russia into one super-ministry of security.
- New Russian spy agency (SVRR) lead by Yevgeny Primakov[102] with an army of 12,000 agents around the world continued the business as usually.[103] He was Breznev's advisor for the Middle East. His Section I (information) maintains the database SOUD loaded with information about all the countries of former Eastern Europe. Ninety percent of STASI[104] personal files are stored there. The same applies to files from Czechoslovakia.
- FSB RF-Ministry of Security of Russia — was led by Viktor Barannikov,[105] probably the most powerful man in Russia at that time. All sections of the former KGB are operating inside MBR even though some had to undergo cosmetic changes. The official report to the Russian parliament said that FSB personal was cut by thirty-eight percent. Not so.

"The society will realize that we are necessary," says FSB spokesman Andrej Cernenko in a interview for *Playboy* magazine. "We are not asking people to love us. Only idiots can love the secret police. But we are asking for respect. And only idiots would not respect us."

Those who devoted their lives to fight Communism are, of course, deeply disappointed because they didn't expect this to happen under KGB supervision. But maybe both sides should be satisfied. Those who were in the power in the past can be happy that they didn't lose and those who were manipulated in the past can be happy that, while still being manipulated, they are manipulated in a more civilized way. In Czechoslovakia, the play written by Ronald Reagan and Mikhail Gorbachev was cast by Václav Havel, Petr Pithart, Jiři Dienstbier and other so-called "Communist fighters."

The image of a Velvet Revolution was shattered by a leak of information revealing facts about the students' demonstration on November 17, 1989. It became clear that the whole conflict was organized by StB. It turned out that the student Růžička leading demonstrators in the clash with heavily armed police and killed by police — falsely identified later by BBC as Martin Šmíd[106]) — was an StB agent, Ludvík Živčák, who later surfaced alive and well. The traffic on the street where this incident occurred was stopped two hours before the demonstration started. Charta's leadership and their families left Prague in the afternoon and returned the next day. Two of the top-ranking KGB officers were "accidentally" on an official visit in Prague at that time. The protesters' slogans were developed in June and posters for the December presidential election promoting Václav Havel's presidency were printed during the summer 1989 as well.

For this action, Živčák was later sentenced to 16 months in jail but was released after serving just eight months. Miroslav Štěpán,[107] a chairman of Prague's Communist party bureau and commander of People's Militia, was also sentenced to two and a half years in jail. He was released after serving 23 months and later became the founder of the new Czech Communist Party.

"I don't call that change in 1989 a revolution, but I am not going to explain why because nobody would believe me yet," Miroslav Štěpán said in an interview for *Region Daily*. He continued, "I believed Gorbachev wanted to save socialism. Today we all know that it was a great trick and he is a criminal. What actually happened in November 1989? We would have to work with objective documents but, unfortunately, nobody wants to show these documents. I would point out two facts. First of all, secret documents from the Czechoslovak Intelligence Services stated that the American administration had a problem in Czechoslovakia — in contrast with other countries in Eastern Europe — to find anybody who would qualify as a leader after the coup. Secondly, it was a result of an agreement between George Bush and Mikhail Gorbachev. On November 2, 1989, we received information that Bush wanted to solve the problem in Czechoslovakia and Eastern Germany before his official visit to Italy. So, the most important fact is that there was an agreement between Washington and Moscow.[108] So, we all knew, but we couldn't do anything about it. Some KSČ members hoped that this change would bring them new opportunities. They were those who were later involved in the roundtable negotiations, like Adamec,[109] Čalfa,

Poledník, Kučera, and others. Even Václav Havel later admitted that he was surprised what the 'Godfathers' offered during the negotiations. He didn't expect that. On the other hand we knew since 1988 what the other side was after and we tried to sabotage Gorbachev's agreements with the U.S.A. I told my Soviet friends just one day before the coup that I don't want to be put in the same bag with Ladislav Adamec. The Soviets asked me to call up a press conference on November 17 and announce that there is no conflict between Adamec and myself. If I did that I could be in the roundtable negations a couple of days later instead of on the way to the jail. I should tell you also that one KGB representative suggested to me that Václav Havel should be made a Minister of Culture. I told him that I don't know any Havel and that the Minister of Culture wouldn't be someone who didn't achieve anything. The decision was made in the meeting with the Interior Minister Kincl on December 9, 1989, that Mirek Štěpán must go to jail so he can't complicate the negotiations and that comrade Adamec in the spring, when he will become the new president, would pardon me. I am saying this to make it clear that I wasn't put in the jail by the Civic Forum but by Communist traitors."

In the same interview, StB officer Ludvík Živčák said, "We had some information, for example that the West was trying break up the Eastern block. We also knew that in the KGB headquarters people were working for the CIA and they are cooking something together, but StB worked under KGB command... I worked for the 2nd division StB watching activities of western intelligence agencies. For example, all the leaders of Charta 77 were connected to the CIA or other western intelligence services. I was personally in touch with Václav Havel. I said this already in my interview for the BBC: Havel was intensively watched but he was no way a number one person inside Charta 77. His reputation was created artificially by western media. But we made a contact anyway and worked together with him on preparations for the November 17 campaign."

Then advisor to U.S. President, John Whitehead, announced after returning from his 12-day trip in Eastern Europe that the political situation allowed the takeover to proceed. The date of November 17 was chosen because it was an International Day of Students Holiday and also because the time was running out before the Gorbachev — Bush meeting in Malta.

The concept of the Civic Forum was agreed on half a year before the coup and it was approved by Rudolf Hegenbart.[110] When this was publicly announced by Václav Havel in Realistic Theater in Prague, StB officers were driving Charta 77 members to the meeting.

The fall of Communism in Czechoslovakia wasn't an internal issue of Czechoslovakia or anti–Communist forces lead by Václav Havel but an integral part of the Soviet-American political concept for Europe.

All those who, after November 17, 1989, entered any position of power were somehow tied up with the KSČ, StB, the former government, or directly to the KGB.[111] We can logically assume that if there were any honest people in the government, a conflict on the issues of punishment of Communist criminals, confiscation of property and compensation to the victims of Communism would have had to arisen during these past 13 years. None of that happened.

Former Communists are still keeping the power in their hands. Opposition is negligible and disoriented. The "revolution" failed because of inability, or unwillingness, to establish a functioning legislative and judicial system. The uncovering of symbiosis between the U.S.S.R. and U.S.A., which was kept in secret for so many years, is opening a new dimension in new global politics.

Economy

Václav Klaus' priority after becoming Prime Minister was to quickly privatize the public sector. He dismissed the moral arguments favoring restitution of state property to its former owners on the grounds that it would slow down the process. Speed was the most important. Jews were not included because the property confiscated by Germans during World War II was excluded from the restitution. He introduced a voucher scam. Every citizen had the right to purchase one book of vouchers for 1,000 Czech crowns and in turn they could use these vouchers to buy shares in companies during a public auction. That's when Viktor Kožený entered the scene. Kožený founded Harvard Capital and Investment Consulting, an investment fund which promised a 1,000 percent return within a year to those who turned their vouchers over to his firm. More than 800,000 Czechs sold their voucher books to Kožený for $37.20 apiece.

The government was not prepared to deal with men like Kožený. No legislation had been prepared on how to control the funds. By the end of the first round of the privatization, over 8,000,000 Czechs purchased vouchers and the privatization scheme was declared a great success. They called it "the Czech economic miracle."

The power of funds like Harvard was indisputable. At some point Kožený was holding a 13 percent stake in the Czech Savings Bank, 18 percent in Komerční Bank, and he was influencing the management of 85 percent of the Czech banking branches. According to some sources, Harvard's portfolio reached a value of $640,000,000 and Kožený himself took $50,000,000 in fees.

In 1995, Kožený's Harvard Funds and Dingman's Stratton Group, a Cyprus-based company, announced that they secretly bought shares of eight leading industrial companies in the Czech Republic. Later they created a new holding firm, Daventree Ltd. On the board of trustees you can find names like John Sununu or Thomas P. Stafford. Viktor Kožený and his Harvard Investment Funds resulted in a net loss of almost one billion U.S. dollars for the Czech Republic.

Cracks in the Czech economy became evident to the public in 1997. It was clear that "the Czech economic miracle" had come to an end. Eight more banks failed because of fraud and incompetence, making a total of 12 since 1994. The amount lost was the equivalent of one month's salary for every citizen of the Czech Republic. For example, the Kreditní Banka in 1996 lost $450 million. Investment funds, the engines of the privatization, were starting to go bust and some fund directors fled the country to avoid prosecution. In March 1997, 75,000 shareholders lost $79 millions in two investment funds alone and by 1997 750,000 Czechs had lost their investments in investment firms governed by bad legislation. In this scheme, most of the population lost the last of their savings. The trade deficit in 1997 reached six billion U.S. dollars.

In 1989, after the revolution, the government's debt was 170 billion crowns. Today (2002) the debt of the Czech government is continuing to rise. Compared to the previous year of 2001, it's 36 percent bigger. In the second quarter of 2002, it rose to 390.8 billion crowns and is expected to rise over 400 billion. The government's loans are almost 19 percent of GNP, and half of the annual budget. It's estimated that next year it will reach over 600 billion. The government's help to failing banks crossed over 500 billion crowns — the sum that could finance the education for six years! All these losses have to be paid by taxpayers.

The strength of corruption has become overpowering. It became obvious that top party people and people with close ties to the StB had rigged privatization to favor their friends. One quarter of Czechs believe that corruption is a necessity of life and apathy seems to prevail.

In 1990, after 42 years of Communist dictatorship, everybody lined up at the start line. When the majority of people came with scooters, others were already waiting there in their Mercedes limousines ready to race.

Notes

1. One of the central figures of the Czech New Wave. As one of the first graduates from FAMU, he made documentaries until 1957 when he directed his first feature, *September Nights*. Some of his other films are *Cassandra Cat* (1963), *All My Good Countrymen* (1968) and *Which Side Eden* (1999). After Jasný left Czechoslovakia, he taught filmmaking in Germany and Austria and since 1984 at Columbia University in New York. He also shot a documentary, *Why Havel?* (1990), but the film is not permitted to be shown in the Czech Republic because President Havel is portrayed as the person he really is—a womanizer, a chain smoker, a man who likes to drink. Even though Havel himself liked the film, he never made any effort to help it get released back home, and later he stopped communicating with Jasný entirely.

2. One of the leading Czech directors, best-known for his films *The White Dove* (1960), *The Devil's Trap* (1961), *Marketa Lazarova* (1967) and *The Valley of the Bees* (1968).

3. Film Academy of Fine Arts in Prague (Filmová Akademie Múziských Umění), founded in 1947.

4. One of the famous directors of Czech New Wave (1931–88).

5. A Czech filmmaker who found suc-cess within the American film industry. He played a major role in shaping the Czech New Wave in the 1960s when he shot films like *Loves of a Blonde* and *The Fireman's Ball*. After the Soviet invasion of Czechoslovakia in 1968, he stayed in the U.S. He received his first Oscar for *One Flew Over the Cuckoo's Nest* in 1975. Since then he's shot many successful films like *Hair, Ragtime, Amadeus* and *The People vs. Larry Flynt,* to name just a few.

6. The Barrandov Studios were built by Miloš Havel, uncle of the Czech president Václav Havel, in 1932. During the World War II, Germans added the interconnected stages totaling 37,000 square feet of the shooting space. During the Communist era, Barrandov Studios produced up to 80 films a year. After the fall of Communism, the production dropped dramatically. At the present time Barrandov Studios have ten sound stages, the biggest 18,000 square feet.

After privatization, Barrandov Studios was turned into a service company. The majority shareholder is Northern Moravian Třinec Steel Works with 79.7 percent shares. The business at the studios picked up in the last couple of years. At the present time, foreign productions are spending up to $200 million annually in Prague.

187

7. Charta 77 was officially born on January 1, 1977, as an informal group of people concerned about human rights in Czechoslovakia, when the first 217 people signed the Charta 77 declaration. One hundred fifty-six of them were former Communists. The authors of the proclamation, Jiří Hájek, Václav Havel and Jan Patočka, appealed in this document to the leaders of the nation to comply with the Helsinki Human Rights Agreement. The document was never published in the media. The Interior Minister Jaromír Obzina* said in 1979: "The Charta was written by the best brains of the 'opposition.' It has been written in such a clever way that if we were to make it public, 90 percent of people would not understand what it was about. This represents a danger that some 2,000,000 additional people could sign it." In November 1989, the Charta 77 group became the base of the Civic Forum (OF) and joined with representatives of the Communist government to achieve the monopoly of power.

The intelligence analysis of the KSČ screenings during 1969–70 stated that after November 17, 1989, approximately 800 Communist party officials were expelled and transferred to so-called reserves for future needs later — like Charta 77 and other variations for future development. The report also states that approximately 1,120 Communists emigrated — were sent abroad — to work in opposition movements there and collect intelligence data. The whole operation was partially under KGB control. At the end of 1977, it was decided in the meeting between KGB and StB that some members of ÚV KSČ would be kept out of the picture. Only 12 select members of ÚV KSČ in Czechoslovakia were partially informed about these actions.

During the period 1980–89, Charta Foundation paid $376,000 to finance Charta 77 activities in Czechoslovakia and $1,341,000 for personal expenses of Charta 77 members. This amount doesn't include individual awards dissidents received abroad. An additional $6,000,000 was transferred to the personal accounts of Charta 77 leaders. The Charta's account — Charta Foundation — was managed by Prof. Janouch in Sweden. Janouch came from a prominent Communist family and his wife had Soviet citizenship. When the account reached millions of dollars and some investment strategy was necessary, money was transferred to Kommerzbank in Hamburg, Germany.

Around 1974, the KGB established in Czechoslovakia a new base of 7,000–8,000 citizens who were not in StB files. Charta 77 was operating all the time with the blessing and under the control of StB and KGB. The system of managing Charta's activity was quite complex. It was executed by the KGB following instructions from the U.S. In charge of the whole operation leading to the "coup" in November 17, 1989, was Rudolf Hegenbart from the thirteenth division of ÚV KSČ with the help of StB colonel Josef Vostarka.

Acceptance of new Charta 77 members ended November 17, 1989, when membership reached approximately 1,900. The majority of them had no idea about the function and goals of this organization. The management of Charta was in the hands of 70–85 people, mostly former Communists. At the present time some 180 of their family members are holding high positions in the government and economy. This group was selected and approved in the beginning by both Soviets and American sides.

During the 13 years of its existence, Charta 77 never achieved any political influence. It was not anticipated. The pur-

---

*Obzina was interior minister during the Normalization era for ten years and chairman of the State Committee for Investment and Development in 1986–88. He is being sued for the operation "Asanace" that he launched in 1977 to force some dissidents out of the country. For years he has refused to come to court, claiming he is ill.

pose was to make Czechoslovak citizens familiar with people that otherwise nobody would know anything about in November 1989. The danger of being the dissident depended on who was one before. The opinion of general public was, more or less, that Chartists were just a bunch of nuts. Overall 43 StB officers were involved overseeing Charta's activities. Each of them supervised five to seven field agents.

When new Interior Minister Dr. Richard Sacher discovered in March 1990 that some materials regarding activities of Charta 77 and personal files of some of its leaders were compromised, the danger arose that the connection between Charta and the former Communist government could leak out. On April 2, 1990, at the request of President Václav Havel, he ordered the removal from archives all documents about the President, members of the cabinet and members of the Parliament. It was ordered that these documents be sealed in metal containers, and that the Interior Ministry be informed immediately whenever anyone sought information about these people. He also appointed Jan Ruml* to the position of deputy director at the Interior Ministry. Within six weeks after his arrival 15,000 personal files disappeared (for example, audio recordings from Charta representatives meetings with foreign diplomats that Charta routinely passed on StB). Also missing were the personal files of Charta 77 leaders Václav Havel, J. Diensbier, Zuzana Diensbierová, Petr Uhl, Jaroslav Šabata, A. Šabatová, L. Hejdánek, Václav Benda, J. Gruntorad, M. Palous, Kantůrek, Eva Kantůrková, Vlasta Chramostová, Marta Kubišová, Z. Jičínský, M. Motejl, Dr. Danisz, Zdeněk Richetský, Peter Pithart, J. Urban, P. Kučera, I. Fišer, Jiří Hájek, A. Marvanová, P. Šustrová, Jan Ruml, R. Slánský, W. Komárek, Miloš Zeman, Václav Klaus, V. Dlouhý and others. All documents re-

garding the negotiations about the transfer of power in December 1989 disappeared as well as files about intelligence organizations activities abroad.

8. Miroslav Müller, the chief of the cultural division of ÚV KSČ during the Normalization era. His biography is unknown.

9. His biography is unknown — all the files have disappeared.

He was an unsuccessful filmmaker. Between 1957 and 1959 he directed six industrial films and documentaries. He became the chairman of the Czechoslovak–Soviet Friendship League. In the mid-60s he moved to the Soviet Union. During his stay in the Soviet Union, he married a high-ranking KGB officer. He surfaced back in Czechoslovakia after the Soviet invasion in 1969 in the position of the Chief Dramaturg at Barrandov Studios and earned himself the nickname "the grave digger of Czech cinema." It became a common practice that filmmakers had to pay him kickbacks of up to 50 percent of their royalties in order to get their scripts approved and their film produced. Between 1970 and 1977 his name appeared in credits as a co-author on 19 motion pictures produced under his leadership. He survived all attempts of ÚV KSČ to remove him from that position.

He died in 1988 in his hotel room in Karlovy Vary. The story goes that while totally drunk, he choked on his own vomit.

10. One of the biggest personalities of Czech literature, a chief representative of the playful, uniquely Czech school of Poetism and a member of the Avant-garde movement in the 1930s (1900–58).

11. One of the legendary figures of Czech poetry. His work was first published in 1930 and by the end of the decade he had established himself as a poet of unparalleled complexity. He wrote several

---

*Ruml, son of a high-ranking communist and a former foreign correspondent for *Rudé Pravo* newspaper, served as the Interior Minister after the Velvet Revolution. His StB file was closed and sealed in 1987.

large collections of poetry and was active as a translator as well (1905–1980). Unlike Nezval, he became deeply disillusioned by the Communist regime and from 1950 to 1960 lived in hermetic seclusion. He is best known for his *Night with Hamlet,* published in 1962. He was nominated for the Nobel Prize in 1969.

12. Civic Democratic Party. The ODS was born after Civic Forum had split in 1992.

13. A founding member of the Communist Party of Czechoslovakia in 1921. He participated in the Communist seizure of power in 1948 and became the First Secretary of the Czechoslovak Communist Party (KSČ) (1905–75) in 1953. He became the President of the Czechoslovak Republic in 1957. During the so-called "Prague Spring" in March of 1968, he was forced to resign.

14. One of the conspicuous officers of the StB who later became a screenwriter. A member of the Communist Party since 1939, he was arrested in 1942 and spent the rest of World War II in the concentration camps Terezin, Natzweiler and Dachau. He started his career working for Prague County National Security office in June 1945. A couple of months later, he was transferred to its Second Division (ZOB 2) which specialized in intelligence conspiracy. This division was under full control of the Communists. Their activities focused on the interrogation of former Gestapo and Abwehr agents with the intention to rebuild the intelligence network of these Nazi agencies. In February 1948, as a lieutenant, he became a deputy commander of the counter-intelligence section at the Interior Ministry (OZ) and at the same time a commander of its Fourth Division. He was in charge of the surveillance focusing on the U.S. and other western agents operating in Czechoslovakia. In 1951 he became the commander of the whole OZ Section. This section was spying on western embassies and diplomats (tapping their phone lines) and recruiting captured foreign agents. During his tenure, the department became infamous for brutal in-

terrogations sometimes leading to death. In 1952 he was removed from this position, promoted to captain and became the chief of the Second Division of StB. He quit in 1953 and came to Barrandov Studios, where he worked as an adviser. In 1962 he was arrested, interrogated in Ruzyne prison for two months and then released. After the 1968 Soviet invasion, he became the General Manager of Short Film Studios (Kratký Film Praha). During a business trip in 1972, he was arrested and interrogated in Paris and then expelled from France. In 1980 he received a decoration of "Merited Artist" from President Gustáv Husák. He retired in 1989.

15. Krátký Film Praha

16. A Polish national, born in Paris, France, director-producer-actor Polanski studied film at Lodz Film School in Poland. In 1962 he directed his first feature film *Knife in the Water,* for which he received an Award of Critics in Venice Film Festival. He moved to Los Angeles and became a successful director. He received the Golden Globe Award for Best Director in 1974 for *Chinatown* and the Los Angeles Film Critics Award, Best Director in 1980 for *Tess.* He is currently living in France.

17. Czech dramatist, writer, politician, President of the Czech Republic. Between 1959 and 1999 he wrote 90 plays and published some 19 books.

He comes from a prominent entrepreneurial-intellectual family in Prague. His grandfather Hugo Vavrečka, a former ambassador to Hungry and Minister of Propaganda in 1938, was a Nazi sympathizer and one of the Bata's managers during World War II. Václav's uncle, Ivan Vavrečka, was allowed to legally immigrate to Argentina in 1949. Václav's other uncle, Miloš Havel, the former owner of Barrandov Studios, traveled to Western Germany in 1951 and opened a Munich restaurant. The place became a popular hangout for the employees of Radio Free Europe. All this didn't create any trouble for Václav. He studied at Economics Faculty in Prague in 1955–57 and in 1962–66 dramaturgy at DAMU (Theater Academy).

In 1964 he married Olga Šplíchalová and in May 1968 he traveled to Western Europe and the USA, where he met Jiří Voskovec, František Peroutka and Pavel Tigrid. In 1969 he wrote the *Ten Points* proclamation addressed to the government and ÚV KSČ as a protest against the current trend in the politics. In 1975 he wrote an open letter to the President Gustáv Husák analyzing the state of the society and politics in Czechoslovakia. He was one of the inciters of the Charta 77 proclamation, which he signed on January 1, 1977, and one of its first spokesmen (together with J. Patočka and J. Hájek). He was jailed between January 14 and May 20, 1977, and then again from January 28 to March 13, 1978. In May 1979 he was arrested and then sentenced to four and half years in prison. He was released from prison in May 1983 for health reasons. He was arrested twice again in 1988. On January 16, 1989, he was arrested and sentenced to nine months in prison but released on May 17, 1989. Then he was arrested for a couple of days in October 1989. He negotiated a smooth transfer of the government by promising Communists they would not be punished and in December of 1989 he became the President of Czechoslovakia. When the Czech Republic was formed on January 26, 1993, he was elected its first President. In 1997, one year after the death of his wife Olga, he married in a secret ceremony actress Dagmar Veškrnová. In 1998, presidential election Václav Havel was re-elected by a margin of one vote in the second round of voting. The presidential vote was conducted in the absence of the Republican Party Chairman Miroslav Sládek, who was stripped his parliamentary immunity and arrested on charges of inciting racial hatred. The election took place on January

20 and Sládek was acquitted and released on January 23. However many Czechs were not bothered by the legitimacy of Havel's one-vote victory.

Havel was the highest paid official in Czech Republic with the monthly salary of 167,000 KC. Before the end of his presidency, the Czech Parliament (in a February 27 meeting) failed to pass a new law about the presidential retirement benefits. The proposal for Havel's monthly retirement benefit called for: salary 69,700 KC, expenses 46,500 KC, office rental 40,000 KC, free car and free secret service detail. Only 58 representatives supported the proposal. Havel retired January 31, 2003, with one-time bonus of 800,000 KC.

In 1990, Havel said he knows how to bite (addressing the Communists), but later he chose to forget the Communists' criminal past. He also didn't do anything about policies discriminating against emigrants. Restitution of emigrants' properties and their return to the Czech Republic would definitely affect political development in the country. This way he became the guarantor of continuity between former Communist and new post-communist power.

18. The period that followed the Soviet-led Warsaw Pact invasion on September 21, 1968, until the so-called Velvet Revolution in November 1989. The Normalization regime under the leadership of the President Gustáv Husák took a tough stance toward Czech intellectuals. It was the darkest period in the history of Czechoslovakia, also labeled as a period of cultural genocide.

19. He studied political economics in Prague and graduated in 1969. He joined the Communist Party during the Prague Spring in 1968. After the Soviet occupation he was expelled from the party. He worked for the Institute of Prognosis.* He

---

*This special division of the Academy of Science was created in 1984 to find a way to switch from a socialist economy to a market economy. The institute, under the leadership of Valtr Komárek, worked under KGB supervision and employed many later successful politicians: Václav Klaus, Josef Tošovský, Vladimír Dlouhý, Miloš Zeman, Tomáš Ježek, Jan Mládek, Karel Dyba, Vladimír Rudlovčák, and Miloslav Randsdorf. One *(cont.)*

emerged as a political figure during the Velvet Revolution in 1989 when he joined the Civic Forum and became a deputy of the Czechoslovak Federal Assembly in 1990. In 1992 he re-launched the Czechoslovak Social Democratic Party. After the 1993 split of Czechoslovakia, he became the chairman of Czech Social Democratic Party (CSSD) and he remained in this position until his retirement in 2002. From 1996 to 1998 he was the chairman of the Lower House of the Czech parliament and in 1998 he became the Prime Minister. His run for President in the January 2003 election was unsuccessful.

20. His father's name was Pruzinsky and he came to Czechoslovakia from Russia. Klaus studied economics at Prague and later received scholarships in Italy (1966) and the U.S. (1969). Until 1970 he also worked in the economics section at the Academy of Science and in 1971–86 at the State Bank. He also worked for the Institute of Prognosis and during that period frequently lectured at Universities abroad. Between October 1990 and February 1991 he was the chairman of the Civic Forum (OF). He was a co-founder and (since April 1991) the chairman of Civic Democratic Party (ODS). In December 1989 he became the Minister of Finance, in October 1991 the Vice-Premier of Czechoslovak government and in June 1992 the Premier of the Czech government. He resigned

from this post in November 1997. In 2002 he resigned from the post of chairman of ODS. Despite failing to get a majority of votes in his run for the presidency in the January 2003 election, he was elected in the office in the third round of election by majority of one vote and became the second President of the Czech Republic on March 7, 2003.

Two days after his inauguration, President Václav Klaus said in his speech to the nation (televised by TV NOVA), "We will not allow to waste time on never ending disputes about how to interpret our past, especially the past of the last decade!"

21. The coupon privatization was a great rip-off of Czech citizens. Masterminded and executed by fellows from the Institute of Prognosis under the leadership of Václav Klaus, it allowed transformation of the national property to the hands of former Communists (StB and KGB agents) and swindlers. The bill for privatization between 1990–2000 reached 2,385 billion KC ($75 billion)— 460,000 KC for each taxpayer!

22. The secret police and spy agency, a backbone of the Soviet police state, was founded by Felix Dzerhinsky in 1917. The KGB was officially abolished in October 1991 by Mikhail Gorbachev and, after many cosmetic adjustments, was replaced by the new Ministry of Security (FSB). In the end, the KGB that the West so naively

---

of the experts in the Institute of Prognosis, not by accident, was Karel Köecher, the famous spy arrested in the United States and exchanged later for Soviet dissident Natan Shcharansky. Köecher joined the Communist Party in 1958 and began work for the intelligence service in 1962. When his training ended he "emigrated" to Austria in 1965 and was granted a visa to the United States, where he arrived in December 1965. In 1967 he started to work for Radio Free Europe and studied at Columbia University. In 1972, on the recommendation of Zbiegniew Brzezinsky, he got a job at the CIA as a translator and analyst. In 1975 he was promoted and transferred to New York. The FBI started to suspect him of espionage and he was arrested on November 27, 1984, a few hours before his departure to Switzerland. Köecher's lawyer, Robert Fiera, asked President Gustáv Husák for help, and on a directive from Mikhail Gorbachev, the HGB started to negotiate an exchange with the CIA. On February 11, 1996, he was exchanged for Soviet dissident Anatoly Shcharansky on Glienicke Brucke bridge in West Berlin. After his return to Czechoslovakia he worked in the Institute of Prognosis. After the coup in November 1989, he worked as an adviser to the finance minister Václav Klaus.

dismissed with a simple "goodbye" has managed to remain true to itself. It still employs 50,000 officers, 90,000 technicians, 240,000 special army troops and 10 million informers. Its Sixth Division became a financially powerful holding company controlling almost 80 percent of investment in banks and the stock exchange. Andropov's Institute of Foreign Services in Moscow with the capacity of 300 students is considered the best spy school. The Soviet government was the biggest mass murderer in the world. During the period from 1917 to 1987, 65 million people were killed in the Soviet Union.

23. Secret Police of the Czechoslovak Communist Party. Its purpose was to defend and reinforce the unlimited power of the Communist party. To achieve these goals, this organization created and maintained an atmosphere of fear and permanent danger within society using physical terror, torture, murder, unlawful imprisonment and threat. Between 1948 and 1989, 248 people were executed, 4,500 died in the prison, 327 were killed when attempting to cross the border and 205 were sentenced to jail; almost 200,000 defected. Who knows how many people were interrogated, barred from jobs, high schools and colleges.

After the Velvet Revolution, the StB was "dismantled" and replaced by BIS — Security Information Service (Bezpečnostní a informační služba).

24. A Czech ice hockey player drafted by the Pittsburgh Penguins in 1990. He won an Olympic Gold Medal in 1998, and was the CZ and NHL Player of the Year for the 1999–2000 season.

25. A Czech ice hockey goaltender, drafted by the Chicago Blackhawks in 1983. He was NHL Goaltender of the year in 1994–95, 1996–97, 1997–98, 1998–99 and 2000–01, NHL Player of the year in 1997–98, and Olympic Gold medal winner in 1998.

26. A film directed by Jan Svěrák. Academy Award winner for Best Foreign Language Film in 1996.

27. A 1999 film directed by Jan Hřebejk.

It's comedy placed in the period of the "Prague Spring" and the Soviet invasion.

28. One of the greatest Italian filmmakers (1920–93). He directed films from 1950. He is known for *La Strada, La Dolce Vita, 8½* and *Amarcord*, just to name a few.

29. This French filmmaker made 15 features during his career (1901–99). In his early films, he developed the severe, formalistic style with which he came to be identified for the rest of his career.

30. An independent and uncompromising American independent filmmaker best known for *Stranger Than Paradise* (1984) and *Years of the Horse* (1997).

31. Probably the best-known and one of the most significant Czech writers, Habal started as a poet (1914–97). It wasn't until 1963, when he was 49, that his breakthrough as a writer of prose came with the collection of short stories *A Pearl on the Bottom* (Perlička na dně). Between 1963 and 1968 he published eight original works. After 1968 he was banned from publishing until 1975. During his lifetime, nearly three million copies of his book were printed in Czechoslovakia, and he was translated into 27 languages. His work has led to eight film adaptations.

32. Czech writer, born in Prague, survivor of Theresienstadt, Auschwitz and Buchenwald. He has twice won the National Jewish Book Award in addition to being honored with an Emmy and numerous other awards for his film and television scripts. He lives in Washington DC and he has been professor of literature at American University since 1973.

33. A Czech writer. Since 1975 he has been living in France and has published 12 books, some fictions and some non-fiction. He is best-known for his books *The Joke* (Žert), *The Unbearable Lightness of Being, The Book of Laughter and Forgetting, Immortality,* and *Life Is Elsewhere*. He writes in French.

34. A Czech writer (1890–1938) best-known for his books *The Insect Play* (Ze života hmyzu), *War with the Newts* (Válka s mloky) and *R.U.R. (Rossum's Universal*

Robots), which introduced the word *robot* to the world.

35. He was the producer on Jiří Menzel's last project, an adaptation of Bohumil Hrabal's novel *I Served the King of England*. The project never materialized. During pre-production, Sirotek secretly negotiated a sale and sold the rights to another production company without informing Menzel. In 1998, at the Karlovy Vary International Film Festival, Menzel beat his producer in public with a big stick in front of TV cameras. The stick was later auctioned to his admirers.

36. The film fund for the development of Czech Cinema was set by legislators to award grants to individual film projects. However, it was designed to award only up to 30 percent of a film's budget. The funds don't cost the government any money because it's financed from revenues coming from a tax added to cinema tickets, videocassette rentals and from films produced in the 60s.

37. With the fall of Communism, the Communist Party of Czechoslovakia didn't cease to exist. KSČ was re-named the Communist Party of Czech and Moravia (KSČM) in 1990. While in 1989 most people supported the idea of outlawing the Communist party once and forever, it didn't happen. With the passing of years, the resurrected Communist party gained popularity and its power is now higher then ever. At the same time they are refusing to take any responsibility for the crimes of the past regime.

When representative Jiří Payne was explaining principles of NATO in the foreign relationships committee of the Parliament, Communist representative Jaromír Kohlíček came to him after the meeting and said, "You will end up in the jail when we get back to power. I will personally take care of it!" In the next elections, representative Payne was not re-elected but the Communist Kohlíček was.

When Vladimír Špidla, the Chairman for Social Democratic Party, announced that he will not invite Communists to participate in the new government, Communist representative Zuzka Rujbrová threatened him, "We will teach you what the democracy is about, Špidla!"

In the magazine *Týden* (6/24/2002), Dalibor Balšínek wrote,

It is alarming how easily the Czech general public accepts the fact that communists are re-gaining the power. Czech communists are evil because they proliferate evil.
It's like that pre-election joke:
"Who are you going to vote for?"
"Communists, who else."
"I know that, but from which party?"

Half of the representatives in Social Democratic Party are former Communists and their Chairman Vladimír Špidla now believes it would be non-democratic to exclude communists from posts in the Parliament when 20 percent of voters support them.

Communist Party of Czech and Moravia (KSČM) received in the 1996 election 10.33 percent, in 1998, 11.33 percent, and in 2002, 18.51 percent of the votes. They are now holding 41 seats in the 200-member Parliament. They spent 15,000,000 KC on the election campaign, while receiving the 88 million campaign contribution from government. Communists as a lighting rod of dissatisfaction pulled to its side a quarter million voters from social democrats.

After the November 1989 revolution, a half million Communists quit the party. That left KSČM with roughly 300,000 members. But the common hope that the Communist Party would disintegrate and vanish didn't happen. They still have more members than all other political parties combined! Václav Havel's hope that the Communist Party will evolve in a modern western type leftist party, as happened in Poland or Hungry, didn't come through.

"We are different from them!" was a slogan of Velvet Revolution. But the Communist Party wasn't outlawed and foreign observers are puzzled by the paradox that a party whose activities are clearly in variance with the law (§ 260) can exist. On the Communist Party web pages you can read that "the capitalism bring the suffering to the whole world and it's necessary to change this 'inhumane' system." As Miroslav Schiffera wrote (*Literární noviny,* 6/20/2002*),* "Promotion of communism is an object of dismissed charges, punishable by up to four years of freedom in the Parliament."

Fingers are pointing to President Václav Havel, who helped create this situation. Havel acted illogically, keeping some Communist around and honoring them for their activities while turning his back on others. He appointed many Communists, former Communist and StB agents in his cabinet and positions of judges. The judicial system is suffering the most.

38. A prominent Czech cinematographer (1929–91) and the second husband of director Věra Chytilová. He worked on the films *Cassandra Cat, Daisies, Fruit of Paradise* and *All My Good Countrymen,* to name just a few.

39. The General Manager of Czechoslovak Film Industry (Československý Statní Film) during Normalization era, he is known for his close ties to StB and KGB. His biography is classified.

40. A specialist in dramaturgy — the art or technique of dramatic composition. This position of a "chief screenwriter" doesn't exist in American film industry.

41. The Premier of the Federal Government in 1968. He was a secretary of the KSČ Politburo in 1989. He was charged with treason in 1995, but in September 2002, together with Miloslav Jakeš, he was acquitted.

42. The head of the Prague' Communist party bureau and one of the most rigorous hard-liners in the Communist party and member of the Communist party politburo. In 1968 he was one of the signatories of the letter inviting the Red Army in to invade Czechoslovakia. He committed suicide in May 1990 at the age of 67.

43. The first President of Czechoslovakia (1850–1937). Born in Hodonín, he studied in Vienna and Leipzig. He married Charlotte Garrigue in America in 1878 but came to Prague in 1882 and in 1897 became professor at Charles University. In 1914 he went into exile and managed to get the support of American President Woodrow Wilson for the creation of an independent nation of Czechs and Slovaks. He came back to Prague in December 1918 and became the first President of Czechoslovakia.

44. Chytilová shot her latest film *Expulsion from Paradise* in 2001.

45. A publication listing StB agents (the Communist secret police) in Czechoslovakia published by Petr Cibulka* in 1992. The list wasn't complete, containing some 80 percent of files from 2nd Division StB. David Elder, a member of Civic Committee at the Interior Ministry after

---

*A former dissident and political prisoner, Petr Cibulka, was elected chairman of the conservative political party Right Bloc (Pravy blok) in 2000. Right Bloc is trying to implement the principles of American democracy and freedom into the Czech political system. In the mid-sixties Cibulka participated in the underground movement, and later he was involved in Charta 77. Between 1978 and 1989 he was arrested five times and spent a total of 59 months in communist prisons. After his last release on November 26, 1989, he immediately started to work for the Civic Forum (OF) in Brno and became a director of its Press Center (ITC). In 1990 he launched the Independent Information & Press Center for Support of Democracy, where he later published *Red Cow* (Rudé Krávo) — a partial list of the 2nd division of StB agents. Later he became publisher of *Uncensored News* (Necensurované noviny). His fierce fight against communists and their involvement in new government and economy put him again under heavy scrutiny of the secret police (BIS). He is currently facing three years in prison for making public an Internet database from the Ministry of StB/KGB, the finance elite, and the power structure from the previous totalitarian regime and the contemporay Czech business.

the revolution in November 1989, originally acquired the files by unknown means. He later died in Croatia under suspicious circumstances — a sportsman and a good swimmer, he was found drowned in two feet of water.

46. A screenwriter, producer and CEO of Barrandov Studios after its privatization.

47. Czech cinematographer. He shot all of Miloš Forman's films until *Valmont* in 1989 (*Hair, Ragtime* and *Amadeus*, to name a few). He also shot *IF, Slaughterhouse-Five, Awakening* and other films. He was twice nominated for Academy Awards: in 1981 for *Ragtime* and in 1989 for *Amadeus*.

48. The General Directorate of the Czech State Film was disbanded in 1990 before any rules or guidelines for privatization had been defined. Studios and Film Laboratories remained the state property for one more year. In 1991 they were sold for 500,000,000 crowns to a company called Cinepont and renamed AB Barrandov. In 1994, 42 percent of AB Barrandov's shares were acquitted by the investment fund Silas Group, 16 percent was owned by some Czech filmmakers (among them also Miloš Forman), and the remaining shares (42 percent) were owned by Barrandov's CEO Václav Marhoul. AB Barrandov was transformed in 1996 into a holding-type company by establishing three main subsidiaries: Barrandov Studios, Barrandov Biografia and Barrandov Panorama. The process by which this happened is quite intriguing:

The letter from the Civic Forum Organization of Barrandov Studios sent to Václav Havel on December 12, 1989

Dear Mr. President,
We are writing this open letter to you on the day of your inauguration because this is extremely urgent.... We, the filmmakers of Barrandov Studios, are asking you, Mr. President, not just as head of our state, but as a representative of Czech culture, to support the quick formation of new legislation about cinema, which would guarantee a national identity and the future development of Czech cinema.... We believe that you will personally help keep our cinema an important part of our culture.
Thank you
For OF: Hynek Bočan, Jaromil Jireš, Dušan Klein, Zdeněk Svěrák, Václav Šašek

The reply from the President's Office on January 5, 1990

Dear friends,
We don't understand your worries about the negative impact of changes in our economy on Czech cinema. If somebody says that President Václav Havel wants to commercialize Czech film, to sell Barrandov Studios to western capital, he is a liar. If somebody takes such lies seriously and believes in it, he is a fool.... It is crystal-clear that all filmmakers will be involved in forming new legislation about Czech cinema, to put our film back in the spotlight of world film production.
For the President Václav Havel:
Saša Vondra* and Jiří Křižan, advisers

Reply to President's office on January 6, 1990

---

*Saša (Alexandr) Vondra, born in 1961, graduated from Charles University in 1984, where he studied geography. He was a protégé of communist Rita Klímová. In 1985–87 he worked at Náprstkovo Museum in Prague. In July 1987 he signed the Charta 77 proclamation and worked as a computer programmer. He was a spokesman for Charta 77 from January 1989 till January 1990 and a co-founder of the Civic Forum in 1990. During 1990–92 he was an adviser to President Havel. In 1992 he was appointed first deputy for foreign relationships, in charge of diplomatic services. From 1992 to 1997 he served as the first deputy to foreign minister Josef Zelieniec, and from 1997 to 2001 as the ambassador to the United States. In 2001 he was appointed a special emissary of the government for the NATO summit in Prague.

Zelienec is a former communist and a Soviet citizen of Polish nationality. His father worked for Kominterna in Moscow. His family moved to Czechoslovakia, and he met Václav Klaus during his study of economics in Prague. There are periods in his life (*cont.*)

Dear Mr. President, dear friends,
We are deeply disturbed and offended by the tone of the letter we received from your advisers Saša Vondra and Jiří Křižan. We sent you our letter believing that you would support our cause. We are stunned by the arrogant answer coming from your office. Not even the office of totalitarian president Gustáv Husák would act like that.

OF, Barrandov Studios

Facts

• The federal government, acting on recommendations from President Havel's advisors, decided in July 1990 to dissolve the General Management of Czechoslovak Film starting December 31, 1990.

• In January, 1991, a legislative vacuum began for Barrandov Studios, Short Film Studios, Central Film Distribution, Film Laboratory, Filmexport, etc. Because legislation for the film industry wasn't created yet, the Ministry of Culture took over management of the Czech film industry. The old model, somewhat functional, was dissolved and the upcoming illegal situation opened the door for many individual interests to arise.

• On January 1, 1993, Barrandov Studios were privatized. CINEPONT consortium acquired Barrandov Studios for 500 million crowns ($20 million). This no interest loan had to be paid back to the government within the next ten years.

• In 1994, 42 percent of AB Barrandov's shares were acquired by the investment fund, Silas Group, 16 percent was owned by some Czech filmmakers (among them Miloš Forman) and the remaining share (42 percent) was

owned by Barrandov CEO Václav Marhoul.

• In 1996 AB Barrandov had been transformed into a holding type company by establishing three main subsidiaries: Barrandov Studios, Barrandov Biografia, and Barrandov Panorama.

• The latest attempt by Moravian Steel Works to sell their majority stake in Barrandov Studios to the Canadian consortium Kodiak Group was not successful.

The transfer of the Barrandov Studios property, with an estimated value of 3 billion crowns, to CINEPONT for 500 million didn't represent just a lost for the national cinema. It was a clear signal from the government that they have no intention of supporting Czech film. The decision as to how Barrandov Studios would be privatized was made a long time before plans for privatization became public. The official document of the Ministry of Culture in August 1991 says that the film industry will be privatized with 30 percent–51 percent involvement of the state. It shows that the whole project was kept secret by Igor Ševčík, the adviser to the minister.

Barrandov Studios and what next?
Record of the discussion about the situation at Barrandov Studios at the meeting of FITES on June 16, 1997.

STANISLAV MILOTA: Barrandov Studios are now in the hands of some steel corporation. What was actually sold and to whom?

VÁCLAV MARHOUL: In April, 1995, I was fired from Barrandov Studios and went to search for money. I wanted to buy shares of Barrandov because I believed, and I was right, that shareholders care only about money and not about the future of

---

when he disappeared for a year, nobody knows where. In 1990 he tried to become the director of the College of Economics, but students voted him down. In 1992, still bearing a foreign passport, he became the foreign minister of the Czech Republic before receiving his Czech citizenship. In 2002 he was an emissary representing the Czech Republic in the European Union Parliament.

the studios. I went to the Czech Saving Bank and Komercni Bank. They both kicked me out saying I was crazy. Finally, with a help from one architect, I was connected to people from SILAS. They were from Trinec. SILAS was a medium size company. They were leasing some furnaces in steel mills. They lent me the money. I borrowed 137.5 million crowns from them and with this money I bought 74 percent of shares from 18 shareholders. But then I had a problem as to how to pay off my loan. So I sold 46 percent shares out of those 74 percent I had back to SILAS for the same price. That's how SILAS got into the Barrandov Studios. I had a veto right, which was important to me. A year later SILAS wanted to increase the capital in AB Barrandov by 100 million. It was possible, but because I had no money to match it — I would have to add 25 million to keep my veto right — my shares went down to 20 percent. I could veto this whole transaction back then, but why would I do that? If they wanted to invest in the studios, why not?

STANISLAV MILOTA: But you shoot yourself in the foot.

VÁCLAV MARHOUL: But if I didn't do that then there wouldn't be a 50 million investment in the facility. That was important. I asked myself what was more important. It would look like I was pushing my own financial interests if I didn't go for it.

STANISLAV MILOTA: And how much did you make on it?

VÁCLAV MARHOUL: I bought it for some 40,000 crowns and left with some 6 million.

STANISLAV MILOTA: 6 million, it is a nicely tunneled out amount of money. That's exactly what FITES was saying in 1992 would happen. It's terrible. All those people who used to work there. Czech filmmakers will never shoot films there again and you are acting like a savior of Czech cinema!

VÁCLAV MARHOUL: I don't pretend to

be a savior, but my conscience is clean Mr. Milota.

JIŘÍ KREJČÍK: What actually happened? How did Třinec Steel Corporation became the owner of Barrandov Studios? Is Mr. Marhoul a victim of dark forces or did he put these dark forces in motion?

VÁCLAV MARHOUL: I will explain it briefly, because it is important to se the whole picture. In 1995 the Czech government decided to privatize Třinec Steel. Moravia Steel Group offered 2,65 billion crowns ($100 million) for 51 percent shares and they got it. To borrow $100 million in the Czech Republic was almost impossible, however they got the money from FNM (Fund of National Property) because they promised to pay it of in four months. And that's where the problem for Barrandov Studios started before anybody knew it. To pay off the loan to FNM they borrowed $100 million from ING Bank in Holland and from the City Bank. But they had to pay this loan off in six months again! The problem didn't go away. They bought Třinec Steel but they needed to change the short-term loan for a long term loan. They looked at the Barrandov Studios and they saw a company without any debt. They made a deal with Czech Spořitelna to use Barrandov Studios as collateral for the long-term loan of 2.7 billion crowns.

Barrandov Studios were used by Moravia Steel to buy Třinec Steel.

49. He graduated from the Charles University faculty of Law. A political scientist by training, he is also a signatory of Charta 77, a member of Civic Forum and later a member of the Christian Democratic Union–Czech People Party. He was a member of the first post–Communist parliament in 1990 and served as Prime Minister from 1990 to 1992. He was a senator in 1996–98 and he became Speaker of the Senate when he was re-elected to the Senate for the term 2000–06. He unsuccessfully ran for the presidency in the January 2003 election.

50. Emma Destinová was one of the

greatest dramatic sopranos of the twentieth century and one of the most sought-
after singers before World War I in Europe.

51. The birthday of T.G. Masaryk,
(Tomáš Garigue Masaryk) the first President of Czechoslovakia, born in Hodonín
on March 7, 1886.

52. A Czech Communist career politician, Premier and Interior Minister. He
studied law at Charles University in
Prague in 1945–49. Beginning in 1948, he
worked for the Communist party. In 1958
he became a member of the Politburo (ÚV
KSČ) and he remained there until 1989.
He served as the Minister of Agriculture in
1959–61 and the Interior Minister in
1961–65. He was the Secretary of ÚV KSČ
in 1965–1970. Since 1970 he served as the
Prime Minister. He resigned from this
post in October 1988. He was the candi-
date for the post of the General Secretary
of ÚV KSČ in November 1989 and in
1990 he was expelled from the Communist
party. In December 1999, charges were
filed against him for his activities during
1961–65 when he served as the Interior
Minister. He was acquitted of all charges
in 2002.

53. A former chief ideologist and secretary of state in Communist Czechoslovakia and now the only surviving signatory of the letter to Leonid Brezhnev
requesting Soviet intervention in Czechoslovakia in 1968. He is indicted on several
charges, including treason.

54. *Production*
Production of Czech films today is approximately 20 films a year depending
more and more on Czech Public Television. The government funds set up to help
finance Czech films contribute to less than
50 percent of the films produced and only
with moderate amounts.

Distribution
In 1989 there were 1330 movie theaters
and 52,000,000 people went see movies.
In 2002 there are only 750 movie theatres
and approximately 9,000,000 people see a
film annually. American films dominate
the market.

The state support for cinema
The volume of state financial support
to Czech cinema was recently reduced due
to austerity measures. The Ministry of
Culture budget — which subsidized Czech
Film Clubs, Czech Film and Television
Union FITES, local film festivals including IFF Karlovy Vary, and the magazine
Film a doba by an amount of around
40,000,000 crowns — suffered drastic cuts
as well.

Czech filmmakers depend on funds
from abroad. Eurimages contributes some
1,700,000 FRF annually to Czech film
production and distribution.

The Film Fund for the Development of
Czech Cinema awards grants to individual
projects covering only up to 30 percent of
the budget. That's why television has become a funding source for films.

55. An actor-producer-director, he
studied acting at DAMU where he graduated in 1987. In 1998 he co-produced
The Manor (Panství), a feature film star-
ring Peter O'Toole.

56. Irish actor. He studied acting at the
Royal Academy of Dramatic Arts together
with Albert Finney and Richard Harris.
His credits include *Lawrence of Arabia,
Becket, How to Steal a Million, Casino
Royale,* and *My Favorite Year.* He has re-
ceived three Academy Award nomina-
tions.

57. A screenwriter and son of the political prisoner executed during Klement
Gottwald's era in the 1950s. He studied
screenwriting at FAMU and then worked
at Barrandov Studies. Ironically, he received a Klement Gottwald Award for his
work from Gustáv Husák's totalitarian
government in 1988. After November 17,
1989, he became Václav Havel's security
adviser and in 1992–96 he served as a
Deputy to the Interior Minister, Jan
Ruml. He is listed in the StB files under
the code name "Mánes."

58. Czech pop star, politician and entrepreneur. He was Chairman of the Parliamentary Committee for the departure
of Red Army from Czechoslovakia in 1990.
His code name in StB files was "Muk."

59. American director who became famous after his adaptation of H.G. Wells' *The War of the Worlds* was broadcast on radio in 1938. His films include *Citizen Kane* (1941), *The Magnificent Ambersons* (1942) and *Touch of Evil* (1958).

60. This founder of pedagogy, also known as Comenius, was a thinker, philosopher, writer and educator. He spent the last 15 years of his life in Amsterdam where he published his *Opera Didactica Omnia* in 1656.

61. In the fall of 1971, many pedagogues were fired (Evald Shorm and Bořivoj Zeman, for example), and the Directing Program's Chair Otakar Vávra was replaced by director Antonín Kachlík, StB agent code name Blackbird (Kos).

62. Written by Homer around 800 B.C., the stories of *The Iliad* and *The Odyssey* are an integral part of ancient Greece, and thus of Western culture.

63. Poems about legendary King Arthur date from the dawn of British history to the fifth century. They start with the Welsh, in the Cornish town of Carmarthen, reputed birthplace of Merlin. Poems were later recorded in the manuscripts *Black Book of Carmanthern, Book of Taliesin* and *Red Book of Hergest.*

64. *Song of the Nibelungs* is the German epic poem composed in the thirteenth century, but drawing on earlier material. Its theme is the disastrous rivers following Siegfried's killing of the Burgundian princes Nibelungs and his seizure of the treasure. Together with the Nordic saga *Old Norse Volsungasaga* (related to the same events), it is a complex tale where characters are not clearly good nor obviously evil and change sides during the story.

65. Son of a Czech diplomat, politician, philosopher and the first President of Czechoslovakia, T.G. Masaryk. He served as the Ambassador to Britain between 1925 and 1938 and as a Foreign Minister of the exiled government in London (1940–1945). In February 1948 he didn't join in the resignation of the democratic ministers and remained in Gottwald's cabinet. He died under suspicious circumstances in March 1948.

66. A pop singer and a strong supporter of ODS.

67. Cinematographer and director of documentary films. He's worked for Short Film Studios since 1957. During his career, he has directed or photographed over 100 documentaries.

68. He was the general manager of Barrandov Studios between 1963–69.

69. The official daily newspaper of the Communist Party of Czechoslovakia.

70. Russian director and screenwriter best-known for his films *Andrej Rublev* (1969), *Solaris* (1972), *Stalker* (1980), *Nostalgia* (1983) and *Sacrifice* (1987).

71. A 1981 feature film (based on the novel by Klaus Mann) directed by István Szabó. The film received the Academy Award for Best Foreign Language Film in 1982.

72. A Czech surrealist poet. In 1968 he immigrated to France, where he has been living since.

73. One of the famous directors of Czech New Wave (1935–89).

74. Films banned in 1969–70: *All My Countrymen* (Všichni dobří rodáci); *Birds, Orphans, and Fools* (Vtáčkovia, siroty a blázni); *Case for a Rookie Hangman* (Případ pro začínajícího kata); *Deserters and Nomads* (Zbehovia a pútníci); *Dogs and People* (Psi a lidé); *Dull Sunday* (Zabitá neděle); *The Ear* (Ucho); *Elective Affinities* (Spřízneni vlobou); *Firemen's Ball* (Hoří má Panenko); *The Fruit of Paradise* (Ovoce stromů rajských jíme); *Hammer Against Witches* (Kladivo na čarodejnice); *How Bread Is Made* (Jak se peče chleba); *Larks on a String* (Skřivánci na niti); *Mourning Party* (Smuteční slavnost); *Nakedness* (Nahota); *The Seventh Day, the Eight Night* (Sedmý den, osmá noc); *Pavilon No.6* (Pavilon č.6),; *Prison Guard* (Hlídač); *Reformatory* (Pasťák); *Report on the Party and the Guestd* (O slavnosti a hostech); *The Visits* (Návštěvy).

75. He worked as a technician until 1965. From 1966 to 1969 he was an artistic director of the Experimental Theatre in

Olomouc. He also worked as a producer, screenwriter and choreographer. He was also a Communist party member between 1962–69. From 1989 to 1993 he was artistic director of the Musical Theatre in Olomouc; from 1990 to 1992 he was an MP in the Federal Assembly of Nations, first for Civic Forum and later for CSSD. In 1996 he was elected to the Parliament and in 1998 re-elected. He is the Minister of Culture since 1998.

76. The Association of Czech Film and Television Artists fites@quick.cz

77. A natural object found by chance, an artifact.

78. In 1989 he was the most powerful politician in Czechoslovakia. Considered a hard-line Communist, he was the general secretary of the Communist party. As one of the government officials who sent a letter to Leonid Breznev in 1968 inviting the Soviet Army into Czechoslovakia, he was charged with treason in 1995 together with six others representatives of the Communist government. After lengthy court proceedings he was acquitted in September 2002.

79. Italian film producer. Worked for Lux Films in Rome from 1945 to 1949. In 1950 he began a successful partnership with Dino de Laurentis producing, for example, Federico Fellini's *La Strada* (1954). He produced many successful international projects with directors such as Vittorio De Sica, Jean-Luc Godard, Michelangelo Antonioni and David Lean. Some of his best known productions include *Dr. Zhivago* (1965), *Blow-up* (1966), *The Verdict* (1974) and *The Cassandra Crossing* (1976). His 1957 marriage to Sophia Loren led him to taking French citizenship in 1964.

80. After the fall of Communism, Ivan Passer was invited to FAMU for a special presentation of his diploma. After the ceremony he quietly left the room, leaving his diploma on the table.

81. A leading experimental novelist who belonged to the Czech avant-garde circles of the '20s and '30s (1891–1942). Although considered one of the most important Czech personalities of the twenti-

eth century, his work is known mainly through film adaptations by František Vláčil (*Markéta Lazarová*) or Jiří Menzel (*Capricious Summer*).

82. Czech novelist, humorist and journalist (1883–1923). He grew up in Prague and became known as an anarchist and satirical personality in bohemian circles. During World War I he served in the Austrian army but soon deserted to Russia, joined the Communist party in 1918 and became a political commissar with the Red Army in Siberia for two years before returning to Prague. Between 1921 and 1923 he published in four volumes his *The Good Soldier Svejk* (Osudy dobrého vojáka Švejka).

83. A Czech writer, screenwriter and publicist. He received a Ph.D. from Charles University in Prague. In 1969 he emigrated to Canada with his wife and helped her run 68 Publishers in Toronto. He was awarded with the White Lion Award by President Havel in 1990.

84. The leader of the Soviet Union between 1964 and 1982. He authorized the Soviet-led invasion of the Warsaw Pact Armies into Czechoslovakia in September 21, 1968, to crush the so-called "Prague Spring" movement.

85. The last president of the Communist Czechoslovakia. A lawyer, politician and President of Czechoslovakia during the "Normalization" era. He was involved in the leftist movement since he was young. At the age of 16 he joined the Communist Youth League and as a student in 1933 he became a member of the communist party. By 1947 he was in charge of StB operations in Slovakia. In February 1951 he was arrested and in April 1955 sentenced to life in prison. He became the victim of the system he helped to build. He was released in 1960 and became a supporter of Alexander Dubček. After the Soviet invasion he became the First Secretary of the Communist party in 1969 and the General Secretary in 1971. In May 1975 he became the president of Czechoslovakia. After November 17, 1989, he had no other option than resign. He died in Bratislava at the age of 78.

86. Poet, writer and playwright. The most conspicuous and at the same time one of the most controversial cultural and political figures of Czech history in the second half of the twentieth century. He was an ardent Stalinist in the 1950s, a reformist Communist in the 1960s, a dissident in the 1970s and an emigré in the 1980s. He is particularly highly regarded in the German-speaking parts of Europe.

87. Born in 1946 in London into the family of Czech diplomat Pavel Kavan and British teacher Rosemary Kavan. The family returned to Czechoslovakia in 1950. His father was later arrested and became one of the key witnesses in the process with Rudolf Slánský (accused of treason and executed). Jan studied in the 60s at the Charles University and was active in politics. After the 1968 Soviet invasion he immigrated to Great Britain. He studied at the London School of Economics, Oxford and Reading. He started the Palach Press Agency, which published information about dissidents' activities and illegally shipped forbidden literature to Czechoslovakia. In 1979 he was stripped of Czech citizenship.

He returned to Czechoslovakia in November 1989, became a member of Civic Forum and in 1990 chairman of the parliamentary committee for foreign affairs. In 1991 he was indicted on charges of collaborating with StB during the 1969–70 period. The file documenting Kavan's relationship with StB (code name Kato) was first discovered by the interim director of BIS Stanislav Devátý. During the period of investigation, Kavan went to the U.S. to teach at Adelphi University in New York and Amherst College in Massachusetts. In 1996 the court concluded that Kavan, regardless of his contacts with StB, was unaware who he was dealing with and all charges against him were dismissed. After his acquittal he became a senator and the vice-chairman of the Helsinki Committee for human rights in Czech Republic. In 1998 Kavan became a Vice-premier and Minister of Foreign Affairs. But the whole affair didn't go away thanks to the book

Kato — the Case of the Real Man (Kato — Příběh opravdového člověka) by John Block and Přemysl Vachalovský, published by J.W. Hill in 2000. The BIS agents were buying the book in bulk from the bookstores to keep it from reaching readers. Kavan's career in the Ministry of Foreign Affairs was full of scandals: in 1998, a driving accident under the influence of alcohol, leaking to the press information about an Iraqi agent, secret trips of his officers to Iraq, and cheating of the lustration law (*lustrace*, the screening of undesirables from government posts); later, the discovery of a large amount of cash in his office's vault and the arrest of his deputy Karel Srba (indicted on corruption charges and murder-for-hire charges to cover some illegal activities). At the end of his term, Kavan managed to convince his colleagues in the cabinet to put aside 118 million crowns ($4,000,000) to finance his U.N. office in New York. On July 8, 2002, he became a Chairman of the UN General Assembly. At the same time he also served as a deputy in the Czech Parliament. By February 10, 2003, he still hadn't obtained the security clearance required by law in Czech Republic for all government employees.

88. The government responded to Charta 77 on Friday January 28, 1977, with a media extravaganza. All personalities of Czech culture — actors, writers, directors, musicians, architects — together with politicians (including the secretary of ÚV KSČ Josef Havlín, the chief of the cultural division of ÚV KSČ Miroslav Müller, and the Vice Premier Martin Lučan) gathered in the National Theatre and in front of live television cameras denounced the proclamation. Actress Jiřina Švorcová in her speech "For new creativity in the name of the socialism and peace" denounced all those who "betrayed the nation and became a tool of subversive activities of the anti-human forces of imperialism." At the end, everyone in the theater came forward and put their signatures under the simple sentence "I agree with the declaration of Czechoslovak Art

Associations." (The signers included Jan Werich, Karel Höger, Ladislav Pešek, Eduard Haken, Jiří Sovák, Miloš Kopecký, František Filipovský, Rudolf Hrušínský and Radovan Lukavský.) Over 7,000 artists added their signatures.

There was a follow-up event one week later (February 4) in the Music Theatre where comrade Müller and Minister of Culture Milan Klusák invited all pop music artists (singers, composers, conductors). Eva Pilarová made the introductory speech. Many others followed including Karel Gott, Karel Svoboda, Karel Vágner, Ladislav Štaidl and Jiří Korn. At the end, the same as the previous week, all added their signatures to the proclamation, which became known as Anti-Charta.

As Eva Kantůrková wrote, "All the faithful boosted their strength in faithfulness and assured themselves it is OK to be an opportunist. And until today cowards never forget they acted cowardly." The same as with Charta 77, the full content of the Anti-Charta proclamation was never made public.

Only a few artists had the courage to publicly apologize after the fall of communism for signing the Anti-Charta document (Jiří Ornest, Michal Pavlata and Zdeněk Svěrák, for example).

President Václav Havel, in his speech at the meeting marking the 25th anniversary of Charta 77, said, "As I remember, we never felt bad about those who signed Anti-Charta. To be angry with them would mean to be angry at our history and to be angry at the archetypes of Czech behavior. It would be like being angry at the Czech nation and at the Czech society as a whole."

89. SS Intelligence Chief. He was appointed by Adolf Hitler in 1941 as Reich Protector of Bohemia-Moravia. On May 27, 1942, he was assassinated in Prague by an SAS Czech commando trained in Great Britain. As a result, the town of Lidice was destroyed and all residents executed.

90. *Parliamentary Parties:* Social Democratic Party (CSSD), Civic Democratic Party (ODS), Freedom Union-Demo-cratic Union (US-DEU), Christian Democratic Union-Czech Populist Party (KDU-CSL), Communist Party of Czech and Moravia (KSCM).

Other Parties: Green Party, Independent Alliance (SNK), Right Block, Republicans, The Hope , Life Salvation Party, Civic Democratic Alliance (ODA), Liberal Social Union (LSU), Balbin's Poetic Party, Open Society Party (SOS), Civic Movement (OM), Czech Communist Party (KCS).

91. Czech writer, journalist and politician (1917–2003). He went to London in 1939 and worked for the BBC. He returned to Czechoslovakia in 1945 and worked for the Foreign Ministry. After the 1948 Communist coup, he emigrated to West Germany, working as a program director for Radio Free Europe until 1952. Between 1952–60 he lived in the U.S. and studied at Columbia University. In the 60s he was sentenced in abstentia to 14 years in prison for treason. He strongly promoted the Czech dissident movement abroad and returned to Czechoslovakia in 1990, serving as President Havel's adviser until 1992. He was Minister of Culture between 1994–96 and the adviser of the President's office for Czech-German relations between 1997–98.

92. A famous Czech actor, writer and comic (1905–1980).

93. The head of the Institute of Prognosis.

94. The coalition of opposition groups created in November 1989 to negotiate the new government with the Communist regime. In May 1992, Civic Forum had split into several competing factions.

95. Born in the Soviet Union, he immigrated to Germany at the end of the 70s or the beginning of the 80s and later moved to the United States. He worked as a babysitter in Albuquerque but after three months moved to Cambridge with the wife of his employer. She supported him during his studies at Harvard University and they got married in 1984. The same year he received his Green Card (# A245 996 68) but he never became a U.S. citi-

zen. He tried to make friends with scientists working at Rockwell on the Star Wars program and was investigated by the FBI. His wife left him in 1985 and in 1987 they got divorced. After his graduation from Harvard with a degree in economics and a recommendation from Prof. Stephen Breyer, a future Supreme Court Justice, he moved to London in 1989 and worked for five months for Robert Fleming Co. He returned to Prague at the age of 27 without any money and founded Harvard Capital Investment and Consulting. He involved some high-ranking officers from ODS in his business. While promising to restructure Czech industry, he funneled off $45,000,000 by 1995 from Harvard Consulting. When the dust settled Harvard Consulting filed for bankruptcy and Koženy walked out with a fortune estimated at between $200–700,000,000.

In December 1992 he was involved in a bizarre case involving an StB agent, Václav Wallis, who was arrested for selling secret government documents to Koženy. Koženy fled the country to avoid prosecution, sold Harvard Consulting to a company owned by his mother, acquired Irish citizenship and since 1994 has lived in Lyford Cay in the Bahamas. His neighbors are Sean Connery, John Templeton and Michael Dingman.

On December 20, 1997, he threw a party in his $19,700,000 Peak House in Aspen, Colorado. He invited 150 people to raise money for his new investment adventure, an oil company Socar in Azerbaijan. His guests invested over $20,000,000. Investors include former Senator George J. Mitchell, Richard Friedman, Aaron Fleck and Rick Bourke. Mitchell invested $200,000 and agreed to serve as vice chairman of Koženy's Oil Rocky Group Ltd. Fleck admitted that he introduced Koženy to Mr. Cooperman, a chairman of Omega Advisors in New York who signed off an investment of $125,000,000 for Koženy's venture. Koženy bought privatization vouchers on the free market for 40 cents apiece and sold them to his investors for $25 apiece. Azerbaijan president and

KGB general Heydar Aliyev stalled the deal at the end. The vouchers expired in August 2000. Cooperman and AIG are suing Koženy (now in London) for fraud, asking $160 million in damages.

Czech police are unable to summon Koženy to court because the Czech Republic has no diplomatic relations with the Bahamas. They are also pending charges against his top executive Boris Vostrý, a former StB agent living now in Belize — another country without diplomatic ties with the Czech Republic.

In his interview for *MF Dnes* newspaper (November 4, 2002), Koženy claimed he is innocent, saying he is a victim of extortion, and he is suing Azerbaijan and its president Hejdar Allijev for $4 billion. When asked what his plans are for the future, he said he wants to return to the Czech Republic and become a politician.

96. Economist Ježek worked at the Institute of Prognosis in 1985–89. He was an adviser to the finance minister in 1990 before becoming one of the leaders of privatization. He is famous for his concept of "run ahead of the lawyers." He was a Chairman of the National Property Fund between 1992–94.

97. An entrepreneur of Russian origin. The place and date of his birth were deleted from his personal files. In 1969 he graduated from Charles University, where he studied sociology. He worked in Czech television in the late 60s and before 1989 as an editor of *Technický Magazine*. In 1990–91 he was a spokesman for Civic Forum and in 1991–92 a spokesman for the President's Office and adviser to the Premier Petr Pithart. He was the General Manager of TV NOVA — the first commercial Czech television — starting in 1993. Owned by U.S. businessman Ronald Lauder, TV NOVA became the most popular station in the Czech Republic, capturing 70 percent of the audience. Železný's troubles started in 1998 when CME (Central European Media Enterprises) tried to oust him from the position of General Manager. He found some indigenous financing and started his own TV NOVA

MARK 2 station instead. CME filed the lawsuit against Železný for "hijacking" the station and the International Court of Arbitration ordered Železný to pay Lauder back $27 million. When Železný refused to accept the court decision, CME filed the other lawsuit against the Czech Republic asking $500 million for failing to secure their investment and won. Since then, Železný was accused of tax and custom duty evasion and harming a creditor, owing the government some 7,000,000 crowns in taxes. After the Fall 2002 election he became a senator and the police intensified their investigation, asking the Senate to strip Železný of his legislative immunity.

Saga of Železný's Investigation

- 2/19/2001 The French government blocked Železný's property in France
- 2/22/2001 Prague's court blocked Železný's property in Czech Republic
- 2/27/2001 American court blocked Železný's Citibank account
- 4/12/2001 Arraigned in court and charged with fraud and tax evasion
- 7/30/2001 Brno's court blocked the sale of three companies tied to Železný
- 8/23/2001 Salzburg's court confiscated four cubist paintings owned by Železný
- 11/04/2001 Železný's lawyer Rozehnal arrested
- 11/13/2001 Železný arrested and interrogated
- 1/14/2002 Železný arrested and interrogated again
- 6/14/2002 A coup in TV NOVA: Rozehnal took over and fired Železný from the job as a station's general manager.
- 10/26/2002 Železný was elected a Senator of Southern Moravia region, where he never lived before. This post granted him immunity against prosecution.

- 1/23/2003 The Senate voted to strip senator Železný's immunity to allow the investigation proceeds.

- 3/17/2003 The International Arbitration Court found the Czech Republic guilty and ordered the Czech government to pay $269.8 million plus interest to CME — a total of $353.4 million. While the Czech government is struggling, pointing fingers who is to blame, the interest is adding $67,000 every day to the bill. In his weekly TV NOVA talk show Volejte Řediteli (March 17, 2003), Vladimír Železný proclaimed that "this is the price we have to pay for the sovereignty of our country."

98. Andropov (1914–84) joined Komsomol in 1930 and the communist party in 1939. He was an Ambassador to Hungary in 1954–57 and was involved in suppression of the 1956 Hungarian uprising. In 1962 he became a Secretary of the Central Committee and in 1967 he was appointed head of KGB and became a member of Politburo. In 1982 he was transferred from the KGB to the Secretariat, a move supported by Gorbachev. In November 1982, after Brezhnev's death, he became General Secretary. In 1983 he was elected Chairman of the Presidium of the Supreme Soviet.

99. Born 1931. The last President of the Soviet Union. His name was connected with "perestroika" and "glasnost," which led to the dismantling of the non-functioning Communist system in the Soviet Union and Eastern Europe. He joined the Communist party in 1952. In 1955 he graduated from the faculty of Law at Moscow State University and in 1967 from the Faculty of Economy of the Sevastopol. Between 1970 and 1990 he served as Deputy of the Supreme Soviet. During his career he relied on the same base of support that Andropov has used, which included the KGB. In 1984–85 he served as Chairman of the Foreign Affairs Committee. In 1985 he became a member of the Presidium of the Supreme Soviet and General Secretary until 1991. In 1990 he received the Nobel Peace Price. Since 1997 he is the President

of International Foundation for Socio-Economic and Political Studies (The Gorbachev Foundation).

100. Former Foreign Minister and Soviet Interior Minister. He became the last head of KGB after the '91 Putch. Mikhail Gorbachev signed a decree abolishing the KGB on October 24, 1991.

101. Born 1931. In June, 1991, he was elected the first President of the Russian Federation. In August 1999, he appointed the former KGB agent Vladimir Putin to the position of Premier. He retired in March 2000.

102. Born 1929. He joined the Communist party in 1959 and became the foreign correspondent for *Pravda* newspaper in the Middle East, a job frequently used as a cover for espionage. He later became a foreign policy adviser. In 1990 he was named to head the foreign intelligence section of the KGB. After the dissolution of the USSR, he continued to run the Russian successor of the KGB. In 1996 he became the foreign minister and in 1998 Russia's Premier.

103. The Germany and US reported a 12 percent increase in intelligence collection effort by Russians between 1991–93.

104. The infamous Ministerium fúr Staatssicherheit, the East German secret police. It was established in April 1950 based on the structure of NKVD (predecessor of the KGB). In the late '80s the Stasi had nearly 175,000 official informants, roughly one informant for every 100 people, and maintained a force of over 90,000 agents. In coordination with the KGB, it collected intelligence on occupational forces in Berlin, the U.S. and NATO forces in West Germany, and other Western European countries. Vladimir Putin,* the KGB operative (and later President of Russia), was stationed in Berlin during the '80s until the fall of the Berlin Wall. In 1995 the unified German court stated that former Stasi officials could not be prosecuted.

105. As Yeltsin's first minister of security, he left most of the former KGB officials in place. He was sacked by Yeltsin in July 1993 and replaced by Nikolaj Golushko. Later that year, Yeltsin disbanded the Ministry of Security and replaced it with a new agency, the Federal Counterintelligence Service (FSK).

106. It was psychologist Žantovský who delivered misinformation about the death of student Martin Šmíd to the BBC after the riots on November 17, 1989. His parents worked at the Information Ministry during the 50. He went to Canada in 1968 and was deported back to Czechoslovakia in 1971. After his return he wasn't tried in court for "illegally leaving the country" as anybody else would. Instead, he finished his degree at the University and worked at the Experimental Psychiatric Institute in Bohnice. He also worked as a personal translator for President Gustáv Husák and in 1988 he worked for the Reuters Press Agency in Prague. In December 1989 he became a spokesman for the President's Office and President Havel's adviser. In 1992–96 he served as an Ambassador to the U.S. and after his return he became a member of the Czech Senate. In the files of Second Division of StB, his code name is "Michaela Žantovská."

107. The youngest of the Communist bosses in the Politburo. He was a general

*Vladimir Putin became president of the Russian Federation in 2000. From his graduation from the state university in St. Petersburg, he worked at the KGB Foreign Intelligence Service, mainly in Germany. In the 1970s he was expelled from West Germany as a spy and moved to East Berlin. He came back to Russia in 1990. In 1994 he was a deputy mayor of St. Petersburg, and in 1998 he was appointed head of the Federal Security Service (FSB)—the successor of the KGB—replacing Nikolai Kovalyov. Subsequently he was appointed head of the Security Council. He is described as an ally of Anatoly Chubais, the architect of Russia's privatization program.

secretary of Prague's Communist party bureau and the only Communist party official sentenced to two and half years of jail for suppressing the students' Prague demonstration in November 17, 1989. He is the founder of the Party of Czech Communists, which was renamed in 2000 the KSČ (Communist Party of Czechs).

108. From the testimony by Kenneth R. Timmerman before the House International Relation Committee, Hearing on U.S. Policy toward Russia: Warning and Dissent, Washington DC, October 6, 1999

> As members of this committee know well, the architect of this administration's policy toward Russia, Strobe Tallbot, was a journalist as I am. Mr. Tallbot jump-started his career after a brief stay in Moscow in the summer of 1969, where he had gone with his Oxford roommate Bill Clinton, and met up with a well-known KGB asset named Victor Louis. Victor Louis's job for the KGB was to serve as a talent scout and what we would call today a spin doctor. He planted stories in the Western press that were favorable to the Soviet leadership and to the KGB, and many reporters got to know him.
>
> According to Dr. Joseph D. Douglas, a specialist for state security and a former employee of the Ministry of Defense, American citizen Mark Rich played an important role in developing the new economic system in the Soviet Union. Mark Rich left the U.S. in 1983 to avoid prosecution. Headquartered in Switzerland he helped the Russian Mafia and KGB loot their country, leaving it bankrupt. He was pardoned by President Bill Clinton on the last day of his presidency.

Mark Rich and the Russian Connection by Christopher Ruddy, **NewsMax**, Feb 19, 2001

109. Between 1987–90 he was the last premier of the Communist government. He started the dialogue with Civic Forum in November 1989.

110. Personal data unknown. As the chief of the 13th division of ÚV KSČ, he was one of the top officials in the Communist party leadership and a Vice Premier in 1987–88. He was in charge of coordination between Charta 77 activities and groups abroad, leading to the management and personal politics of Civic Forum. In his open letter to President Václav Havel in July 2000, he wrote, "I was a part of the past political system, a servant who was helping its development. I wanted to make my experience public but, unfortunately, when I tried to publish my book about the past and the present situation I was informed while walking at the main square in Žďár nad Sázavou that the truth will never become public. I was strongly advised to forget all about it and move into seclusion. Otherwise an accident could happen to me like, for example, 'falling' into the Orlík dam. I wish the best to all those starving for power and money. Let them enjoy their rise in the society, fogging reality, and manipulation of people. I am just asking not to be put in the same bag with you and all the others who are taking part in the present devastation of our society. At the same time I am asking you to make public all information related to the collaboration of your pre–November opposition movement with Gustáv Husák and StB. Nobody likes to think about stolen billions. As the President you possibly could not see the corruption of some individuals and groups, great financial bubbles, and your part in all that…."

111. The Parliament approved a law to open StB archives to the public. If anybody thinks they can finally find the "truth" about all agents StB, he will be surprised. The archives were ransacked twice in 1989–90: first by StB officers who took out files by the bag loads and then by the management of the Interior Ministry. What disappeared were files of high-ranking StB officers and files of people who landed high posts in politics after the November 17 revolution and who are active in politics even today.

What actually happened with the StB archives in 1990 came out only recently when the first non–communist Interior Minister JUDr. Richard Sacher was forced to testify in the court regarding the operation "Decontamination" (Asanace) — the StB action to run dissidents out of

JUDr. Richard SACHER

V Praze dne 2. dubna 1990
č.j.: OV-0017/X-90

Výtisk číslo: 2
Počet listů : 2

P o k y n

federálního ministra vnitra k zajištění ochrany údajů v eviden-
cích statisticko evidenčního odboru vnitřní a organizační správy
federálního ministerstva vnitra

V zájmu zajištění stability politického vývoje nařizuji
s okamžitou platností:

1. Vyjmout z ústřední evidence SEO VOS FMV evidenční karty, které
   se týkají
   a) prezidenta republiky,
   b) členů federální vlády, vlády České republiky a vlády Sloven-
      ské republiky,
   c) poslanců Federálního shromáždění,
   d) poslanců České národní rady, Slovenské národní rady a před-
      sedů politických stran.

2. Vyjmout archivní materiály uložené v operativním archivu SEO
   VOS FMV, které se vztahují k výše uvedeným osobám.

3. Uložit registrační protokoly do plechových obalů a tyto zape-
   četit. Změny v registraci řešit náhradním způsobem s využitím
   lístkovnice a na počítači.

4. Evidenční karty, archivní materiály a registrační protokoly
   uložit do zvláštního fondu SEO VOS FMV.

5. Okamžitě signalizovat ministru vnitra ČSFR všechny případy,
   kdy lustrace směřuje do okruhu osob, uvedených v bodu 1 tohoto
   pokynu.

Ministr vnitra ČSFR

164

The Fund Z memo was an internal memo issued by Minister of the Interior
Richard Sacher, which sealed the personal files of all members of President
Václav Harvel's government.

Czechoslovakia in the late 70s and early 80s.* During the hearings, Sacher admitted that he created a Fund "Z" where all the files of legislators, members of the government and officials from the State Attorney's office were compiled. "I also requested a compilation of all StB files on Charta 77 members. In April 1990 I passed all the materials to representatives of Charta 77," he said. (They are not yet identified.) "They promised to return the materials to the State Archives after reading them over. I have no knowledge if they returned these files or not."

Viliam Ciklamini was the First Secretary of the first Federal Interior Minister Richard Sacher. He served in this position for only four months before he was dismissed from his job by Sacher. Ciklamini insists that he was fired because he didn't agree with the plundering of StB archives and with illegal lustrations. He now lives in Bratislava, the capital of Slovakia. He claims that President Václav Havel personally participated in "wild" lustrations, which had to cover connections of some of the top politicians and dissidents with StB.

Mr. Ciklamini answered questions in the interview for *Super* magazine:

As the First Secretary you were in charge of intelligence services, pretty much everything in the former StB.

CIKLAMINI: Yes, I was handling very sensitive matters. At that time everything was about what direction the country would go. The issue was who will be the next President, Havel or Dubček⁺. Mr. Sámel, another secretary in the Interior Ministry who was in the Havel's group, came to me and said, "If you will side with Havel, instead of Dubček, you could become the Interior Minister." I refused and thus became undesired.

Why did they stand against Dubček?

In January 1990 they believed that Dubček was an obstacle for them. Havel was ready to become the president and go to the Castle but people would like to see Dubček there. But Havel's presidency was fixed already. As you

---

*According to the executive order by Interior Minister Jaromír Obzina from December 21, 1977, the goal was "to achieve a total isolation of Charta 77 leaders from other members of the movement and force selected individuals to leave Czechoslovakia." The operation partially succeeded, forcing some twenty Chartists to emigrate. Karol Sidon, Jarolav Hutka, Vladimir Třešnák, Svatopluk Karásek, and Pavel Landovský were just a few of those who left the country. So far only four employees of the Interior Ministry have been sentenced to probation for participation in this operation, and former interior minister Obzina is claiming immunity, saying he is too ill to appear in the court. The trial with eleven StB officers involved in the operation finally started, after six years of preparation, in May 2002. After ten minutes of hearing, the case was indefinitely postponed.

⁺Dubček's parents met as immigrants in the United States, but they were deported to Europe after his father refused to serve in the army during World War I. Alexander was born in Slovakia in 1921, but his family moved to the Soviet Union, where his father joined the Communist Party and became active in politics. Dubček joined the party in 1936 and moved back to Slovakia in 1938. He was appointed to the Central Committee of the Slovak Communist Party, became a full-time politician and studied politics in Moscow. In 1964 he became the chairman of the Slovak Communist Party. He became one of the key personalities during the so-called "Prague Spring" movement and replaced Antonín Novotný as the leader of the Czechoslovak Communist Party in 1968. His attempt to create "socialism with a human face" ended with the September 1968 Soviet invasion. After the revolution in November 1989, he became a leader of Social Democratic party (CSSD) and served as a speaker in the Czechoslovak parliament. He was one of the key witnesses against Jakeš, Lenárt and others charged with treason after the Velvet Revolution. His career ended abruptly in November 1992 when he was killed in a car accident.

know, as the First Secretary I was in charge of intelligence....

Are you saying that Havel needed a loyal person at the Interior Ministry to control the ministry and intelligence services?
Yes.

But why?
Sacher and Havel privately ran a lustration of politicians. In the process they found out that half of the Parliament and the federal government are communist agents. Then they created a special Fund "Z" where they put all those selected for important posts, mostly dissidents. They wanted to control the situation.

Do you have evidence that Havel was involved in pulling out StB files?
Zdeněk Formánek, director of intelligence then, first found out that Sacher was checking files and pulling files of some of the individuals out. He went immediately to the President's Office to inform Havel. He told his secretary he wanted to report an illegal lustration. Havel immediately called Sacher telling him that there was a leak. Then Sacher blamed the whole affair on Formánek.

How do you know that Havel really knew about it?
Havel refused to see Formánek but the secretary Sámel admitted that Havel knew about it.

What did Formánek actually find out?
Formánek discovered that 20 people in the interior ministry were going through the files, day and night.

Was it on Sacher's request?
Yes, it was on Sacher's and Havel's request. I mentioned this at the press conference and I wanted to bring it up in Parliament but they didn't let me. Then Sacher fired me.

So they took names of politicians and government officials and checked them against StB files?
Yes.

And if a name matched the name in the archive, the file was pulled out and put in the Fund "Z"?
Yes, that's correct. But not everybody was sheltered in this special fund. Only those who were considered potential politicians. Those selected to participate in politics in the future. In any case, it was illegal.

Who was specifically affected?
That's difficult. I didn't have an access to names.

Sacher was in London when you found out this was going on. What did you do?
I immediately asked the chief of the Office of the Interior Ministry Jiří Novotný for explanation. He admitted that 20 people were checking the files for over a week. Quite a job they had to do. They had to go through 130 thousand files of the StB Second division!

Did they do it by hand?
Yes, it wasn't in computer files yet.

And what about files of other divisions of the StB, and what about army intelligence and counter-intelligence?
Fortunately they didn't make it so far....

How do you see that time period now after years passed by?
It was a struggle for power. If I would compare it to something, it would be a situation I experienced during my intelligence work in the mid-eighties in Africa. We treated democracy here like we did in developing countries.

The Parliamentary commission in charge of lustration discovered that they were not the first to look at the files. The StB archives were compromised and there was evidence that some files were photocopied before being destroyed and thus they still exist. The commission also found that 13 government officials who previously obtained clearance were indeed registered agents of StB.

Bibliography

Related Reading

Boček, Jaroslav. *Looking Back in the New Wave*. Czechoslovak Filmexport, 1967.
_____. *Modern Czechoslovak Film*. Brno: Artia, 1965.
Dewey, Langdo. *An Outline of Czechoslovak Cinema*. London: Infomatics, 1971.
Hames, Peter. *The Czechoslovak New Wave*. Berkeley: University of California Press, 1985.
Liehm, Antonín J. *Closely Watched Films: The Czechoslovak Experience*. New York: International Arts and Science Press, 1974.
Liehm, Mira, and Antonín J. Liehm. *The Most Important Art: Eastern European Film After 1945*. Berkeley:University of California Press, 1977.
Skvorecky, Josef, and Peter Martin. *All the Bright Young Men and Women*. Toronto, 1973.

References

Bittman, Ladislav. *The Deception Game: Czechoslovak Intelligence in Soviet Political Warfare*. Syracuse NY: Syracuse University Research Corp., 1972; [pb] New York: Ballantine, 1981.
Gevorkian, Natalia. "The KGB: 'They Still Need Us.'" *Bulletin of the Atomic Scientists*, January 1993.
Keane, John. *Vaclav Havel: A Political Tragedy in Six Acts*. Bloomsbury, 1999.
Kessler, Ronald. *Spy Versus Spy: Stalking Soviet Spies in America*. New York: Scribner's, 1988.
Kohout, Lubor. "Viktor Kožený-náš vzor." *Český deník*.
"Kozeny Facing Charges," *Lidovky* (Prague), September 7, 2001.
Lewis, Charles, and Bill Allison. *The Cheating of America*. New York: William Morrow, 2001.
Ruddy, Christopher. "Mark Rich and the Russian Connection." *NewsMax*, February 19, 2001.
"Uncensored News (Necenzurované noviny)," www.cibulka.net/nnoviny/
Wallace, Charles P. "The Pirates of Prague." *Fortune*, December 23, 1996, v134 n12 p78.

Many of the Czech New Wave films are distributed with English subtitles on VHS or DVD by Facet's Multi-Media, Inc., Chicago (www.facets.org).

Index